FRONTISPIECE
Under the shadow of Blea Moor, Stanier Class 5 4–6–0 No. 4509 leaves a swirl of smoke haze as it emerges into the sunshine in May 1962. (Photo: D. Jenkinson.)

Rails in the Fells

RAILS IN THE FELLS

A Railway Case Study

An account of the origins, characteristics and contribution of a railway to the landscape; together with an attempt to evaluate its past and present influence on the area through which it passes.

David Jenkinson

with a Foreword by
The Rt Rev Eric Treacy, Lord Bishop of Wakefield

Peco Publications and Publicity Limited
BEER . SEATON . DEVON . ENGLAND

Published by
Peco Publications and Publicity Ltd.
Underleys Beer Seaton Devon EX12 3NA
First published in 1973
Second edition, revised 1980
© David Jenkinson

Printed by
Sidmouth Printing Works Ltd.
Set in 10 on 12pt Old Style

ISBN 0 900586 53 2

Contents

List of Maps, Drawings, Diagrams

Introduction to the Second Edition

When an author is fortunate enough to be told by his publisher that a second edition of his book is in prospect, he can be faced with contradictory emotions, aside from the satisfaction of knowing that the first effort was reasonably successful. On the one hand, he can take the self-satisfied view that there is no scope for improvement and therefore leave well alone or, on the other, he can take the opportunity to re-write the whole thing so as to be in effect an almost new compilation. I have felt prey to both these temptations but, in the end, have decided to compromise, I hope not unsuccessfully.

The first problem was of a practical nature. Since this book was first published I have continued to receive a steady supply of additional pictures, many of quite unique nature, which it seemed a pity not to include. This inevitably meant discarding some of those which were included the first time—unless the price of the book was to be increased considerably beyond that caused by the natural ravages of inflation. I hope I shall be forgiven for this since I honestly feel that the revised selection is of considerably enhanced historical interest, albeit of probably less technical excellence.

The second problem stemmed from the fact that the book was initially written in the shadow of what seemed to be the likely closure of the Settle-Carlisle line in the very near future (i.e. related to 1972–3). Indeed, my last chapter was almost in the form of a farewell eulogy before sentence of death was passed. Happily this never happened, and I would like to think that some of my ideas advanced in 1973 may have had some slight influence on the latter day change of heart. Be that as it may, however, the happenings since 1973/4 can give us cautious grounds for belief that the worst of our collective insanities regarding the British railway network are, at last, behind us. The railways as a whole seem a good deal healthier than they did a few years ago and, above all (in the context of this book), the Settle and Carlisle is still there. It therefore seemed sensible to re-write the last chapter in order to update the story.

Finally, during the interval between first publication and today, that great and godly man, my friend Bishop Eric Treacy, died at Appleby in 1978. He had just photographed the departure of 'Evening Star', on which I was about to ride to Ais Gill, and I received the sad news as I got down from the engine at Garsdale. Happily, he lived to see steam back on his favourite railway line and to me, in spite of the almost Wagnerian symbolism of his death, he is still very much alive in spirit. I have therefore left his foreword exactly as he wrote it, and I would like to dedicate this second edition to his memory.

D.J.

Harrogate 1979

Foreword

by the Rt Rev Eric Treacy, MBE, LL.D
Lord Bishop of Wakefield

I came to Keighley in 1945 after 5½ years in the army; prior to that I had worked on Merseyside. At first, I was not very excited about the line which wound through the Aire Valley. No Pacifics there; none of the cavernous majesty of the Lime Street cutting and, it seemed, relatively little traffic.

However, two things soon changed my attitude. One was that I started to explore the country north of Skipton and discovered the rural charms of places like Bell Busk; the rugged splendours and impressive loneliness of Ribblesdale with its three peaks, its potholes and rushing waters; the placid beauty of Dentdale; the magnificence of Wild Boar Fell dominating Ais Gill and the kindness of the Eden Valley. And through it all, there ran the most marvellous railway which seemed as much at home as the rocks and rivers.

Up this line there struggled steam engines whose eruptions somehow reflected the savagery of the setting—and there were times when it could be very savage up there. Re-built Scots, Jubilees, Black 5s had it almost to themselves until in the latter years of steam they were joined by the Britannias and Gresley's A3s. These double chimneyed A3s scarcely noticed the gradient; they panted effortlessly to the top, even though they were coming to the end of their days.

For the photographer, weather permitting, this was a marvellous hunting ground, but the weather didn't often permit! They were friendly people who lived in those hamlets and they welcomed strangers.

The other thing that changed my attitude to this bit of line was that I got to know the men at Holbeck shed and often I was allowed to ride on the footplate with them and to take my turn with the shovel up the 'Long Drag'. So I came to feel possessive pride in the old Midland line. I have 'footplated' often, but nowhere have I found it as thrilling as labouring up the hill from Settle to Blea Moor, under the brooding shadow of Ingleborough; and bucketing down the hill from Ais Gill to Appleby—perhaps on a fierce 'Scot'—through that lovely red sandstone country of the Eden Vale.

The thought that this line may soon be closed fills me with gloom, but I have to admit that it must be a very expensive railway to maintain with all its tunnels and bridges.

Whether this comes to pass or not, railway lovers the world over will treasure David Jenkinson's book, at the same time both scholarly and entertaining. It is written with a deep affection; not only for the line but for the area which it serves. Is it too much to hope that it may convince the authorities that there is a strong case for the retention of this line; strongest in terms of human and social need?

ERIC TREACY

Preface

This work was originally conceived as far back as 1962 as a straightforward geographical case study of the Settle and Carlisle Railway when, in the Spring of 1963, a plan for the 'Reshaping of British Railways' was presented to the Nation by Dr Richard Beeching (now Lord Beeching), at that time the chairman of British Railways. The 'Beeching Plan', as this document soon became known, laid down detailed methods by which it was felt that the chronic ills of the railway system might be cured. Most controversial of these were the proposals to close a large part of our railway system, if not altogether then at least to local traffic. One such proposal was to threaten the 72 miles of main line railway between Settle and Carlisle.

The British have a somewhat illogical regard for their railways and it was not to be expected that such sweeping proposals as were made by Beeching would meet with universal acclaim. Although we might never even consider actually travelling on our trains, stopping them altogether was, apparently, unthinkable. Words and phrases like 'hardship', 'social need' and 'invaluable and indispensable assets' became part of our vocabulary; but this time to little or no avail. The Ministerial 'Seal of Approval' on closure after closure seemed to be more of a rubber stamping of predetermined policy than a genuine attempt to analyse the true merit of any objections. Then, in late 1964, along with one or two other services, the Settle and Carlisle was given at least a temporary reprieve on the grounds that withdrawal of its local passenger services would cause grave hardship in the area through which it passes.

To the writer, this was a paradoxical decision, for if any railway was built in Britain with less thought of bettering the local area than was the Settle and Carlisle, it would be hard to find. It therefore seemed that the geographical case study of this railway might well be enhanced by attempting to evaluate its influence in the surrounding area; for it would seem that its very future existence as a feature of the landscape might well, in the end, depend on factors which were possibly the least important at the time of its building. However, various events conspired to bring the author's work on the project to a virtual standstill during the later 1960s—which was just as well; for in 1970 the paradox seemed complete when the six year old reprieve came to an end with the final cessation of local passenger services on the line. At the same time, it also had the effect of increasing the desire to produce a detailed study of the line—hence this book.

The Settle and Carlisle Railway was a comparative latecomer in the field of English main line routes, not carrying its first passengers until 1876, several years after most authorities are agreed that the main pattern of the British railway system had been established. Yet, in many ways, it represented the only logical outcome of that characteristic approach to transport problems which bedevilled the growth of a harmonious integrated transport system during the 19th Century and which desirable ideal we are only now beginning to fully appreciate.

In many ways, this line was not necessary from the national point of view; and yet it was built at considerable expense and difficulty through some of the most sparsely populated and inhospitable terrain in England solely in order to overcome the many problems which faced its promoters, the Midland Railway Company. But if the reprieve in 1964 was correct (regardless of subsequent events) then one is faced with the fact that the railway's main long-term contribution to our national story could have been a pure accident of its own existence. It will, therefore, be one of the objects of this work to investigate in some depth the truth or otherwise of the assertion that the line has been (and maybe still is) a vital factor in the life of the surrounding area—despite the fact that it was almost never built at all. In short, to what extent can it be truthfully claimed that, although the line's main purpose could have been otherwise achieved, from the local point of view it was and is necessary.

The main emphasis will be geographical; but since the geographer is essentially interested in a synthesis of causal factors, it is first necessary to devote a little space to an examination of these factors before placing the line in its geographical setting. It is therefore felt entirely relevant to include a brief historical resumé since, without it, the line would not exist at all as an element of the landscape. Similarly, the nature of the economic role it was designed to fulfil is a vital factor in the precise fitting of the railway into the physical environment. Appreciation of the latter is impossible without a knowledge of the former. Indeed, it is worth noting from the outset that in making the line suitable for its primary purpose, it was, in terms of precise location, rendered somewhat less effective in the local role than it might otherwise have been.

It should, however, be made clear that this book in no way attempts to emulate or even ape the pattern of traditional railway histories. Not only is this not my purpose but, in the case of the Settle and Carlisle, it would be superfluous. Like many others, I attribute a great deal of my fascination with the line to the inspiration of that marvellous book 'The Story of the Settle-Carlisle Line' by Houghton and Foster, published way back in 1948 but happily reprinted since. I count it as a great privilege to have subsequently met one of the authors.

Nor could I hope to improve on the monumental history researched in such detail by Peter Baughan in 'North of Leeds'. In fact, when, in the early 1960s, I began work on my own detailed study of the line and discovered that Mr Baughan was also researching in the same field, I almost decided to abandon my project, so thorough was his work! However, it soon became clear that our activities were not in conflict and, in the event, his book has been of great help to me.

Thus, to those who want the detailed history of this magnificent railway I would say: 'Read Houghton and Foster, and Peter Baughan'— there are no better in the field. Other, less lengthy but still eminently reliable sources are the Dalesman paperback 'Settle-Carlisle Railway' by Joy and Mitchell and the relevant chapters of 'Main Lines Across the Border' by

O. S. Nock and Eric Treacy. I have gained inspiration and knowledge from all these sources and would hope readers will do the same.

Despite the number of sources I have consulted and which are listed in the Bibliography, this work is nevertheless very much a personal document. I am, above all, interested in the sheer fact of the railway's existence and the effect this has had upon the surrounding landscape and its human society. I have, therefore, tried to present this study as an honest and objective portrait of a railway in its setting. However, as well as being a professional geographer, I am also a railway enthusiast in the more familiar sense. With the publisher's blessing, the railway enthusiast part of my personality has occasionally been allowed to intrude—particularly, but not exclusively, in the area of illustrative material. Furthermore, I have also included a section devoted to the trains themselves which, although not strictly relevant to my main theme, will, I hope, help to round out the total picture of the railway. It will also, perhaps, give the enthusiast some traditional fare and the modeller more data for his files.

In this latter respect, I would like to offer my especial thanks to those photographers who have willingly given of their time and talent to help illustrate my work. The Settle and Carlisle is a very photogenic line and I count myself fortunate indeed that some of the most eminent railway photographers in the country have felt able to offer their advice and encouragement and to let me choose from the pick of their collections. Their names are credited with their pictures and any artistic merit which the book may have is in no small measure due to the efforts of these gentlemen.

This, then, is my own personal portrait of the Settle and Carlisle Railway—personal because it is beyond the power of any one individual to do full justice to the subject matter and much must needs remain unwritten. My best hope is that it may add a little to the sum total of recorded railway history and, perhaps for a few readers, gently draw attention to a different way of looking at our railway system. If it does no more than this I shall be well pleased.

D. J.

Harrogate, 1973

AIS GILL SUMMIT

A. D. Whitehead

PART I

The Historical Background

PLATE I RIBBLEHEAD

To many people, Ribblehead symbolises the Settle and Carlisle more than any other single location. It is a wild place and much legend has grown around it and its celebrated viaduct whose vital statistics alone are impressive enough.

Here was a 2000 strong shanty town in the 1870s; from here the navvies not infrequently set off on the long trek to Chapel-le-Dale to bury their dead comrades killed during the construction of the line; here the local parson for many years conducted monthly church services in the station waiting room—which had a harmonium just for that purpose; here the stationmaster sent daily weather reports to the Met. Office and here the trains were, and are, frequently battered to a halt by the driving gales; and wagon loads, including even the sacred motor car, are prone to be blown unceremoniously onto the ballast. Here one could buy magnificent bowls of piping hot curry at the Station Hotel after a cold day in the biting wind and here one could also bask in the warm sunshine on one of those rare days of high summer and listen to the sound of the curlew, lapwing and skylark. Here, in short, was the Settle and Carlisle in all its many moods. . . .

This magnificent study of Stanier Class 8F 2-8-0 No. 48074 captures the entire spirit of the Settle and Carlisle as it battles north from Ribblehead viaduct with a down through freight on 4th November 1967. (Photo: Gavin Morrison.)

Chapter 1

Origins

It is clear beyond doubt that the establishment of the
Midland Railway had a profound influence on the
subsequent course of railway development
CLEVELAND-STEVENS. *English Railways, their
development and relation to the State* (1915).

To understand the Settle and Carlisle Railway
one must understand the Company that built it.
Without the Midland Railway there would, it is
virtually certain, be no Settle and Carlisle—at
least in its present form. Therefore, in a very
real sense, the very existence of the line as an
element of the landscape of North West England
is only explicable in the context of the railway
company whose position in the English Midlands
was to make it essential to find this outlet to the
north.

The Settle and Carlisle was but one product of
the extremely complicated political and legal
manoeuvres of railway growth in the 1850s and
1860s which, even today, are only partly analysed.
It would be well outside the scope of this work
to discuss the whole of the second 'Railway
Mania' but several aspects of it are relevant to
the issue. Of these, two notable trends seem to
emerge; firstly that of railway policy in general
with particular reference to the attitude of
Parliament and of the other interested railway
companies and secondly, the nature of the
Midland Railway itself. These two considerations
overlap considerably and cannot readily be
separated, but they must not be entirely divorced
from a third, although in this context a less
important factor in the shape of the local landowners and the general trend of public thought in
the area concerned. Railway history was closely
connected with all aspects of national development in the 19th Century, not the least of which
being the forceful personalities and idiosyncracies
of many leading men of the day. With this
background to the story, the Settle and Carlisle
was almost a foregone conclusion sooner or later.

Origins of the Midland drive for Scotland

The whole growth of railway communication in
mid 19th Century Britain took place against a
background of almost pathological fear in
Parliamentary circles of 'Railway Monopoly'.
Almost any proposal between two railway

companies to amalgamate tended to be regarded
with some distaste, if not outright hostility.
Union of an 'end on' type being reasonably
natural, was tolerated and often inevitable, but
union of parallel competitors, although it went
on, was disliked, considered unnatural and was
the cause of many doubts and fears of consolida-
tion. In consequence, mid-Victorian Britain saw
the promotion, with full Parliamentary approval,
of many competing lines whose legacy this
century has been to severely hinder the attempts
of railway management in trying to create a
viable economic system against the background
of competition unthought of at the time of
construction of the railway. The Settle and
Carlisle was possibly the most striking of such
competing lines and its origins go back well
before the date of its promotion in Parliament in
1866.

The roots of the idea can be traced back to two
amalgamation attempts in 1852/3. The first of
these, between the Midland and the London and
North Western Railway, came to nothing because
the Midland chairman, John Ellis, was not
satisfied that his company was getting a fair
bargain from the LNWR. The second attempt
was, however, much more comprehensive. In
this proposal, the two companies, together with
the Great Northern Railway, tried to amalgamate
into one very large single concern. The prospect
of this development, amongst many other
controversial railway matters, so alarmed Parliament that on 15th April 1853, Caldwell's
committee moved:

That no railway or canal bill containing any powers of
amalgamation, purchase, lease, working arrangement or
any other combination of interest between different
companies heretofore incorporated, be read a second
time

—unless, of course, the promoters agreed to
strike out all such powers!

This, as it did to many promising schemes
elsewhere in the country, sounded the death knell

for the Midland/LNWR/GNR amalgamation and, although probably not apparent *as such* at that time, by helping to force Derby and Euston apart, almost certainly formed the first seed from which grew the Settle and Carlisle plant. Certainly, from this time on, the Midland was to become more and more of a force to be reckoned with in railway politics as it freed itself from domination by the LNWR, which company had been, to some extent, a restricting influence during the first few years of the Midland's existence.

Had the amalgamation gone through, it would have given the Midland a major stake in a company controlling two main routes to Scotland and would have provided the answer to many of the company's problems. However, it might reasonably be asked why the Midland should need a Scottish outlet. To appreciate this aspect, it is necessary to go back even further to the formation of the company itself. Established in 1844 by the amalgamation of the North Midland and the constantly bickering Birmingham and Derby and Midland Counties Railways, the Midland in 1847 formed the essential central link in the original, somewhat circuitous route from London to Scotland via Rugby and York. Consequently, the Derby directors were, to say the least, reluctant to lose their share of this traffic. However, the completion of the 'West Coast' route by the opening of the Caledonian Railway in 1848 and the establishment, after a tremendous Parliamentary and legal battle, of the GNR in the East in 1850, had the effect of by-passing the Midland on both sides. Thus, the 1852/3 amalgamation foiled, the Midland was faced with the prospect of degenerating into a minor provincial railway unless it could develop fresh outlets.

The company occupied some very strategic ground right in the centre of England but it is one of the ironies of British railway history that this same central position was also to be the root cause of most of the Midland's problems. That the Midland pursued an aggressive policy during the 1850s and 1860s can hardly be denied but in many respects it had little choice:

The position of the company . . . compelled by the very nature of its central position to be constantly fighting for outlets, necessitated a fighting policy . . . and the Midland Railway lived by competition which at all times stimulated the company to efficiency while prompting it to strike out further and further from the centre
CLEVELAND STEVENS p.244

From this general standpoint, it is possible to trace the particular growth of the Settle and Carlisle idea from the breakdown of the amalgamation attempts. Railway politics at this time were often complex and frequently somewhat dubious so it could well be argued that the Midland was well out of an over close association with the LNWR, a somewhat disreputable railway in the 1850s, led as it was by that 19th Century railway pirate, 'Captain' Mark Huish. At all events, shortly after the breakdown of the 1853 amalgamation proposal, relations between Derby and Euston became somewhat strained as a result of overcrowding on the LNWR main line south of Rugby. The Midland traffic was the one which suffered and the eventual solution was provided when the Midland promoted a south-ward extension of its own line to Bedford and Hitchin. By exercising running powers from this latter point the Midland reached London via the GNR, abandoning its reliance on the LNWR in 1858.

Unfortunately for the Midland, the problem of Rugby was not to be an isolated incident. At Manchester, the GNR and LNWR had, for some time, been in a state of open hostility over traffic and most of the standard obstructing tactics such as trucks left blocking platforms and signs painted out, had been employed. When the Midland became an ally of the GNR in 1858, it was not entirely surprising that it too used Manchester as a further point at which to irritate the LNWR. The significant difference was that in this case, the better solution (for the Midland, at all events) seemed to be to build a new line through the Peak Forest which may, uncon-sciously, have set a pattern for the future since, in the South, conditions were again deteriorating. The GNR main line between Hitchin and Kings Cross was becoming, if anything, even more crowded than had been the case only a few years earlier at Rugby and again, inter-company relationships became strained. Once more the Derby company felt that the only solution was to have its own line and the London Extension to St Pancras was opened in 1868, only one year after the line to Manchester.

While the Midland Railway had gradually freed itself in the South and at Manchester, the same could not be said of the North West. In 1852, John Ellis had acquired for the Midland, control of the nominally independent 'little' North Western Railway which ran from Skipton to Lancaster with a branch to Ingleton. This line provided a natural extension of the Midland's Leeds and Bradford Railway but unfortunately at Ingleton it made an end-on junction with the Low Gill branch of the Lancaster and Carlisle section of the LNWR. The Lancaster and Carlisle was again a nominally independent concern but leaned heavily on Euston for support so in effect the Midland had to hand over its northbound traffic to the LNWR which was frequently disposed to treat it in somewhat cavalier fashion. In view of the Midland's own policy, one cannot put all the blame onto Euston but matters at Ingleton seem to have been more than usually bitter. The classic statement attributed to the Midland general manager, James Allport is still worth quoting:

It is a very rare thing for me to go down to Carlisle without being turned out twice. I have seen twelve or fifteen passengers turned out at Ingleton and the same number at Tebay. . . . We have applied in vain for through carriages to Scotland over and over again. . . . They will not book through from Glasgow to London by us. . . . It is only recently that I had a correspondence with a family who particularly wished to come by the Midland; (from Glasgow to Derby) but they were refused and were sent by Crewe
F. S. WILLIAMS. *The Midland Railway* (1876)

The LNWR refused to stop its faster trains at Tebay to pick up Midland passengers, making it difficult for the latter company to compete for express traffic. Passengers had often to find their own way to the LNWR system and Allport complained of being conveyed to Tebay attached to a train of coal trucks. Further unnecessary hindrances took place to the Midland's traffic when it did eventually reach Carlisle and in complaining of this, the Midland was supported by the manager of the North British Railway who is reported to have said: '. . . there has been ill-will. There has been systematic delay'.

The Midland Railway was, however, somewhat more reluctant on this occasion to try what was fast becoming its standard remedy in such a situation—namely the promotion of a new line—for the territory involved was very much more severe than any hitherto attempted. Accordingly, several other proposals were made to improve the Midland's access to Carlisle via Low Gill and Tebay; but the antagonism between Derby and Euston had by now reached such proportions that no satisfactory solution could be found. In 1865, James Allport and John Crossley (the chief engineer) decided that another survey of the Pennines would be in order and having ascertained that one possible route did exist, it was not long before there was introduced a bill in Parliament for:

Enabling the Midland Railway Company to construct railways from Settle to Hawes, Appleby and Carlisle. . . .

It is easy, in retrospect, to feel that things need never have come to this, but in this brief coverage it is difficult to envisage the real hostility between Derby and Euston which is only touched on here. However, the divisions were very real and very deep, frequently lasting well beyond the grouping year of 1923. Even today one can still witness occasional signs of the old antagonisms in the scarcely veiled sneers about the 'other' line by the older railway servants!

The West Coast partners, chiefly the LNWR, but not forgetting the Caledonian Railway, strenuously fought against the bill, concentrating their objections on the use of and access to Carlisle Citadel station by the Midland—a vital part of the project as far as the latter was concerned. The Parliamentary campaign was conducted vigorously by both sides and at first it seemed as if the LNWR might succeed in blocking the proposal. However, by obtaining permission to gain access to Carlisle over North Eastern track from Petteril Bridge, the Midland side-stepped most of the objections from Euston and the bill was eventually passed. The LNWR did try to raise the question of overcrowding at Carlisle but since it had never before raised this issue, Parliament was not convinced of its merit.

There remained the question of what would happen to the Midland's traffic at Carlisle. The North British Railway was keen to take over the Edinburgh portion but the Glasgow and South Western Railway, which would have provided the link to Glasgow, was contemplating amalgamation with the Caledonian. As the Settle and Carlisle Act had now been passed, the attitude of the GSWR was a little disturbing to the Midland. However, after an extensive campaign, the GSWR was finally persuaded in 1867 to agree to amalgamation with the Midland instead.

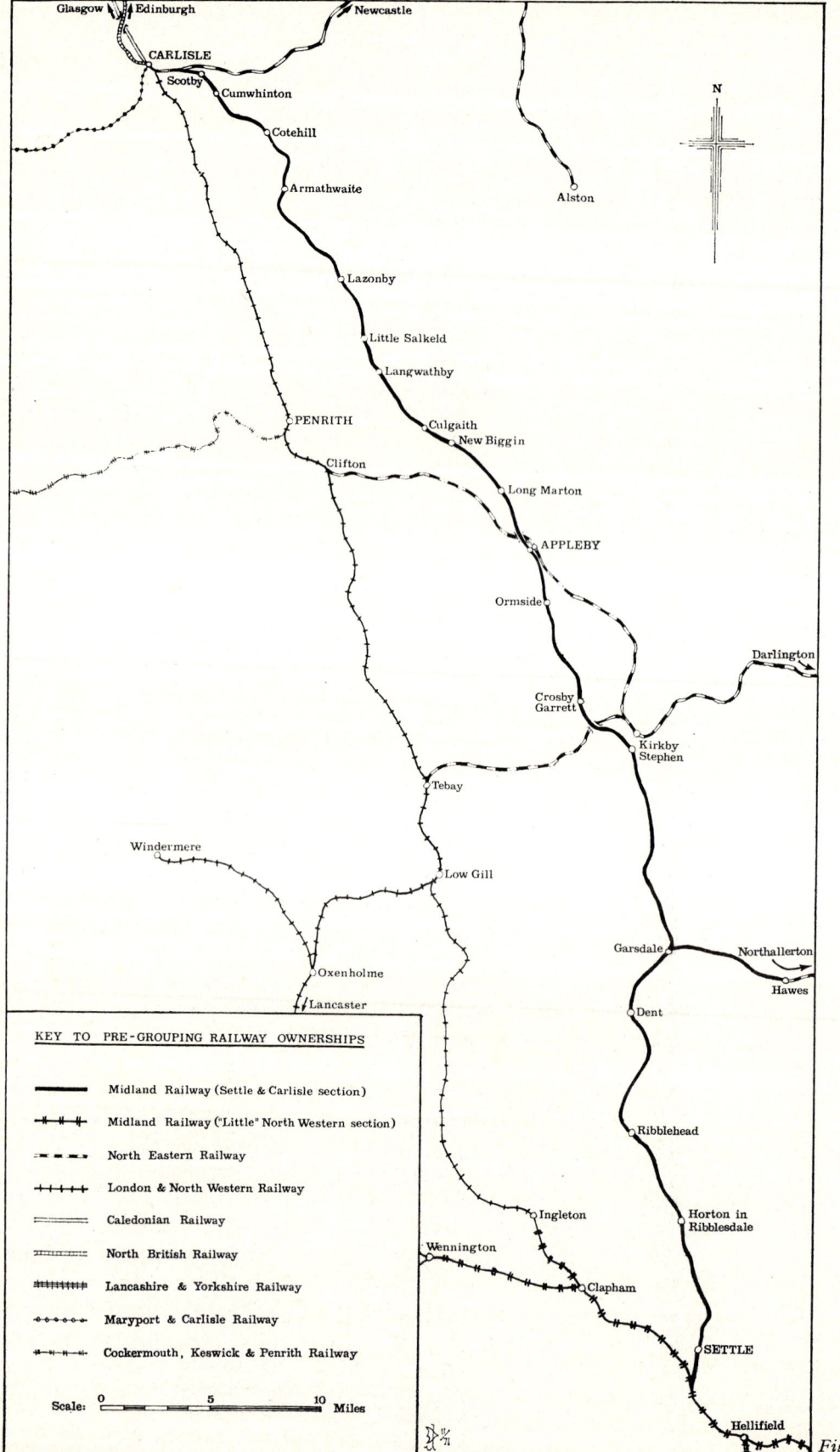

N

KEY TO PRE-GROUPING RAILWAY OWNERSHIPS

Midland Railway (Settle & Carlisle section)

Midland Railway ("Little" North Western section)

North Eastern Railway

London & North Western Railway

Caledonian Railway

North British Railway

Lancashire & Yorkshire Railway

Maryport & Carlisle Railway

Cockermouth, Keswick & Penrith Railway

Scale: 0   5   10 Miles

Fig. 1

This development, however, was rejected by the House of Lords because there was no physical connection between the two railways at that time. Nevertheless, relationships between the Midland and GSWR were not impaired and there was every prospect that the latter company, together with the NBR, would remain loyal to the Midland cause.

The abandonment proposal and its aftermath

Apart from one very short spell of activity in the Autumn of 1867, the Midland seemed strangely reluctant to start building the Carlisle line and the reason for this delay was apparent when, in 1869, the Midland and the LNWR sponsored a bill to abandon the Settle and Carlisle. It seems that the LNWR had offered to review conditions between Ingleton and Carlisle via Low Gill to the increased benefit of the Midland if the latter company would agree to abandon its own line. This rather strange reconciliation between the two companies probably resulted from a somewhat unofficial approach to the LNWR in 1867 by the secretary of the Midland Committee of the Railway Shareholders' Association, Mr W. Sale. It subsequently transpired that neither he nor his association had any official status as far as the Midland was concerned but they did provide evidence that some, at least, of the Midland shareholders were worried about the expense of the proposed new line and to the shrewd management of the LNWR, this may have seemed an opportune moment to re-open negotiations. The Midland was committed to great expense on its London and Manchester extensions and was, probably, more willing than it had been to try and reach some agreement; indeed, one might reasonably hold the view that the whole Settle and Carlisle project may have been nothing more than a gigantic bluff to force the LNWR to give better terms on the Shap Fell route. If this was the case, it proved an expensive bluff for the Abandonment Bill was rejected, largely as a result of strenuous opposition by the Lancashire and Yorkshire and North British Railways who were looking forward to

increased through traffic. This opposition was supplemented by that of influential local residents who wanted the railway in its own right.

The LNWR was now, therefore, faced with the actuality of a rival route to Scotland which, on completion, would almost certainly be followed by a revival of the Midland/GSWR amalgamation scheme. At this stage the cross-currents of inter-company politics became more than usually confused but the outcome was an attempt in 1871 to amalgamate the LNWR with the Lancashire and Yorkshire. Since this coincided with an equally strange marriage of interest between the Caledonian and the North British Railways, the Midland found itself in the somewhat ironic situation of owning a half completed line which it did not really want to build while the two principal objectors to its abandonment were contemplating fusion with the Midland's chief rivals!

Needless to say, the Derby directors were 'forced to consider their Scotch traffic' and the Midland/GSWR scheme was revived along with strenuous opposition to the rival proposals. This considerable jockeying for position in the North of England, combined with other schemes elsewhere in the country, drew public attention again to railways and caused a re-birth of the general feeling that competition was about to vanish. Not surprisingly, in 1872 as in 1853, Parliament again became very nervous and all the proposals, good or bad, were rejected and the status quo was restored.

This attitude on the part of Westminster was absolutely characteristic. As a result of its obsession over the supposed 'evils' of monopoly, Parliament quite failed to appreciate the actual and more damaging 'evils' of unbridled competition and did not seem at all to realise that the need for a comprehensive scheme of development was just as important as the more emotional issues. In consequence of this, railways grew up piecemeal and because control was negative rather than positive, Government policy lacked consistency. Private interests were often protected while the public interest was ignored which might have been more acceptable had the much desired competition materialised, but it frequently did not. The railways were surrounded with so many regulations in the interest of protecting the public that competition in its purest sense could never really exist; while the long term

FIG. 1 *System map indicating the pre-group ownership of railways in the area served by the Settle and Carlisle. After the 1923 grouping, most of the railways on this map became part of the LMS system. However, the North Eastern and North British lines were incorporated in the LNER. (Crown Copyright Reserved).*

PLATE 2 '... one possible route did exist ...' This view of Dent Head, taken in 1962, gives a clear impression of the terrain traversed by the Settle and Carlisle Railway as it negotiates the main watershed of the Pennines. It does not need much imagination to envisage the rail-less scene of over a century ago and to marvel at those Midland Railway engineers who looked across these hills and, without the benefit of any modern aids, planned their route. The train in the distance is the daily southbound pick-up freight. (Photo: D. Jenkinson.)

effect of this attitude to railway legislation was to make the railways singularly unsuited to fight back under 20th Century conditions until very recently—and then only by repealing some of the archaic laws. By entrusting railway matters to Parliament, they were frequently given inadequate attention and although many problems were better understood in 1872 than in 1853, the basic confusion still remained.

That Parliament did not need much excuse to reject any kind of union is well exemplified by the proposed Midland/GSWR amalgamation. This union being 'end-on' could scarcely have reduced competition but would certainly have increased efficiency, especially for the smaller Scottish company, but, although the bill had passed the Commons in 1867, when it was re-introduced in 1872, it inevitably became entangled with all the other emotional issues of that year and never came to fruition.

In many ways, it can be argued that railway policy of the 1870s was fifty years ahead of public opinion and political thought, in which latter case, the whole emphasis seems to have been on preventing possible and even hypothetical evil rather than promoting active good. The paradox is even more complete when one considers that at the same point in time, the North Eastern Railway had obtained what amounted to a virtual monopoly in one area of the country and is generally regarded as having been a very good railway.

One thing does seem certain; the LMS would have been far better able to stand up to the problems of the 1920s and 1930s had it not inherited at the 1923 grouping, not only all the petty jealousies of its constituent companies, but all the unnecessary competing lines as well, of which the Settle and Carlisle was perhaps the prime individual example. It seems more than coincidence too, that the first casualties to passenger services in this area, even before Dr Beeching, were the LYR link to Hellifield and the services on the Hawes branch. Moreover, even before the local passenger closures, the Settle and Carlisle had been diminishing in importance as a passenger line for some time, even if the freight traffic has managed to hold its own to a greater extent.

6

Chapter 2

The Local Aspects

So far, the Settle and Carlisle has been discussed in the context of the Midland's drive, not only for Scotland, but for independent outlets in many different directions. There were, however, local reasons for wanting a railway in these parts for its own sake. In 1865, amongst several other proposals for railways across the Pennines (in general over ambitious and abortive) there was promoted a bill for the North of England Union Railway. The prospectus of this line envisaged a course from Settle to Horton-in-Ribblesdale (where it was to have a junction for a branch to Clapham), through to Hawes (with a junction for Sedbergh), Leyburn, Richmond, Darlington and terminating at Carlton on the West Hartlepool Railway. Considerable traffic was envisaged. Coal supply was estimated from 60,000 to 80,000 tons per annum for the local residents, great play was made of the attractions of the scenery, the economic advantage of the rich pastures, the timber resources, mineral deposits and so forth and every attempt was to be made to accommodate the local residents:

The local traffic of such a district must necessarily be something very large and capable of the highest development. The proposed railway, placing the district upon a Main Trunk line in every direction will afford the most ample facilities for its exports and imports
NEUR *Prospectus* 1864.

Parliament viewed the NEUR proposals favourably and there is little doubt that, had not the Midland come forward with its Settle and Carlisle proposals, a railway would still have been constructed through Ribblesdale. However, when the MR first proposed the Settle and Carlisle line, the promoters of the NEUR promised to withdraw their bill if the MR would agree to provide the same, or similar local facilities on the Carlisle line. This the Midland undertook to do and by adopting the cause of the NEUR probably assured for itself a very wide measure of support for the Settle and Carlisle in the Ribblesdale/Wensleydale area.

Not only did the inhabitants of Ribblesdale and Wensleydale want a railway, but the reactions in the Eden Valley when the Settle and Carlisle bill was passed are worth recording. There was,

apparently, not one opposing landowner along its entire length. 'I have heard of only one dissentient voice in the whole of the Eden Valley' is the comment attributed to a farmer who sent over 5000 lbs of butter annually to Sheffield and who was thus looking forward to the line; and this comment apparently came from a gentleman who had a 'few trees he was partial to'. This could well refer to Sir R. Musgrave of Edenhall who originally opposed the line and then strenuously campaigned against the abandonment. Lord Wensleydale was an enthusiastic supporter and put the case of the local people who were anxious for direct communication, in order to send produce to the industrial areas. Church bells rang in Appleby when the bill passed the Commons and Matthew Thomson of Kirkby Stephen said that there was only one feeling among landowners—that the line would be of 'very great advantage'. It is not, therefore, surprising to note that when the Midland proposed to abandon the venture, local opposition was vociferous and a petition against abandonment was drawn up by local landowners which contained over 1600 signatures. It is one of the more curious tricks of fate that the ultimate destiny of the Midland's magnificent road to Carlisle may well be to do little more than provide a few of the local facilities envisaged by those 1600 signatories.

It is difficult to assess the weighting which Parliament gave to local opposition to abandonment. It must have had some effect but from all available evidence the need to meet local traffic did not alter in any way the alignment of the route itself. The Midland's main intention was to get to Carlisle and if the Abandonment Bill is proof of anything it is that the Midland did not think too much about the local aspects once the company felt it had a satisfactory alternative solution. In fact, during the Parliamentary proceedings relating to the abandonment of the Settle and Carlisle, the Midland's spokesman claimed that the Midland had never represented the scheme as one for local traffic. The Midland's view was that if the Settle and Carlisle was abandoned, Wensleydale would still get its local branch line (presumably built by the North Eastern Railway). As for the local communities in the northern part of the Eden Valley, presumably the Midland felt that they might well revive the idea of a branch off the existing NER Eden Valley line if they needed a railway so badly. One has only to look again at the NEUR prospectus:

The line will be an easy one; there are no engineering difficulties, there will be no tunnels or any other heavy or extraordinary works
Prospectus: North of England Union Railway, 1864–65

Clearly Lord Wharncliffe and his supporters were not envisaging the sort of railway which the Midland had in mind.

The final indication that the Settle and Carlisle was never really thought of by its promoters as a local line is probably the fact that the abandon-

ment proposal was rejected without the need to present the landowners' petition to Parliament. In other words, the rejection of abandonment was based on the broader issues of railway politics rather than local petition. These broader issues may seem, in retrospect, to have been a little trivial but were, apparently, sufficient to convince the Parliament of the day that the Settle and Carlisle was desirable solely as a through route without ever really considering its local desirability.*

It does therefore, seem very clear that the sole reason for the presence of the Settle and Carlisle in its present form was the basic desire of the Midland to reach Scotland. Although the line itself was very nearly not built, the concept of the route was a typically Midland solution to its own peculiar problems. As has been indicated in the case of London and Manchester, and could be equally well exemplified in other areas (e.g. the Erewash Valley), this was the characteristic 'Midland Method'. Therefore, the Settle and Carlisle should not be regarded as an isolated example but more correctly as the most spectacular expression of a policy for independent outlets which had been forced on the company in several other locations as a result of its geographical position in the centre of England.

It was, however, not in the nature of the Midland Railway Company to pursue 'half measures' once embarked upon a course of action; therefore the presence of the imposing structures and buildings 'en route' is not necessarily indicative of any great expectation of local originating traffic. More probably, these features can, in fact, be regarded as an accidental by-product of the Midland Railway's general policy in relation to its status as an enlightened 19th Century industrial concern. Although the Midland Railway conceived the Settle and Carlisle exclusively as a through route, as a result of the NEUR it found itself in duty bound to make some sort of provision for local needs. Being the Midland, it seems entirely in character that it should do so in a somewhat ostentatious way in the context of the likely traffic it might thereby attract. Nevertheless, the facilities initially provided for local traffic do afford some insight into the local geography of the day and will, therefore, be considered in due course.

PLATES 3 and 4 *Local aspects of the Settle and Carlisle. Plate 3 (above) illustrates one of the many private owner freight wagons associated with firms along the route—John Delaney Ltd. of Settle—while below is depicted the celebrated Allendale wolf. This creature escaped from private grounds in 1904 and did so much damage to sheep that hunts were arranged for its capture. After some 40 sheep had been killed, the wolf was finally cut in half by a Midland Railway express near Cumwhinton. It was sewn together for this picture to be taken—apparently minus one leg! (Photos: Author's collection.)*

THE ALLENDALE WOLF.
KILLED ON THE RAILWAY NEAR CARLISLE
DEC: 29TH 1904.

---

*'North of Leeds', P. E. Baughan, Ch. X

DENT STATION   *A. D. Whitehead*

PART II

The Line in its Environment

PLATE 5 DENT IN THE SNOW

    The weather and its antics are an ever present hazard on the Settle-Carlisle and it is somewhat rare for a year to go by entirely free from its influence. Snow is, perhaps, the most spectacular hazard and the isolated outpost at Dent has traditionally been used as a centre for snow clearance works—possibly on the basis that if the line can be cleared here then it can be cleared anywhere!

    Notwithstanding the extensive snow fences on the hillsides, if the snow really gets a grip then nothing can prevent a blockage of the line—as the winters of 1947 and 1963 amply demonstrated. On 16th February 1963 the situation became particularly bad when the Kingmoor snowploughs came to grief just north of Dent Station. This picture was taken by a member of the footplate crew and has been kindly loaned by BR.

Chapter 3

A Brief Discussion
of Methods

An old Yorkshire farmer is alleged to have informed the first surveyors that there was not enough level ground to build a house between Settle and Carlisle, never mind a railway. In many respects this puts in a nutshell the essential problem of building a railway through mountainous areas, namely the finding of a route. In presenting this discussion of the problem, the writer freely acknowledges the fact that it draws heavily on the methodology of J. H. Appleton in attempting to provide answers to the questions 'Where?' and 'Why there?' in relation to the precise alignment of the Settle and Carlisle railway. The only reason it has been thought desirable to repeat the basic principles here is in order to make for a less disjointed narrative than would be the case by making cross-reference to the appropriate parts of Dr Appleton's book.*

General Principles

A railway is, first and foremost an economic element. It represents a flow of traffic, a factor

*'The Geography of Communications in Great Britain', J. H. Appleton 1962

affecting the location of industry or perhaps a significant topic in the study of population distribution. This is well known and therefore the economist *must* consider the railway, albeit from a rather scientific standpoint. The railway is, however, something else. It is, above all, *there*. It forms part of the landscape and its appearance, shape and relation to the land surface are not haphazard but meaningful.

One cannot altogether divorce this second factor from the economic motive. The purpose of the railway, its commercial 'raison d'etre', may have a profound influence on its outward appearance and when discussing the Settle and Carlisle, one cannot ignore this; for the line may have taken on a very different 'look' had the basic motive for building it been different. In fact, as has been seen, it may never have been there at all. The essential terms of reference were to get through to Carlisle and much of the subsequent character of the railway can be explained by the remarkable way in which every possible assistance from an often unfriendly physical landscape was utilised, consciously or

PLATE 6 *This early view of Ribblehead Viaduct under construction came into the author's possession quite recently. It clearly shows the navvy shanty town of Batty Green, the method of constructing the viaduct itself and the bleak nature of the land surface. The authorship of this picture is not known, but it is one of a series taken c. 1872-3, others of which are included later in the book.*

PLATE 7 *This unusual view of Kirkby Stephen was taken on 6th August 1966 and depicts a BR Class 9F 2–10–0 (believed to be No. 92093) heading a southbound freight. The picture clearly shows the pastoral setting of the station (it is more than two miles from the town) and virtually all the structures visible are of MR origin. Note the single storey railway cottages in the right foreground. (Photo: S. E. Teasdale.)*

otherwise, in the achieving of this objective.

In consequence of this and selecting a few examples at random, one finds the line poised 300 feet above and two miles away from Kirkby Stephen and no less than 600 feet above and over four miles from Dent at the stations bearing these names. This by-passing, particularly in the case of Kirkby Stephen, is only explicable in terms of the overall concept of the route and effectively demonstrates, if further proof were needed, that local aspects were largely secondary considerations to the builders of the line. Thus, the way in which the line owes its outward appearance and location to the problem of satisfying one overriding economic consideration is an all-essential aspect in the study of this particular railway landscape.

The *precise* relation of the railway to the land surface reflects, of course, the fitting together of two variables; the railway and the surface itself. While a railway should, ideally, be straight and level, this is rarely the case; the exact nature of the departure from the ideal depending largely on the function of the line itself and the nature of the surface over which it is built. Inevitably, compromises in gradient and curvature have to be made and it is no small tribute to the original engineer of the Settle and Carlisle that there is not one speed restriction along the whole route below the overall limit for the line.* Moreover, although built in 1869–75, the ruling gradient of 1:100 fits in very well with the recommendations for main line railways in the Town and Country Planning Textbook of 1950, some 80 years later.

The Importance of Landforms

When studying landforms and communications, it is important to remember that some of the accepted simplifications—e.g. railways keep to valleys and roads are independent of them—need more critical examination if a true picture is to emerge. A valley provides a means to an end, but it is only when the ultimate objective is known that one can discuss the usefulness, or lack of it, of any specific valley. Indeed it is

---

*'Main Lines across the Border', O. S. Nock and E. Treacy, p. 89

10

not a valley as such which is required but a strip of level and straight land. This can and often does rule out such features as immature valleys with no real floor and interlocking valley side spurs; while an abrupt change in floor level, such as might be represented by a waterfall, or series of waterfalls, could render an otherwise suitable valley quite impossible for a railway line. In the particular case under survey, it is hoped to show that most of the valleys have been, in general, favourable to the line of the railway.

One must also consider the modifications to landforms produced by glaciation as these are often of a vital nature to communications. Nor should one forget the effect of the underlying geology on the structure of the area which, in many cases, can prove the dominant factor in the subsequent shape of the surface landforms—frequently so in the area under discussion. There is a certain inevitable quality to the route of the Settle and Carlisle railway which is all the more remarkable when one realises that the type of approach which the modern student can bring to bear on the problem was in its infancy, if indeed it was born at all, when the first surveyors looked out over the terrain a century ago. It is, therefore, all the more interesting when looked at in the light of modern studies to find that the line does in fact follow the only favourable landforms which Nature provided.

The significance of river systems

Railways almost invariably reflect, in their final alignment, the alterations of upland and lowland areas; and the part played by the evolution of river systems in the creation of these areas is, therefore, of vital importance. Level surfaces are undoubtedly useful but, since a railway cannot, by its very nature, cope with a sudden change in surface level, a more undulating but otherwise favourable surface is frequently better than two perfectly flat plateaux separated by a 200 foot step. This balance between upland and lowland is usually reflected in the drainage system and not infrequently caused by it; therefore the evolution of the rivers in the Pennines is also important and it will be shown how they, too, have played their part.

Visual Aspects

It will be appreciated that the visual appearance of a railway will reflect all the above considerations but, in addition, it will also mirror two further variables. One of these is the extent to which provision is made for local traffic and the other is the architectural style of the structures and buildings along the line—and these two aspects will largely be influenced by the particular company which built the railway.

Although in the case under discussion, the primary objective was Carlisle, thus causing the by-passing of certain settlements, it nevertheless remained true that the Midland Railway was under an obligation to provide local traffic facilities once it had taken over the NEUR proposals. This it did in the grand manner and, employing a distinctive architectural style in the process, produced a chain of stations and structures along the route which add an important element to the total scene.

These, then, in outline, are some of the considerations which must be analysed when discussing the fitting of a railway into the physical landscape. Concluding this discussion of methods, therefore, it would seem to be useful to restate the problems the engineers faced. Their task was to build a through route to Carlisle from the best jumping-off point on the Midland system, as easily graded as possible and to main line standards of curvature. The route had to be as direct as possible with a minimum of detour, bearing in mind that the 'easiest' route over the fells was already occupied by the Lancaster and Carlisle Railway. Overlaying all these considerations, the line also had to provide for the local traffic of the area.

Chapter 4

The Geological Background

The area traversed by the Settle and Carlisle railway falls naturally into two main structural divisions, the dividing point between which lying somewhere near Appleby. At this point, the line in going north, leaves the mountain section and enters upon the Eden valley proper, although it has been following this river from the summit of the line at Ais Gill. The upper part of the Eden valley is, however, much more closely allied to the mountain section from the structural point of view and is more conveniently dealt with in that section.

The Southern Section—Settle Junction to Appleby (Map—Figure 2)

The geology and structure of this part of Northern England has been so comprehensively covered by other writers that there is no reason to repeat it all here. Accordingly, therefore,

attention will be confined in the main to those aspects of structure which have affected the railway.

Including part of the main watershed of England, the area exhibits to a marked degree the control of geological conditions on structural forms which, in places, has proved vital in the alignment of the railway. The flat topped plateau is the characteristic end-product of the structure, but it is fortunate for the railway that it is well dissected by valleys because the lowest plateau which might otherwise be suitable, the extensive surface at about 1300 feet, is too high for the

PLATE 8 (below) *This picture of Rebuilt Royal Scot 4-6-0 No. 46112 'Sherwood Forester' heading past Pen-y-Ghent with the down 'Thames-Clyde Express' not only demonstrates the generally open nature of the upper Ribble Valley, but also clearly indicates the widespread almost level surface of the land at the approximately 1300ft level (partly obscured by the smoke from the engine). (Photo: Eric Treacy.)*

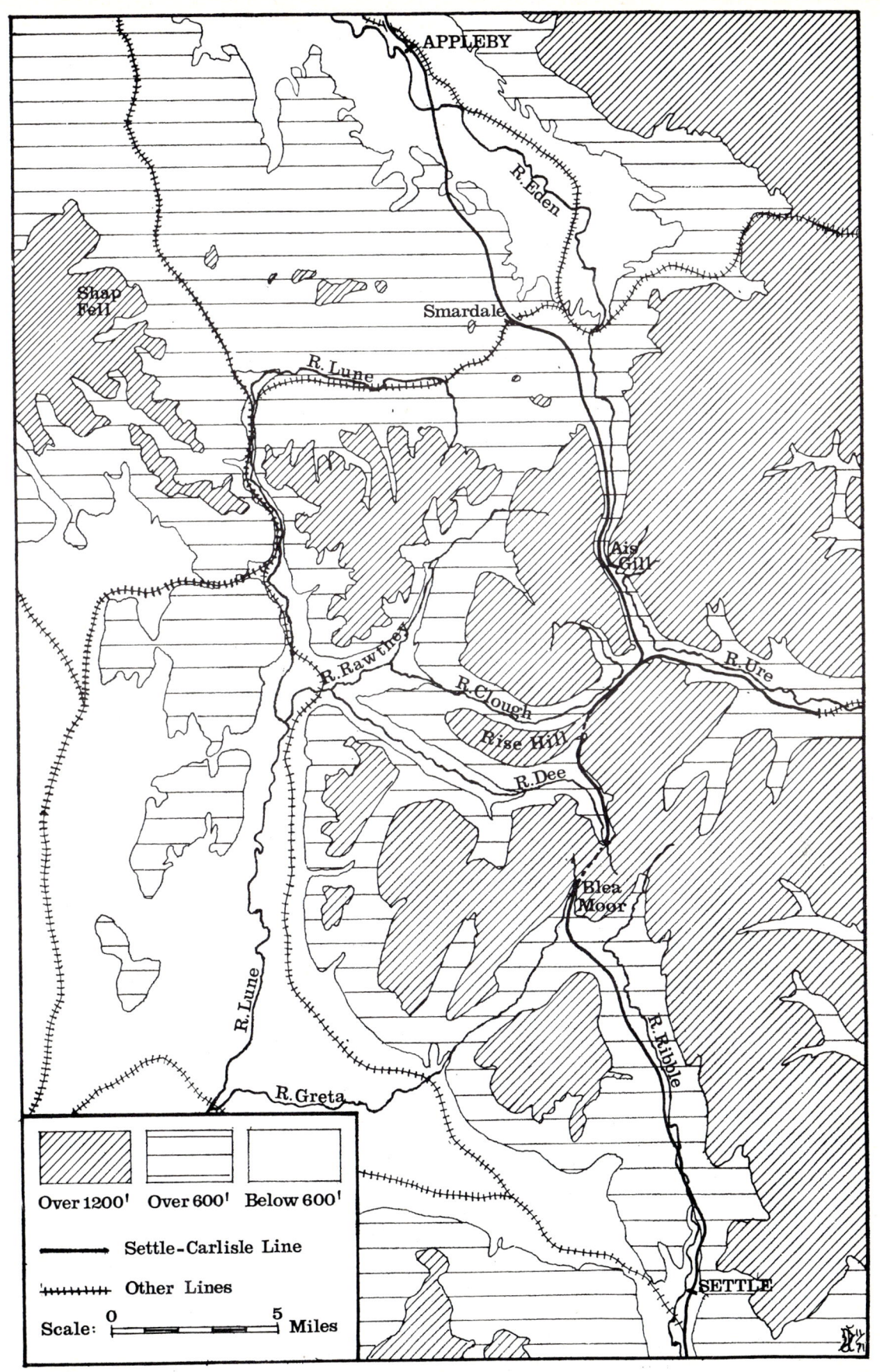

FIG. 2 *Relief map showing the southern portion of the Settle and Carlisle railway in relation to the principal rivers and hill masses.* (*Crown Copyright Reserved*).

railway line (Plate 8). The influence of structure, therefore, is not in the provision of a level surface but rather in the way in which the structure has affected the alignment of the valleys within the area. The many valleys in these parts vary considerably in nature. Swaledale is narrow and deep while Wensleydale is wider and more mature as are, for the most part, the valleys used by the railway. This latter fact, fortuitous though it may have been, is not, however, anything like as important as the orientation of the valleys in relation to the desired route. It is fortunate, therefore, that this critical mountain section of the route traverses a region where the overall structural influence has been a help rather than a hindrance.

The region consists of the major part of the rigid rock mass known to geologists as the Askrigg block which has remained remarkably stable since very early geological times. It is also clear that before the present surface rocks were laid down (the well known Carboniferous Limestone and Millstone Grit series), the Askrigg block had been eroded to an almost level surface.* This advanced stage of erosion has considerably assisted the widespread horizontal stratification of the limestone and later rock systems and in rendering it fairly stable and free from folding has freed the area from the contorted landforms which frequently occur as a result of violent earth movement. The present day rocks, therefore, are still as essentially level as when they were first created.

The surface is not, of course, exactly level and does, in fact, slope very gently towards the east which explains why most of the rivers eventually drain into the North Sea. However, although the area is very stable, it has not remained entirely free from earth movement. In fact, and significantly as far as the railway is concerned, the present drainage pattern has been cut into an uplifted Tertiary peneplain† which has warped slightly.‡ Thus, although the bulk of the surface water does eventually reach the east coast, the slight downwarp in the south has caused the upper valleys of the Ribble, Aire and Wharfe to be aligned much more nearly north-

south than east-west. This north-south alignment in Ribblesdale is of far more value than the precise nature of the valley itself and is one of the key factors in the presence of a routeway at all in an area where the bulk of the surface drainage is in a direction almost at right angles to the desired course of the railway.

Where the line follows the watershed between Ribblehead and Ais Gill is, in many respects, the most interesting area of all, but here, the purely structural influence is nowhere near as strong as it is in the provision of a north-south alignment in Ribblesdale. The route along the watershed owes its course much more to the history of drainage development and will, therefore, be considered later.

Apart from the basic structure already mentioned, the edge of the Askrigg block is marked by a series of faults in the rocks. These vary considerably in their outward appearance in the landscape from the spectacular to the non-existent. Some of these faults lie directly in the path of the railway and therefore impinge on it but not always in the direct physical sense. For example the South Craven Fault gives rise to the tremendous wall of limestone running west from Settle—Giggleswick Scar—but it is fortunate that the Ribble has cut a gap through the scarp near Settle or else the railway would have had a colossal task in surmounting the obstacle and may, indeed, never have been conceived at all. By contrast the North Craven Fault which crosses the Ribble near Stainforth, although producing little in the way of a spectacular feature to the eye, does bring valuable rocks to the surface which have been exploited commercially and hence have provided a source of revenue for the railway. There is a nick point* in the river bed here, associated with the hard edge of the Askrigg block, and the problems of surmounting this feature will be considered later.

North of Horton-in-Ribblesdale, the area is basically free from faults until the upper Eden valley in Mallerstang where Birkett Tunnel was cut through the complex Dent fault which caused comment even when the line was building (Plate 22). However, in the main, the structural influence in the mountains is confined to the provision of a stable, horizontally bedded platform into which the subsequent valley

---

* 'British Landscapes Through Maps—The Yorkshire Dales', C. A. M. King (1960), p. 3
† An almost level surface created during the Tertiary period of geological history
‡ C. A. M. King, p. 10

* A sudden increase in the river gradient associated with a fall in level of the valley

PLATE 9 *The contrast between road and rail engineering of the mid-Victorian period is clearly shown at Dent Head where the massive viaduct pier on the left quite dwarfs the bridge built to carry the road when diverted to make way for the viaduct.* (*Photo: D. Jenkinson.*)

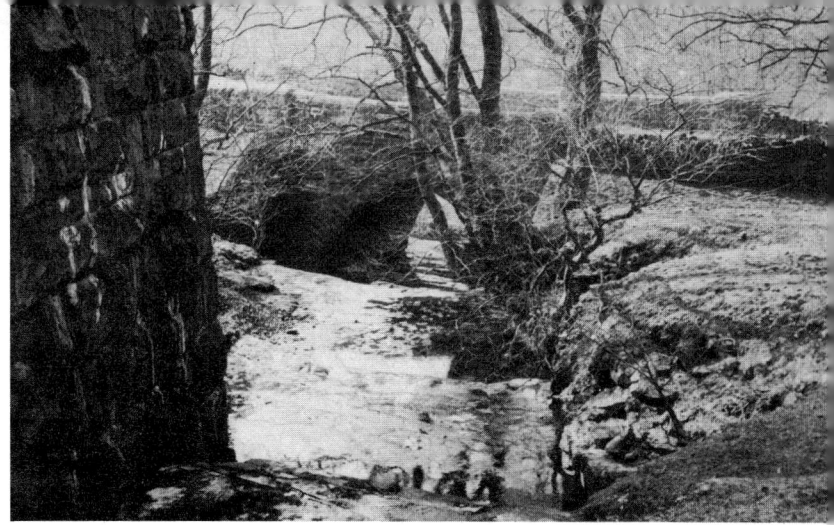

pattern could be incised; the slight flexures in this platform giving rise to valleys orientated in such a way as to be eminently usable by the railway.

The Eden Valley—Appleby to Carlisle (Map—Fig 3)

Here, by far the most dominant structural influence has been the great Pennine escarpment whose outcrop has determined the basic alignment of the Eden valley after leaving the watershed area. This great wall of hills stretches in an unbroken line down the whole length of the Eden north of Appleby and forms a most striking backdrop to the wooded slopes and green fields of this region. On leaving Birkett Tunnel, the railway runs through gradually more open country until north of Appleby, the regional contrast is so marked that it is difficult to believe

PLATE 10 *This photograph, taken between Long Marton and Appleby, clearly shows the continuous nature of the great Pennine escarpment (in the distance) and its dominant position in relation to the Eden Valley. The train itself is the southbound 'Border Venturer' on 13th May 1978 headed by Class 9F 2-10-0 No. 92220 'Evening Star', normally based at the National Railway Museum. This was only the second 'Return to Steam' trip on the line and was the first occasion that 'Evening Star' had traversed the route.* (*Photo: Peter Robinson.*)

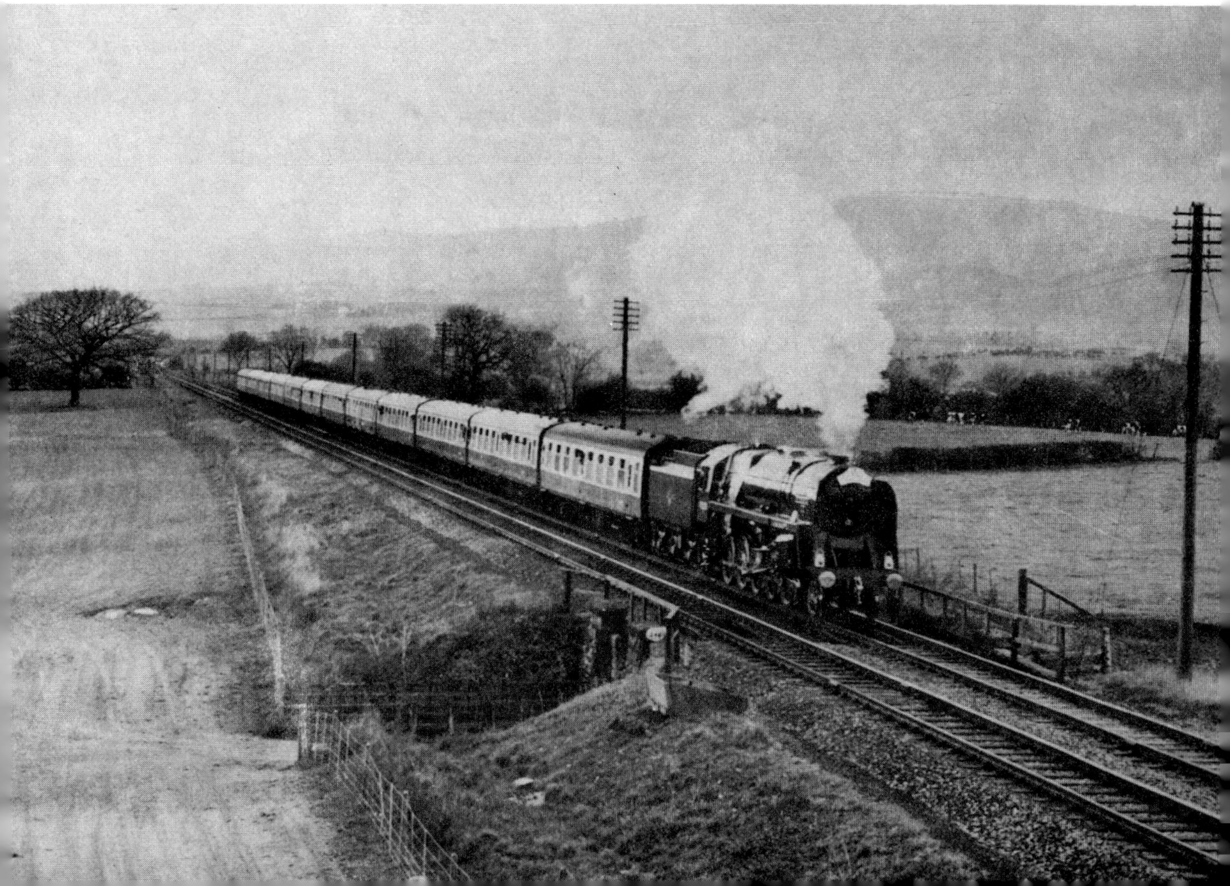

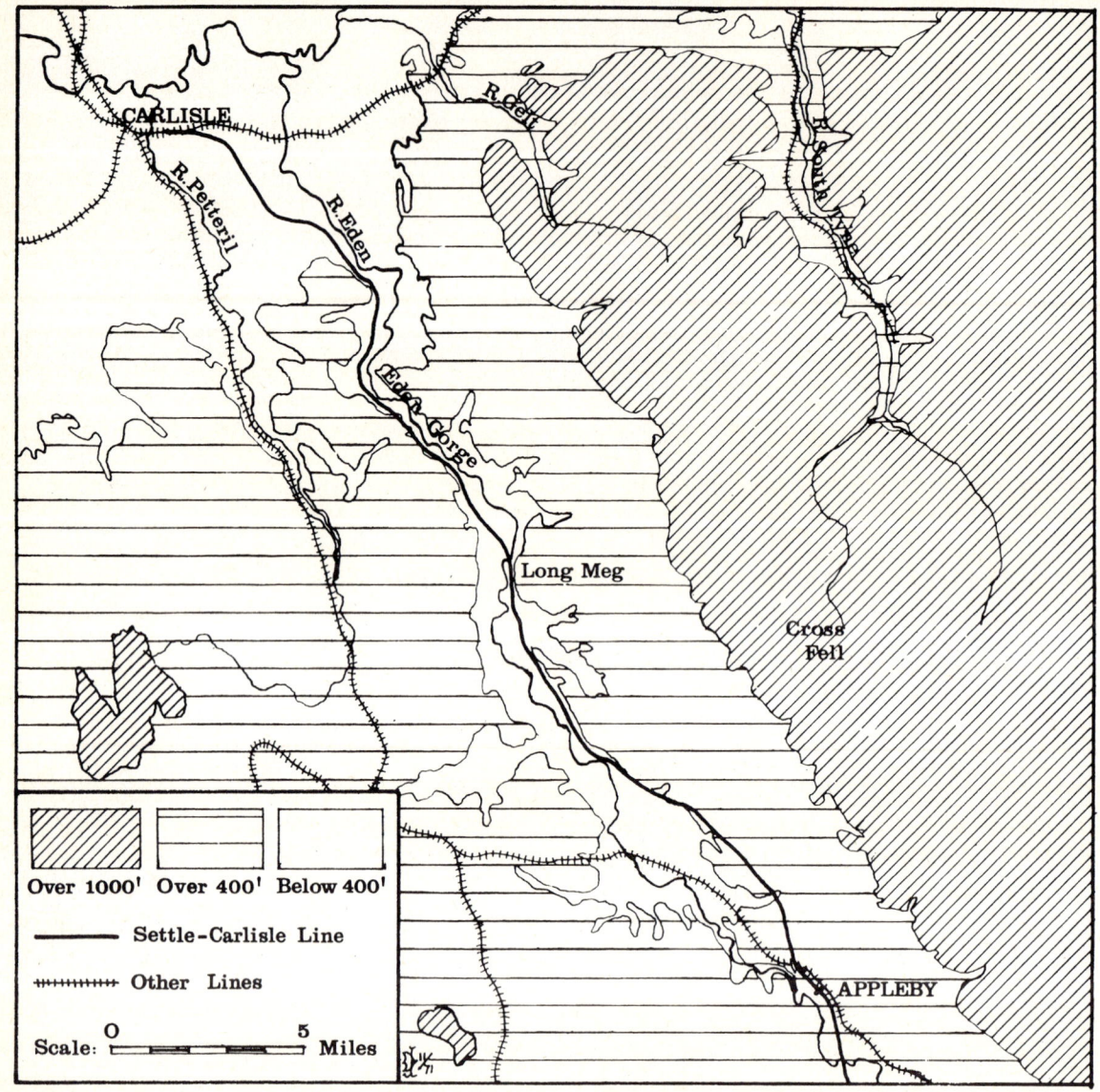

FIG. 3 *Relief map showing the northern portion of the Settle and Carlisle railway in relation to the Eden valley and the Pennine escarpment. (Crown Copyright Reserved.)*

that one is travelling the same route that was so recently characterised by bleak moorland and bare rock outcrops (Plate 11). The Eden valley is, of course, floored by red sandstone, inserted like a wedge between the mountains of the Lake District on the west and the Pennines on the east, but its presence here and hence much of the character of the scenery, is as much a product of the structure as the flat topped mountains hemming in the head of Ribblesdale. The influence here, however, is much less sophisticated than in the southern half of the line, since the Eden valley simply follows the foot of the escarpment—a perfectly orientated route albeit not without its own engineering problems.

In summary, therefore, it seems fair to say that, in spite of the formidable engineering problems and the hilly nature of the country, the structure was such as to render possible rather than bar the provision of a route. The provision of properly aligned valleys was clearly of prime importance but since the main structure can do little more than determine the basic valley trends, it remains to be seen in what way they could be utilised. This aspect is much more dependent on subsequent valley evolution which will now be considered.

PLATE II *The quaint station at Culgaith (now closed) was set in delightfully pastoral country and this high summer picture of a northbound freight headed by a BR Birmingham Type 2 Bo-Bo diesel gives a good impression of the scenery at this point. (Photo: Peter Robinson.)*

PLATE 12 *This view of the Eden valley just south of Armathwaite gives a very clear indication of the generally more lush and less rugged scenery associated with the red sandstone country in the northern section of the Settle and Carlisle. For clarity, the railway is marked with a pecked line in the middle distance. (Photo: D. Jenkinson.)*

ARMATHWAITE STATION

Chapter 5

The Railway in relation to the evolution of Landforms

Before considering individual cases, one must again emphasise the overall concept. Clearly the line was going to have to climb in order to surmount the obstacles in its path, but for how long and to what altitude? Once this question has been answered, the precise location of the line in the landscape can be the more readily interpreted.

It has already been explained how the basic elements of the route, the Eden valley and Ribblesdale, were more or less predetermined by the structure. On this basis, therefore, in order to get out of the Eden valley and link up with the southern portion, the line was going to have to climb to at least 1150 feet at Ais Gill Moor, the lowest point on the watershed at which the line could cross from the west flowing to the eastern orientated drainage systems. The line could not conceivably have crossed the watershed at much less than this height because of the large area of ground at about this 1150 foot level (Plate 13). A summit height of as little as 50 feet less would have involved miles of extra cutting and tunnelling between Ais Gill and Garsdale alone, not to mention probably longer tunnels at Blea Moor and Rise Hill as well—and these were destined to be bad enough as they were. The question, therefore, resolved itself into whether any further climbing would be necessary

from the Ais Gill area in order to link up with the head of Ribblesdale.

If this section between Ais Gill and Ribblehead seems to assume a dominant place in the writings on the Settle and Carlisle railway it is because in it lies the key to the whole line. That the railway was built at all testifies that the project was possible but it is in the way it was achieved in relation to the natural landforms that the interest lies. For convenience, this relationship will be considered in four sections; the lower and upper Eden valley, Ribblesdale and the mountain region, remembering that in the basic sense they are interdependent.

The Lower Eden Valley—Appleby to Petterill Bridge

In many ways, this section presented the least problem to the surveyors. Not that there were no problems, but the lack of necessity for heavy climbing north of Appleby made the finding of a route a little more simple. From Petterill Bridge to Ais Gill is some 46 miles whereas from Settle Junction to Blea Moor is less than 15. Accordingly, the line can keep to a much more level course north of Appleby, falling less than 500 feet in some 30 miles, mostly in the last six or seven miles north of Edenbrows. This in itself is logical since the gradient of the line bears quite a close

PLATE 13 *Ais Gill Moor looking south towards the summit of the line—marked by the overbridge. This picture illustrates the wide tract of almost level ground at this point and demonstrates why the summit of the line could not reasonably have been much, if any lower than its existing height— see also Fig. 12, page 32. (Photo: D. Jenkinson.)*

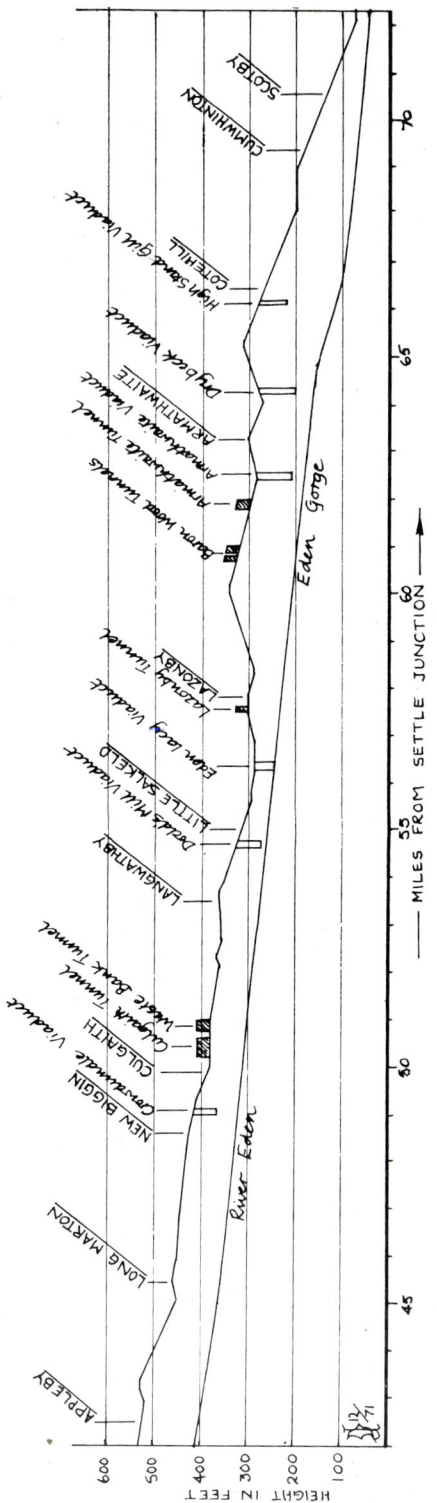

FIG. 4 *Gradient Profile; Appleby-Carlisle. This profile shows the level of the railway in relation to the valley floor level of the river Eden at its closest adjacent point. Note how the railway has to climb further away from the valley floor to negotiate the Eden gorge.*

relationship to the profile of the Eden except where the line crosses a series of minor summits in negotiating the Eden gorge near Armathwaite and Barons Wood (Figure 4). Doubtless the line, coming south from Carlisle, could have climbed higher before reaching Appleby but in so doing would have sacrificed much of the advantage of the valley and incurred rather heavier earthworks. It would also have by-passed most of the intermediate settlements associated with the river, including probably Appleby itself. Although the line was, essentially, surveyed as a trunk route, these Eden valley settlements could be served without detriment to the overall scheme of things and since they gave some promise of originating traffic, it doubtless seemed the sensible thing to pass close to them. In passing it is interesting to note that these intermediate settlements retained their facilities long after the passing stations on the otherwise more important Shap Fell route lost theirs. As it is, therefore, the line closely follows the river and, south of Appleby, the climb to Ais Gill is no worse than that from Settle to Blea Moor. Thus the line gets the best of both worlds. By keeping to the valley it can, for the most part, maintain easy grades *and* keep closer to the intermediate settlements than it can in the hills to the south.

How, then, does the line take its place as a part of the Eden valley scenery? In general, a well established river valley, by having a fairly flat floor, lends itself to utilisation by railways. The river itself probably winds to and fro across the width of the valley in a manner too sharp for the railway to follow, but the floor itself is frequently level across its whole width. Thus, if the railway keeps well to *one side* of the valley floor, it can often gain the advantage of the fairly level valley floor surface without having to cross and re-cross the river by bridge or viaduct. The Eden valley shows just such characteristics, for example north of Little Salkeld (Figure 5), but, somewhat surprisingly, the line keeps to the valley sides some 50–100 feet *above* river level. This, although it has the effect of reducing the amount of bridgework necessary to overcome meanders, at the same time increases the amount of earthworks on the valley sides and, therefore, merits further investigation.

A perusal of the map and the ground itself, makes it quite clear that although the Eden has a flat valley floor, it also has an important secondary

PLATE 14 *This illustration, taken looking north from the flank of Waste Bank, shows the course of the railway between Waste Bank and Langwathby. The valley side 'step' alluded to in the exit is marke by the bank of trees in the middle distance. The Eden can be seen to the left of this bank of trees, some 50–100 feet below rail level. (Photo: D. Jenkinson.)*

PLATE 15 *This picture, looking towards Langwathby from just north of the bank of trees shown in the previous plate, illustrates the generally level nature of the land surface some 100 feet above river level in this part of the Eden Valley. The course of the railway is marked with a pecked line. (Photo: D. Jenkinson.)*

LANGWATHBY STATION

PLATES 16/17 *These two views of Eden Lacy (Long Meg) viaduct demonstrate how the railway utilises the close opposition of the valley side 'steps' to cross the river just south of Lazonby. The approach embankments, although still quite large, are nothing like as big as they would have been had the Eden crossing been made further south. The right hand view (taken looking south) clearly shows that the railway is some 50 feet or so above the level of the river flood plain. (Photos: D. Jenkinson.)*

RAIL LEVEL

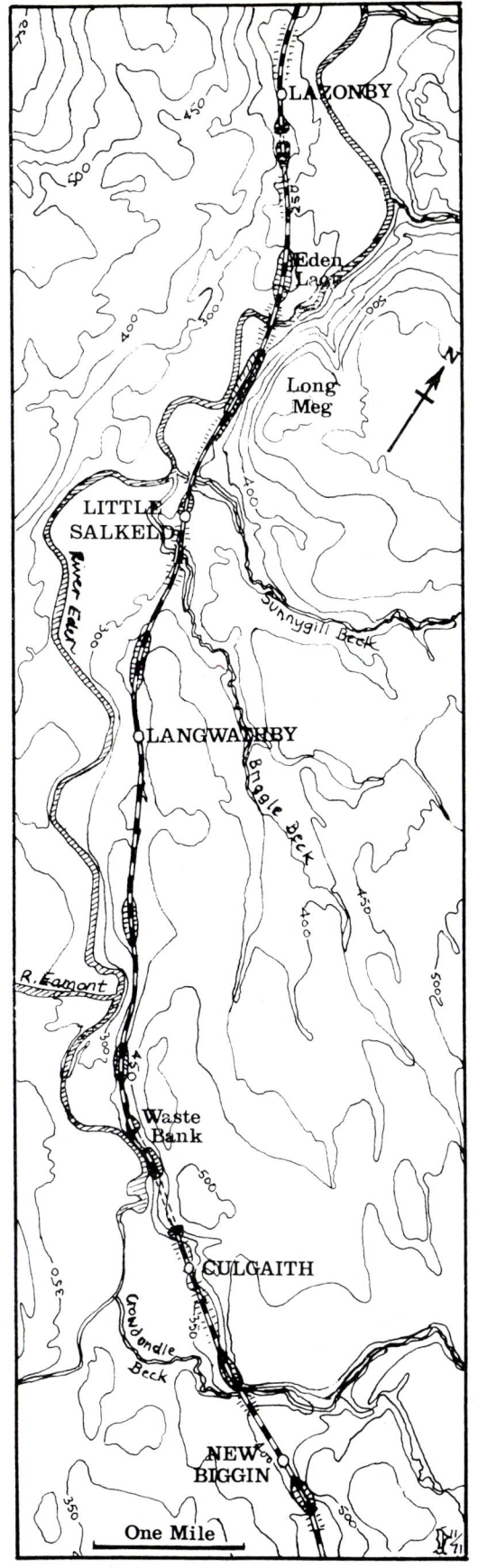

feature in the shape of a step in the valley side quite close to the river. Above this step, the valley levels off again, often for a considerable distance from the river (Plate 14). This fact is mirrored in the way in which many of the settlements such as Culgaith, Langwathby and Lazonby, tend to be sited on this slight bluff some 50–100 feet above the river. Had the railway been built in the conventional fashion, at or near river level, it would have by-passed these villages at a lower level. Furthermore, if the line had kept to the valley floor, it could not have utilised the, in general, more extensive level surface above this valley side step as it does for several miles south of Langwathby (Plate 15). Lastly, had the line kept right in the valley bottom, it would have been faced with a much more difficult problem when leaving the river at Appleby at the start of the long climb to Ais Gill.*

It is, one feels, significant that the line only crosses the Eden north of Appleby where these valley side steps, in the shape of the 300 foot contours, come sufficiently close together for them to be only half a mile apart on the opposite sides of the river (Eden Lacy viaduct—Plates 16 and 17).

Therefore, by using the slightly higher ground, the line still manages to find itself in close juxtaposition to the Eden valley settlements but in a much better position for embarking on the climb to Ais Gill once south of Appleby. This town, therefore, seems to mark a significant change in the relationship between the railway and the Eden valley. North of Appleby, the railway runs in close juxtaposition to the river and while managing to sacrifice none of its main line characteristics, can still manage to pass close to numerous settlements; whereas southwards from this point, the problem of gaining height becomes paramount.

Even so, there are, in this straightforward section north of Appleby, several places illustra-

*F. S. Williams (p. 537) also mentions the prone-ness to flooding of this portion of the Eden valley which may have been an additional contributory factor to the chosen route

FIG. 5 *Sketch map of the railway between New Biggin and Lazonby; contours at 50 ft intervals. The map attempts to portray the valley side 'step' in the Culgaith-Waste Bank area and again nearer to Long Meg. Note how close together the 300 ft contours come on opposite sides of the river at Eden Lacy. (Crown Copyright Reserved.)*

tive of the control which physical features can occasion and these are worthy of further investigation. The first example north of Appleby is at Culgaith tunnel (Plate 18). Cut through the red marl, this tunnel was only built at the cost of encroaching on the river, which had to be diverted, thereby causing a shift in the county boundary.* The problem seems to have resulted from the fact that the village itself is so close to the river that to tunnel further east would have undermined the settlement, while to by-pass the village entirely to the east would have forced the line to climb some 100 feet in half a mile or so north of Newbiggin in order to surmount the steep valley side—or make an even more lengthy tunnel to overcome the hazard. As it is, a fairly hefty viaduct and cutting are needed to overcome the problem caused by Crowdundle Beck cutting a rather steep sided and asymmetric valley as it joins the Eden (Plate 19).

Further north, at Little Salkeld, is another example which emphasises the through nature of the line. Conceivably, the line could have

*F. S. Williams, p. 535

crossed the river to call at Great Salkeld, a much bigger village than the first named. However, the potential traffic was presumably not deemed of sufficient importance to justify the diversion and the line stays on the right bank until Eden Lacy. At this point, some difficulty was, apparently found in getting foundations for the viaduct, but a far more serious problem was presented by the Eden gorge north of Lazonby.

The first surveyors must have had rather a tricky job in deciding the correct alignment

through this part of the valley, for the normally open nature of the countryside near the river changes remarkably between Lazonby and Armathwaite (Plate 20). If the route had been placed too close to the river level, the curvature involved in following the bends would frequently have been very severe but on the other hand, to climb right out of the valley would have involved unduly steep gradients. The line, therefore, compromises at a position on the valley side which allows the ruling gradient to be maintained, along with main line standards of curvature, yet still makes use of the way through provided in the first place by the river (Figure 6). This compromise position was to cause a few problems to the engineers.

Confident predictions had, apparently, been made by the local people to the effect that no railway was possible here but the Midland seems not to have taken over much notice. Unfortunately, no sort of record has been located of the basis on which these dampening predictions were made, or of their authenticity; which is a pity, for shortly after beginning construction, a five acre landslip started, as if to mock the builders. The hillside here, just north of Armathwaite at High Stand Gill and Edenbrows, is on inclined strata and tunnelling through it was, therefore, considered too risky. The landslip was only stopped in the end by covering the hillside with a series of vertical shafts down which rubble was tipped to act as a sort of friction brake to prevent further movement of the rock strata. It is interesting to speculate if this troublesome stretch near Armathwaite could have been avoided. Undoubtedly, the precise course of the railway here is nothing like as closely determined by the topography as it is in the mountain area and the line could have avoided this section by going outside the limit of deviation of the original plans. It seems clear, however, that at the time of survey, there was no particular reason to suppose that this section was going to prove any more difficult than any of the other hilly areas of the line and therefore it probably seemed more sensible to keep to the valley than to make an unnecessary detour with extra gradients. This is, however, only speculation and it would certainly be much more satisfactory if the reported scepticism of the local people was properly authenticated.

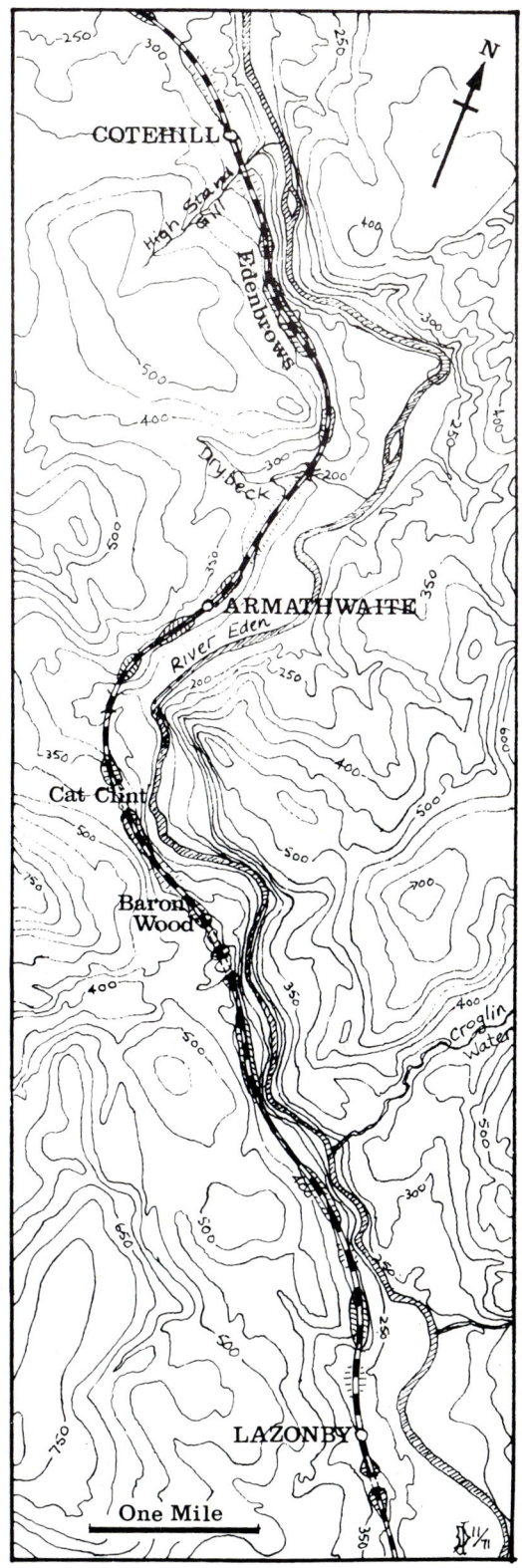

FIG. 6 *Sketch map of the Eden Gorge; contours at 50 ft intervals. The position of the line at an intermediate height on the valley side can be noted. (Crown Copyright Reserved.)*

Once north of the Eden gorge, there are no striking structural or other considerations to materially affect the course of the line and by the time it reaches Carlisle, the surrounding landscape is sensibly level.

The Upper Eden Valley—Appleby to Ais Gill

Once south of Appleby, the line loses its direct association with the Eden valley for a little while, the problem of making height for the mountain crossing becoming the dominant consideration (Figure 7). It is at this stage that the line exhibits the first real feature that can be wholly attributed to the overall concept of the route—the by-passing of Kirkby Stephen by some two miles. Undoubtedly the line could, by continuing to keep close to the Eden as did the NER branch line, have come much closer to the centre of Kirkby Stephen, but it would have been at a height of some 550–600 feet only. This would have then involved a climb to Ais Gill of some seven miles on a gradient of 1:60/65—clearly unacceptable to the Midland directors, notwith-standing the fact that, together with Appleby, Kirkby Stephen is one of the two largest centres on the route. Height, therefore, had to be made

as soon as possible south of Appleby and as a result, the line begins its major ascent immediately Ormside viaduct is crossed, from which point onwards, its relation to the landscape becomes much more striking.

The line is now compelled to leave the main valley and make what use it can of the much less suitable tributaries. The first of these is the Helm Beck whose valley exhibits many of the characteristics which are not ideally suited to railway communication. Before leaving this valley to cut across to the next one at Crosby Garrett, the immature nature of the Helm has given rise to a series of cuttings, embankments and one longish tunnel, all in the space of some three or four miles, which earthworks are for no more spectacular purpose than to circumvent the interlocking spurs of this little river (Figure 8). The line finally crosses the Helm at Griseburn viaduct and from here to Kirkby Stephen has no valley at all to help it on its way and it now has to cross the grain of the country in its quest for height. The streams in this district are mostly characterised by fairly steep sided valleys which play their part where the railway has to cross over them. From Griseburn to the south is no

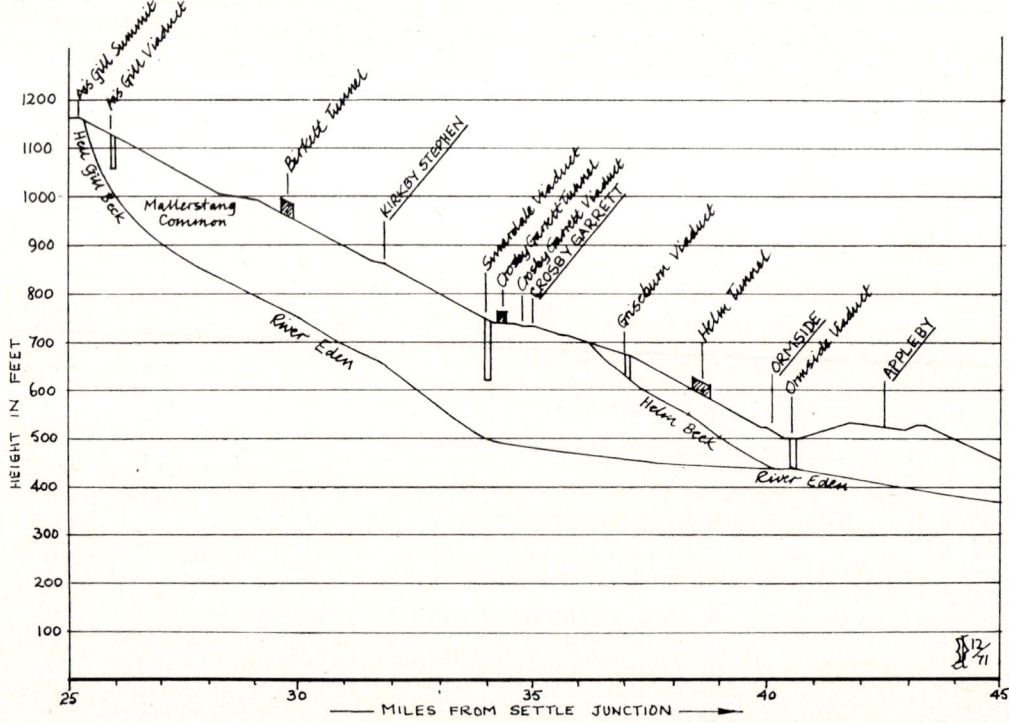

FIG. 7 *Gradient Profile: Ais Gill–Appleby. This profile shows the level of the railway in relation to the valley floor at its closest adjacent point. The swift deepening of the Eden valley north of Ais Gill is clearly shown, hence the position of the line well up on the hillside. Note the effect of the Helm Beck and also the height of Kirkby Stephen station above valley level.*

PLATE 21 (*above*) *Smardale viaduct viewed from the old N.E.R line. This immensely tall and massive structure was necessitated merely to overcome the problem presented by the Scandal Beck. The start of the deep cutting at the approach to Crosby Garrett tunnel is just discernible at the far end of the viaduct. This view makes an interesting visual contrast with Plate 44—page 44. (Photo: D. Jenkinson.)*

FIG. 8 (*right*) *This sketch map attempts to show the difficulty posed to the railway in coming south once it leaves the Eden valley proper at Ormside viaduct. The contours (at 50 ft intervals) illustrate the rather broken nature of the countryside between Birkett Common and Ormside caused, in part, by the after effects of the Dent Fault at the North-West edge of the Askrigg block—page 14. (Crown Copyright Reserved.)*

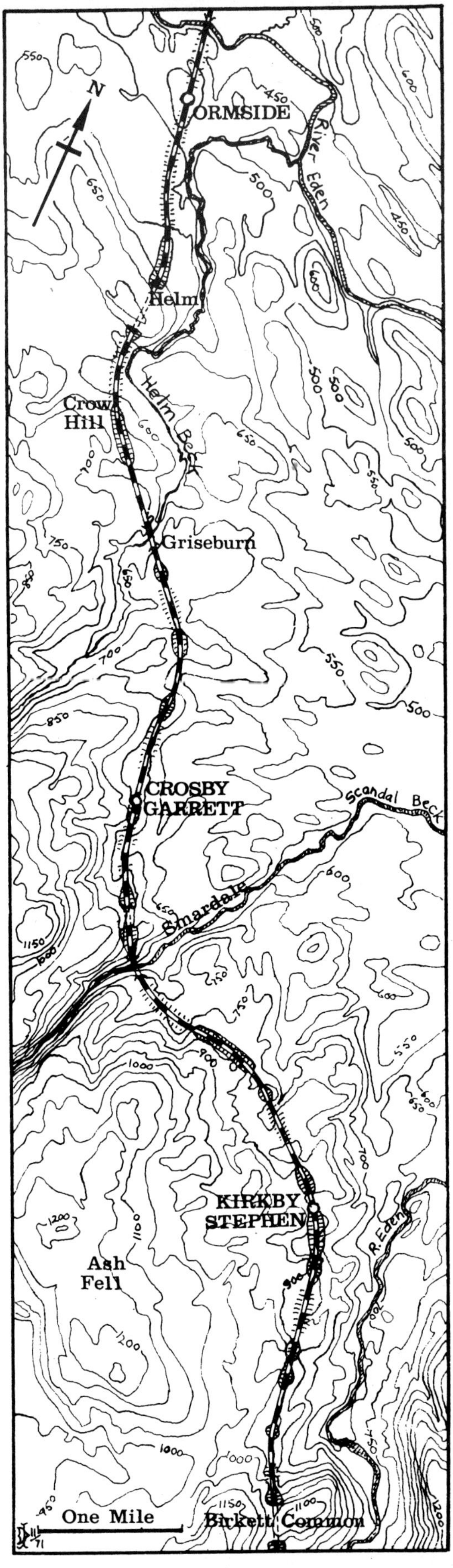

exception. In following this stretch, the line has to negotiate Crosby Garrett tunnel and Smardale viaduct in quick succession—illustrative of the high degree of relative relief encountered in crossing the grain of these minor streams (Plate 21). Nevertheless, contours are followed to a certain extent from Smardale viaduct where the line skirts the north flank of Ash Fell, rejoining the Eden valley at Kirkby Stephen—but not without the need for earthworks (Plate 22).

From Kirkby Stephen to Ais Gill, the railway is greatly assisted by the glaciated upper valley of the Eden and after passing through Birkett tunnel, the line gradually climbs up the valley side, taking advantage of the typically straightened contours of a glaciated valley to avoid speed restricting bends (Plate 23).

PLATE 22 *This view of the up 'Thames-Clyde' relief on 3rd January 1966 depicts something of the broken ground (and the consequent railway earthworks) immediately north of Birkett Tunnel. Once through the tunnel, the line joins the glaciated upper valley of the Eden—below. (Photo: Peter Robinson.)*

PLATE 23 *This view of Stanier Class 8F 2–8–0 No. 8126 approaching Ais Gill clearly illustrates the straight sided characteristics of the glacial flank of Wild Boar Fell (behind the train). Note how, on the right, the valley floor proper is already falling away below rail level. (Photo: W. Hubert Foster.)*

As with the section north of Appleby, the engineers encountered not a few problems occasioned by the physical nature of the countryside. Perhaps the most important here were those of land slipping and working boulder clay. Helm tunnel and the embankments adjacent to it gave trouble in this respect while glacial erratics* of up to four tons caused Crow Hill cutting to take $5\frac{1}{2}$ years to make. A stable foundation for Smardale viaduct was only reached after penetrating 45 feet of clay and the rock falls encountered in the building of Birkett tunnel were in part, no doubt, explained by the presence here of a considerable fault feature which throws shale, Great Scar limestone, grit, slate, iron, coal, magnesian limestone and lead all in close juxtaposition. F. S. Williams mentions this and also the fact that this tunnel was, in part, bored by using the then very revolutionary Burleigh rock drill. Embankments were, apparently, difficult to make and often ended up much bigger than intended as tipping proceeded for many months without any forward progress.

Thus, even in the actual engineering works, the line reflects the nature of the terrain as it climbs from the pastoral landscape of the lower Eden to the more wild and spartan environs of Ais Gill, almost two-thirds of the distance from Carlisle to Settle.

Ribblesdale—Settle Junction to Ribblehead

The height of the line at the head of Ribblesdale was, clearly, going to be of considerable importance. As has been seen, the summit level at Ais Gill was largely predetermined by the overall nature of the topography at this point so the question that faced the surveyors was basically one of whether any further climbing would be needed to cut through the mountains. Blea Moor at the head of Ribblesdale, is only a matter of 14–15 miles from Settle Junction, but provided the line could make a continuous climb from this latter point, approximately the same height could be reached at Blea Moor as at Ais Gill which, with luck, might avoid the need for any further climbing of a serious nature in the mountain stage which was probably destined to be bad enough anyway, without adding to the already considerable mileage to be built on a gradient of 1:100. Thus, before considering the

mountain section it will be as well to see how Ribblesdale lent itself to the achievement of a height of over 1000 feet at its head.

Ribblesdale, like the upper Eden valley in Mallerstang, is basically straight with fairly regular valley side contours following on glaciation and hence it offers a valley form fundamentally favourable to railway communication. Above Helwith Bridge, either side of the valley would seem suitable for the railway to follow but, in fact, it keeps to the west side which is the slightly easier prospect of the two. This may be because of the difficulty in passing too close to Horton-in-Ribblesdale or perhaps to avoid the expense of bridging the more prominent tributary valleys on the east side of the dale. Nevertheless, the writer is inclined to think that the line would almost certainly have gone up this eastern side, problems notwithstanding, had the route through the mountains led this way. It is his view that it is probably just good fortune more than anything else that the only really suitable route through the mountains and along the watershed necessitated the approach in upper Ribblesdale being on the easier western side of the valley.

The major hazard to the penetration of Ribblesdale seems, undoubtedly, to have been the marked narrowing of the valley below Helwith Bridge, consequent upon rejuvenation of the river system.* Sweeting gives evidence that the second rejuvenation stage of the local rivers has been held up by the edge of the Askrigg block and thus, Ribblesdale below the nick point exhibits similar, but not as severe, rejuvenation features to those found at the falls near Ingleton and at Aysgarth in Wensleydale.† The railway, therefore, must climb to overcome this change in river level but, unlike Wensleydale where the branch of the NER could (and did) make a wide sweep to the side of the valley to overcome the barrier of Aysgarth falls by using the non-rejuvenated part of the valley, the Ribble at

---

*Solid rock boulders deposited upon the land surface as a result of moving ice

*In simple lay terms, rejuvenation is caused by a lowering of sea level (or a raising of the land surface) which has the effect of speeding up the flow of rivers. This, in turn, gives rise to more vigorous erosion by the rivers and results in an increased amount of vertical, compared with lateral erosion. In consequence, river valleys tend to become more incised. The term 'nick point' is used to denote the part of the valley at which the river gradient exhibits this sharp increase. In the case of the Ribble, the nick point is located just south of Helwith Bridge.

†Geographical Journal 1950, pp. 63–78

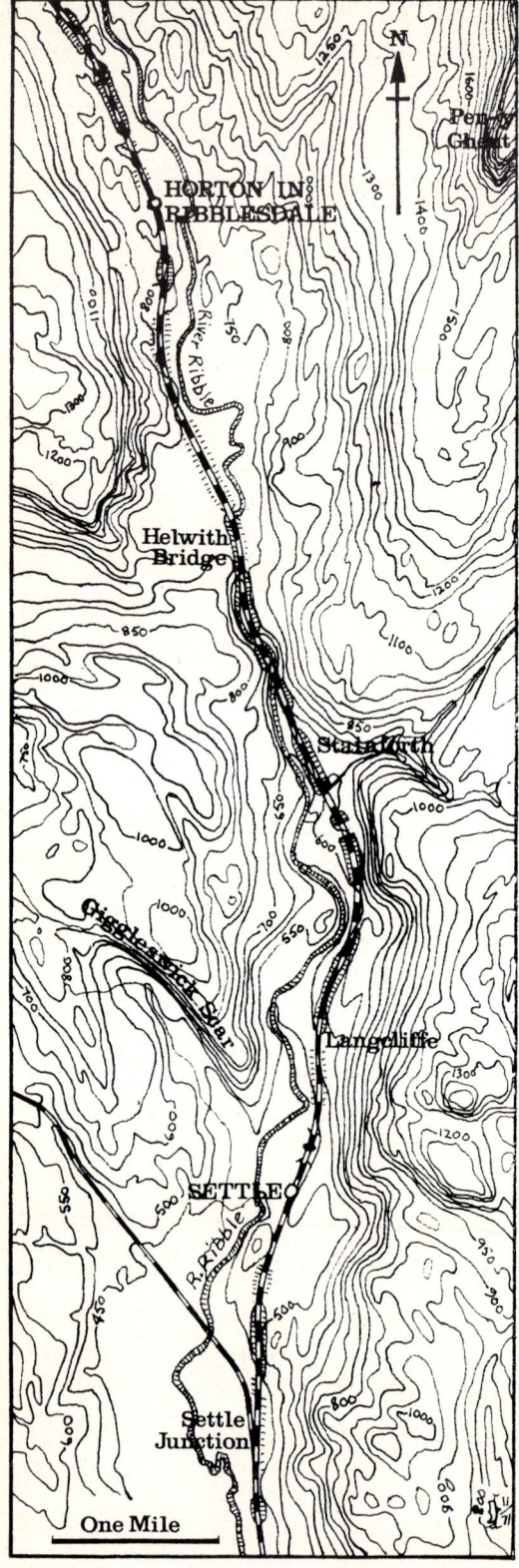

FIG. 9 *The Ribble valley between Settle Junction and Horton-in-Ribblesdale; contours at 50 ft intervals.*
The narrowing of the valley between Helwith Bridge and Langcliffe is very clearly marked. Note how the line is already some 50–100 ft above river level as it enters the narrowest part of the gorge at Stainforth.
(*Crown Copyright Reserved.*)

Stainforth gorge is too constricting (Figure 9). Because of this, the engineers were forced to make the difficult decision whether to keep close to the river using bridges and heavy embankments, or to work further east of the valley and, by using a tunnel, cut through the southern shoulder of Pen-y-Ghent north of Stainforth. Eventually they decided to avoid tunnelling but not without some extensive modifications to the river itself.

Problems of this nature were a recurring issue in the finding of a precise route during the survey and building of the Settle and Carlisle line but, almost invariably, they were resolved more by nature than by deliberate choice on the part of the engineers. In the outcome, the problem of the Ribble gorge near Stainforth was not the question of one of two equally balanced alternatives. The height of the line at Blea Moor proved the decisive factor as in so many cases elsewhere on the line. In order to make the climb from Settle Junction as easy as possible, the ascent had to start as soon as the line had left the 'little' North Western section. Because of this, the line was bound to be at a height of some 650 feet at Stainforth (Plate 24) and would hence enter the gorge some 50 feet above river level to start with (Figure 10). This reduced the problems to a certain extent for the engineers, especially since the alternative solution would have involved a mile long tunnel through even harder rocks than those of the Blea Moor area— a daunting prospect—and the engineers were probably grateful to take advantage of the slight benefit which entry to the gorge at 650 feet might provide.

In order to fully negotiate the gorge, the river had to be diverted for a few hundred yards to enable the railway to utilise the line of the old river bed. North of the gorge above Helwith Bridge, the bed of a dried up glacial lake provides a short level stretch for some few hundred yards as a mild 'breather' in the main climb (Plate 27). Again boulder clay caused problems in construction but, on the credit side, the presence of potholes is recorded by Williams as having assisted in respect of drainage.

Once clear of Stainforth gorge, the line follows the much more open valley of upper Ribblesdale (Plate 28), gradually climbing away from the river until at Ribblehead station it is over 1000 feet above sea level and at least 100 feet

PLATES 24/25 *This pair of pictures clearly demonstrates the effect of the sudden fall in river level caused by rejuvenation of the Ribble at Sheriff Brow. On the left, a rebuilt Royal Scot Class 4-6-0 is seen crossing the much taller and more southerly of the two bridges with a northbound express and on the right, Class 5XP 4-6-0 No. 45593 'Kolhapur' is seen just a few hundred yards to the north re-crossing the river over a much less impressive bridge. The train was the down Birmingham-Glasgow express on 29th July 1967 during the period of summer services which witnessed the last regular rostering of express passenger steam on the line. (Photos: Norman Wilkinson; John Whiteley.)*

PLATE 26 *Once north of the Ribble gorge the land begins to open out again with the railway once more close to river level. This is clearly shown in this fine study of two Stanier Class 8Fs heading north with a permanent way train just south of Helwith Bridge in 1967. (Photo: Gavin Morrison.)*

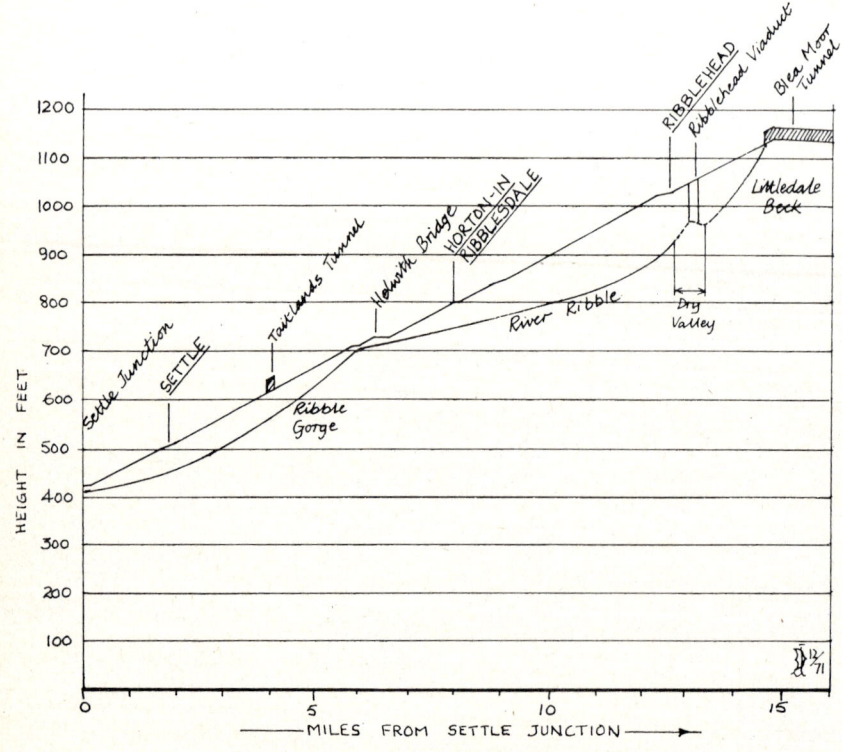

PLATE 27 *This picture of No. 92220 'Evening Star' heading north at Helwith Bridge on 30th September 1978 with the 'Bishop Treacy' memorial train clearly shows the temporary easing of the gradient just beyond the trees at the right hand side of the picture. The train is just about to traverse the old glacial lake bed mentioned in the text. (Photo: David Eatwell.)*

FIG. 10 *Gradient Profile: Settle Junction—Blea Moor. This profile shows the level of the railway in relation to the valley floor at its nearest point to the line. The composite profile of the Ribble caused by rejuvenation is clearly marked as is the dry valley at Ribblehead and the upper part of Littledale. Note the short easing of the gradient of the railway at Helwith Bridge.*

above the river. At this point, the line launches itself over Ribblehead viaduct and, although the climb to Blea Moor is not quite complete, the railway leaves Ribblesdale so its course from here can best be considered with the mountain section.

The Mountain section—Ribblehead to Ais Gill

So much has been written about this part of the Settle and Carlisle of both the authentic and the romantic kind, that it is often difficult to separate fact from fiction. There can be little doubt of its fascination and attraction to any student, not just the railway enthusiast, for at first glance, this territory is a very strange place to find a railway at all, much less one built on the scope of the Midland's Pennine road.

This stretch was, without question, the most critical one as a study of the map will reveal. In direct line between Ribblehead and Ais Gill are the following hill masses at their least heights: Blea Moor (1700 feet), Rise Hill/Widdale Fell (over 1300 feet) and the southern extension of Swarth Fell (over 1500 feet). As F. S. Williams put it, the engineers had one of four courses to take: 'to go over it, or to go under it, or to go round it, or to go through it; go they must'. In fact, in his

contemporary description of this area, although dated in its prose, there is given a very clear impression of the Midland's absolute determination to get to Carlisle over these hills. It is all too easy to be cynical in this modern day and age, but if one can imagine the situation some 100 years ago, it must have seemed a forbidding prospect. Looking at the map today with the line marked 'in situ' and in the light of more recent knowledge and research, the chosen route perhaps seems more obvious than may have been the case in 1866. The remarkable thing is the way in which, consciously or otherwise, it follows the only real path that geology and topography allowed it. That this fact was appreciated at an early stage is born out by Williams' statement that James Allport and his chief engineer knew that there was only one route through and that the engineering was going to be of a high order and of an expensive nature because this was *not* going to be a purely local line. One can, therefore, at least conclude that the Midland went into it with its eyes fully open.

The feasibility of the whole section lies in the interlocking nature of the valley heads, coupled with the nature of the valleys themselves. Dr. Appleton has commented on the valley

PLATE 28 *A mile or two further north than Plate 27, 'Evening Star' is now seen on the short level stretch. Note the wide green valley and flat valley floor. (Photo: David Eatwell.)*

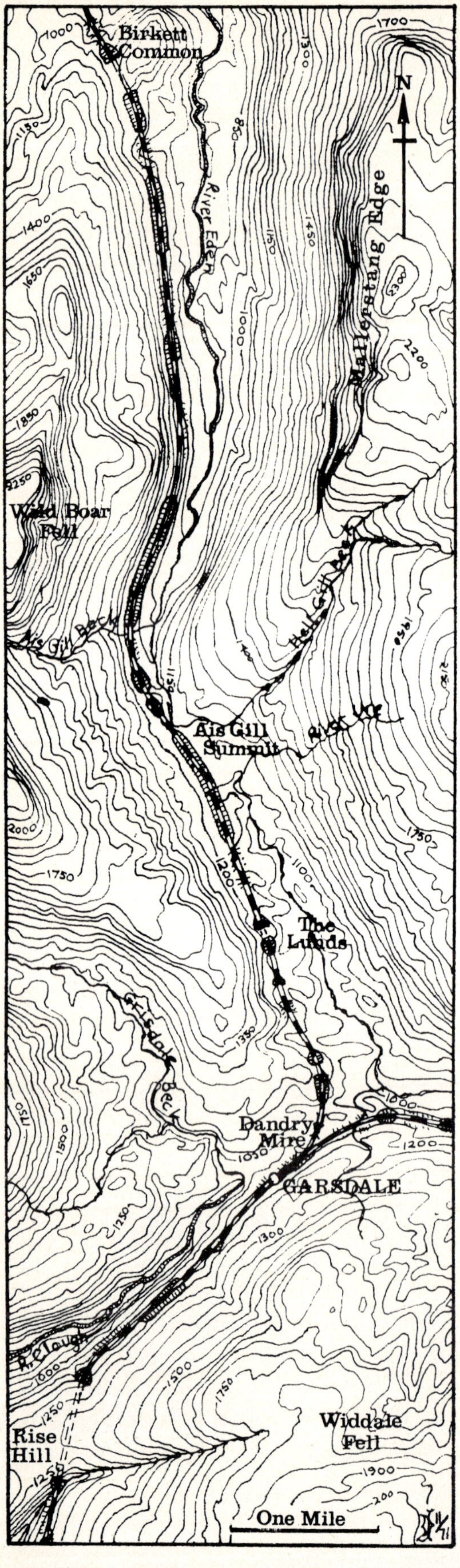

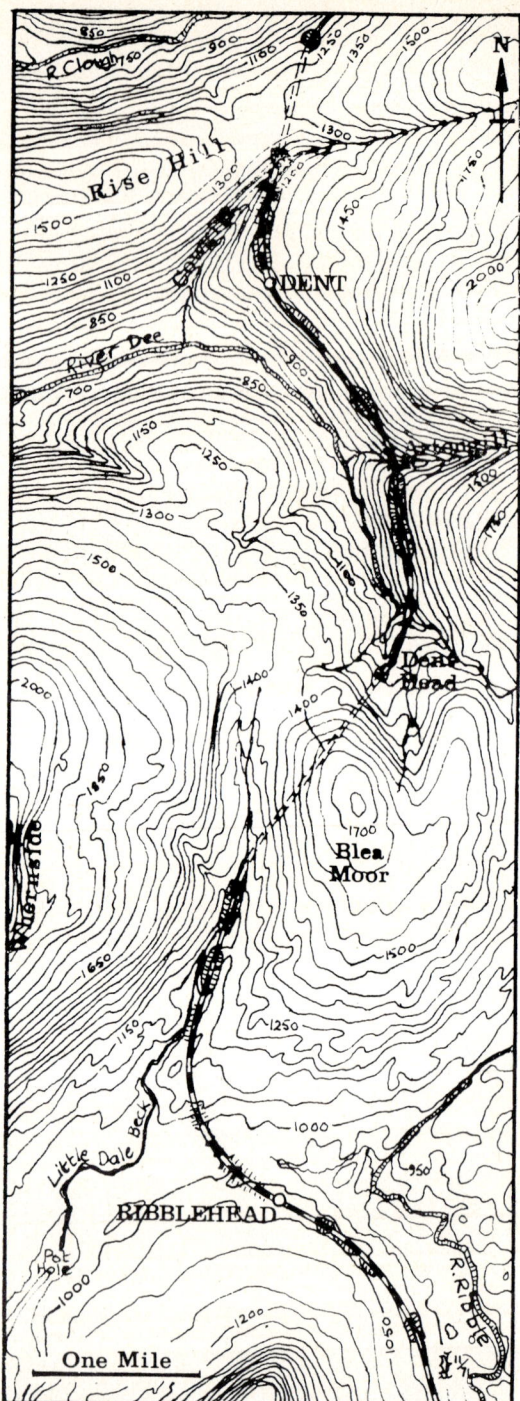

FIGS. 11/12 *These two sketch maps (contour intervals at 50 ft) show the course of the line between Ribblehead and Birkett Common. The typically straightened contours of the glaciated valleys traversed by the railway should be noted. Note also the way in which the line keeps close to the 1150 ft contour between Blea Moor and Ais Gill. (Crown Copyright Reserved).*

PLATE 29 *The sheer size of Ribblehead viaduct is very apparent in this view of a northbound freight climbing towards Blea Moor in November 1967 behind an ailing BR Class 9F 2-10-0. The abandoned valley mentioned in the text is in the foreground.* (*Photo: John Whiteley.*)

head progression of this route, but it is the rather inevitable nature of this progression that will be amplified in this work.*

The line is at 1150 feet at Ais Gill and some 1000 feet at Ribblehead. It has already been explained how it was hardly possible to get any more height at this latter point if the gradient was to be kept to 1 in 100 so the first task was to gain the extra height from Ribblehead and then link up with the Ais Gill area. Clearly, after a long climb to 1150 feet in both directions it would be desirable to reduce further climbing to a minimum if possible. A study of the contour pattern reveals how this could be done. By keeping close to the 1150 feet contour line, a possible route, provided by the succession of valley heads, emerges (Figures 11 and 12). True, it involves tunnelling but this was bound to be necessary; the important thing was to keep it to a minimum in rock known to be very hard. That the route exists at all is a direct consequence of a rather unusual drainage pattern and glacial history which is not without interest.

The key to the whole situation is found in the assymmetric nature of the Pennines. The early part of this chapter made mention of the very gentle eastward and southward slope of the surface rocks of this area. This means that the

highest part of the Pennine range is well over to the west side of the country. In consequence of this, those rivers which drain to the east and south have a much longer journey to the sea than do those which flow to the west, thus causing the law of unequal slopes to apply.†This has resulted in a series of, for the purpose of this discussion, absolutely vital river captures‡ by these west flowing streams.

The first area of note is the probable capture of some of the headwaters of the Ribble by Littledale Beck, one of the headwaters of the Greta. This has left an abandoned valley, or 'windgap', north of Ribblehead station which the railway can cross in order to continue its climb to 1150 feet along the side of the upper Greta valley in Littledale before crossing into Dent Head via Blea Moor tunnel. This through valley is, admittedly, at a fairly low level, as witnessed by the height of Ribblehead viaduct which was built to cross it (Plate 29). However, without this valley, the line may well have met with a

---

*The Geography of Communications in Great Britain, pp. 105–6

†In other words, those rivers with the shortest distances to travel to the sea have steeper gradients and, in consequence, a greater eroding power.

‡River capture is the name given to the phenomenon caused by a vigorously eroding river cutting its valley back into the headwaters of a less vigorous stream and diverting the headwaters of this stream into its own course.

substantial barrier to further progress, probably in the form of a continuous ridge connecting the Ingleborough/Simon Fell upland with that of Blea Moor.

The second area of capture is at the head of Wensleydale where the Ure has lost headwaters to both Clough and Eden. Grisdale beck, a Clough tributary, once flowed into the Ure, but a pre-ice age capture and subsequent partial blocking of the old valley near Blake Mire by glacial drift, has left an empty valley at Dandry Mire which is used by the railway. It is interesting to note in passing that a railway culvert has permanently diverted a north flowing stream into the Ure near this point.* The other capture in the Lunds area is that of the Hell Gill beck, a former source of the Ure but now draining into the Eden, a very active river. Irrespective of any future captures by the Eden, the process has already gone far enough to open up a complete through route out of the head of the Eden valley without recourse to tunnelling except to circumvent glacial drift. Without this capturing, the Eden valley would probably end, like most mountain valleys, in a hillside. Thus there are now no less than three separate valleys, Eden, Ure and Clough, converging towards the Moorcock Inn without intervening high ground to bar communication between them and of this fact the railway takes full advantage (Plate 30). These through valleys at Ribblehead and Garsdale Head are, therefore, of great importance for their presence reduces the need for major tunnelling to but two places, Blea Moor and Rise Hill. Furthermore, if the alignment of these valleys is studied in relation to the contours in those areas where tunnels were to be needed, it is

seen that the tunnels could be bored across almost the narrowest parts of the surrounding hills (Plate 31).

Glaciation, while it occasioned numerous problems in the actual *building* of the line, has actually made the route finding task considerably simpler. Without glaciation, these Pennine valleys, river capture or no, would almost certainly exhibit youthful characteristics with all their associated problems of narrow valley floors, interlocking spurs and so forth. As it is and as a result of glacial action, the valley sides, especially Dentdale and Garsdale, are remarkably straight. This did not eliminate engineering problems, but as in Ribblesdale and along the flanks of Wild Boar Fell, it went some way to make them easier. Even a little sidestream in Dentdale, Cowgill beck, has materially shortened the length of Rise Hill tunnel by cutting well back into the southern flanks of the hill (Plate 32). The value of these straightened valley sides can well be appreciated when one considers the height of the railway above the valley floors (Figure 13 and Plate 33).

Thus, an almost level stretch of railway exists for some ten miles at a height of 1150 feet or thereabouts, its presence being entirely due to the juxtaposition of favourable landforms. Additional benefits, on the operational side of the railway, were also conferred by the nature of this level section. Because of it, Blea Moor and Rise Hill are tunnelled on very easy gradients and the vast majority of the heavy climbing could be done in the open. Furthermore, the level nature of the mountain passage made it possible to lay down water troughs at Garsdale (approximately half-way between Leeds and Carlisle), a valuable asset in the days of steam hauled trains.

*C. A. M. King, p. 11

PLATE 30 *This general view looking north from the coal road connecting Dent with Garsdale attempts to illustrate the convergence of the three valleys at Garsdale Head. The railway as such is not visible but its course, including that of the Hawes branch, is marked by a pecked line. (Photo: D. Jenkinson.)*

PLATE 31 *The southern entrance to Dentdale is rather dramatic. In this view Class 8F No. 48074 heads north out of Blea Moor tunnel in November 1967. A few hundred yards later and it will be almost 100ft above the valley on Dent Head viaduct. (Photo: John Whiteley.)*

PLATE 32 *Another early constructional view shows Dent Head viaduct with its attendant shanty town. The new road bridge in the centre of the picture still carries local road traffic (see Plate 9), but the adjacent farmstead under the viaduct is long gone — probably abandoned when the line was built and the road diverted. (Photo: Author's collection.)*

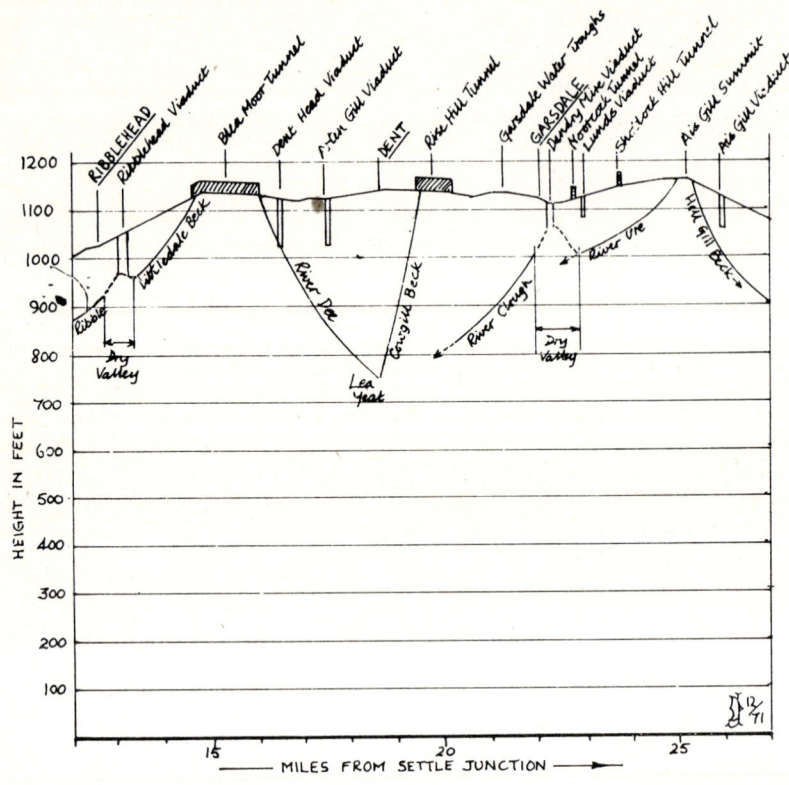

FIG. 13 *Gradient Profile:
Ribblehead—Ais Gill. This profile
shows the level of the railway
related to the valley floor level of
the various valleys traversed in
the watershed area. The contrast
between this section and the
previous gradient profiles is
striking. Note particularly how
the rivers Clough and Eden (Hell
Gill Beck) have steeper gradients
than the Ure, thus paving the way
for the erosion processes
(described in the main text) which
give rise to the dry valley at
Garsdale Head and the through
valley at Ais Gill. This profile
helps to emphasise the critical
nature of the mountain section of
the route.*

PLATE 33 *This picture, taken from the top of the now demolished water tank at Garsdale, shows the lunchtime
Hellifield-Carlisle local slowing down for the Garsdale stop in May 1963. The site of the old North Eastern Railway
shed—see Plate 48, page 50—is in the foreground. (Photo: D. Jenkinson.)*

As throughout the line, the fundamental character of the landscape dominated the engineering response. Within this section are five major viaducts, two long tunnels and sundry large embankments. Two of the viaducts, at Ribblehead and Dandry Mire are used to cross the aforementioned windgaps, although the latter was not planned. Glaciers, having cleared a passage through, also deposited the sort of drift material which would not support the weight of an embankment. Ribblehead viaduct is immense—$\frac{1}{4}$ mile long and over 100 feet high—and said to have foundations 25 feet below the top surface of the glacial overlay.

The making of the tunnels was hindered by the rock structure which, although hard, was affected by the boring to such an extent that both Blea Moor and Rise Hill tunnels had to be lined throughout. The southern $\frac{1}{4}$ mile of Blea Moor tunnel should have been cutting but the rock was insufficiently stable to support the 100 foot depth as planned; while post glacial streams cutting into the sides of the major valleys often necessitated extensive engineering works like the viaduct at Arten Gill (Plate 36). It is

PLATE 34 *The meeting point of routes at Garsdale Head. The famous stockaded turntable is prominent, Dandry Mire viaduct being hidden behind it. The main line swings away to the left, the Hawes branch to the right. The train is the up 'Waverley' in 1963, headed by a BR Sulzer Type 4 diesel. (Photo: D. Jenkinson.)*

PLATE 35 *This view of Shotlock Hill tunnel looking back towards Garsdale, shows the sort of engineering feature caused by glacial drift in the Lunds area. In view of the lie of the land at this point, one wonders why the engineers did not opt for a cutting—perhaps such a feature through glacial drift may have been thought prone to landslips. (Photo: Alan Robey.)*

tempting to go on—as others have done—discussing in great detail all the many examples of massive engineering but sufficient has probably been said to indicate the intense correlation between the natural features and the final response of the railway in relation to them and its ultimate purpose.

It is, perhaps, helpful to consider possible alternative routes between Ribblehead and Ais Gill to fully appreciate the inevitable course of the chosen route. The first alternative would have been to follow Ribblesdale up the east side and tunnel through Gayle Moor into Dent Head but this would have taken the line even further away from what little settlement does exist and would also have meant a rather tricky path through the extensive Ribblesdale drumlin* field followed by an almost certainly longer tunnel into the next valley. An even less probable alternative would have been not to use Dentdale at all but by crossing Newby Head moss, use the flanks of Widdale Fell to enter Upper Wensleydale by Appersett pasture. This, however, would have involved a long detour almost to Hawes and although it would have probably meant only one tunnel (through Newby Head), this would have been a very long one and would still have been approached on the harder side of the Ribble valley. This route too, would have added miles more to a line already destined to be two miles longer than via Ingleton and Low Gill.

*A drumlin is a small rounded hill left behind after glaciation. Generally some 50–100 ft. high, drumlins are generally found together with many others and collectively give rise to a land surface frequently likened to a 'basket of eggs'.

Conclusion

It seems reasonable to conclude that the route chosen was the best and, in fact, the only practicable way through these hills if the basic concept was to be maintained. As it stands, it is a remarkably well integrated example of the way in which natural conditions in relation to the economic purpose of a line can control its route. One hesitates to claim that this control is exercised here to a greater extent than anywhere else in the country, but what seems certain is that once the basic character of the line as an economic element had been established, the course it takes through the countryside was largely fixed by nature. It is doubtful if, even were the line being built today, the chosen route would be very different, fulfilling as it does all the functions one could reasonably expect of a modern main line. This cannot always be said of our British railway system, not least the line over Shap Fell with its far tougher gradients over generally easier territory. For this reason, if no other, the Midland and its servants should command our respect.

Having, then, attempted to answer the question of why the line is located precisely where it is, attention can now be concentrated on the line itself and its contribution to the geographical environment. In a sense this is to reverse the normal procedure but it is hoped that sufficient has been written to make it clear that the final expression of the Settle and Carlisle railway as a finished entity, is so much a product of circumstances, that to describe it without knowing these circumstances would be to present only half the picture.

PLATE 36 *This view of Arten Gill viaduct, taken from the valley below, clearly shows the effect on the relief caused by even quite small tributary streams running 'across the grain' of the main valley. The train is the 'Lord Bishop' memorial special to Bishop Eric Treacy on 30th September 1978, headed by LNER A3 4-6-2 'Flying Scotsman'. (Photo: David Eatwell.)*

Chapter 6

Railway Landscape I
The Line Itself

In attempting to place a railway line in its total geographical setting as a landscape feature, one can distinguish two broad aspects. In the first place there are those features represented by the line itself (e.g. bridges, embankments etc.); while secondly are those elements of the scene which owe their existence to the presence of the railway although not actually forming a part of the structure of the line (e.g. station buildings). In the case of the line under discussion, these two aspects together form an important visual element of the region, many parts of which, prior to the coming of the railway, gave little evidence of human occupation. Certainly, the line and its structures represent a greater proportional contribution to the total landscape than would be the case of, say, a new road or railway added to an already complex pattern of human activity. As such, they inevitably assume a somewhat dominant rôle.

It would be tempting, as others have done, to describe the line chronologically from Settle Junction northwards, but this would not necessarily present the subject in the most fitting way. Having already considered it in fair detail, section by section, in relation to physical control, it would, perhaps, be more useful to evaluate the line from a descriptive point of view on a rather different basis.

As has been stated in the introduction to this work, when studying landscape one is interested in the overall synthesis of causal factors. It is, therefore, somewhat unrealistic to extract one element of the landscape to the exclusion of everything else. A more valid approach, one feels, is to attempt to evaluate the contribution made to the overall landscape as a result of the presence of a railway in it. No attempt will be made to list every example, but by selecting the more important ones, suggest possible lines of approach for the omitted areas. Apart from anything else, mere repetition of similar cases would become tedious and add little to the argument. For convenience, stations and structures have been allocated a separate chapter.

Railways as landscape elements have never really been accorded much treatment—possibly the general attitude to them having been influenced by such opinions as those of the poet Ruskin who accused the Midland of desecrating Monsal Dale with the Peak Forest line. Roads, on the other hand, like buildings, seem always to have played their part in art and literature—perhaps because they have always been with us. At all events one senses that an appreciation of how their function affects their outward appearance has always been felt. That the appearance of a railway line can have as many facets as a road seems not to have been so well understood.

The North of England Union Railway prospectus (p. 8) might have dismissed the engineering problems as trivial but once the Midland had taken over the project, the terms of reference were to be radically changed. The Midland was anxious that the finished railway should be as 'fast' as possible and, as a result, the whole line changed in scope from a local line which would, for the sake of economy, have probably kept close to the surface of the land, to a main line with sweeping curves and easier gradients; although, in truth, there were to be more than enough of the latter. Because of this, the engineering works had to be of a high order of magnitude to the extent that, in places, the railway dominates the landscape even where the latter is at its most rugged. True, the line utilises many of the valleys provided by nature but it cannot follow their every twist and turn if it is to keep to its fast nature and so one has the engineering works which are such a feature of the route.

Railways, therefore, like any other form of transport, reflect their function in outward appearance so again a brief discussion of some general principles seems desirable.

We are familiar with the differences between a picturesque country lane and a modern commercial highway or between a coastal tramp steamer and a super tanker but a railway, although exhibiting the same sort of differences, does it in a more subtle way. Even the lightest of railways is more inflexible than a major road and, as a result, tunnels and bridges in themselves do not necessarily confer main line status to the route. Whereas it is easy to distinguish in appearance between a road of minor status and a motorway, a railway possesses less obvious points of difference. Moreover, lack of direct contact with the railway makes this form of 'road' less easy for the average person to visualise. Even though the railway is frequently a dominant factor, its inaccessibility to the general public makes it more remote—one can neither drive or park a car on the railway!

The first indication of a railway's importance is in the number of tracks provided. There are, it is true, many places in the world where important trunk routes are single track but in Britain, the presence of two or more tracks is the most usual indication of main line status, much as dual carriageways increasingly tend to distinguish the primary trunk roads from their feeder systems. The second point of difference is the matter of gradients where the main line is usually easier graded than secondary and branch lines. Railway gradients are not, as a rule, easy to discern from the line-side—except in the most extreme of cases—and evidence of rise and fall of the route must be sought elsewhere, such as the form and magnitude of the earthworks and structures involved. In general, a secondary line will rise and fall rather more than a main line and probably use steeper grades. Earthworks there will be, but the likely revenue from the line would not be such as to justify the expense of huge earthworks, such as are frequently employed on the Settle and Carlisle, merely to reduce the gradient from, say, 1 in 50 to 1 in 100.

Curvature can indicate the function of a line. Unless a curve is very gentle it will impose unacceptable speed limits for main line work—thus the avoidance of sharp curves is again characteristic of the main line, frequently exemplified by the use of large and expensive earthworks. A secondary line, which usually follows the physical contours more closely, will not exhibit these features to the same extent. Thus, main and secondary railway lines exhibit similar differences as between main and secondary roads but in a more sophisticated way. Overall, therefore, the main distinction between the two

can be seen to be one of scale. A road can be seen to adjust itself to the land surface over quite a short stretch but a railway has usually to be studied over a greater mileage to understand the relationships. It is, however, interesting to note that the modern motorway tends to be landscaped very much on the traditional railway pattern.

If it had been simply a question of engineering in the case of the Settle and Carlisle, the problems might well have been capable of an easier solution since, by the 1870s, considerable expertise in railway building had been acquired in this country. What must further be understood in the case under discussion is the totally unpredictable nature of the physical environment during the actual construction phase of the line. The weather assailed the work on all sides, even during the summer, turning clay into mud, making many of the works almost impossible and frequently unapproachable. Paradoxically, the frost which hardened the surface for the contractors' vehicles made it too cold to go on with the masonry work. Even when the weather relented, the uncertain nature of the heavily glaciated land surface with its considerable deposits of unconsolidated drift material made it difficult for the engineers to predict what they might find to build over. The chief engineer is reported to have said of the glacial drift:

I have known the men blast the boulder clay like rock and within a few hours have to ladle out the same stuff from the same spot like soup in buckets. Or a man strikes a blow with his pick at what he thinks is clay, but there is a great boulder underneath almost as hard as iron and the man's wrists, arms and body are so shaken by the shock that, disgusted, he flings down his tools, asks for his money and is off
F. S. WILLIAMS. *The Midland Railway*

Thus, not only did the engineering works have to reflect the overall main line concept but not infrequently the nature of the land surface itself. The area is remote and, even in the present motor age, difficult of access, but at the time of construction things were probably worse. An early 19th Century writer describes Dentdale as being 'entirely surrounded with high mountains and of difficult access to carriages, having few openings where they can enter with safety'. Into this remote region came the engineers and surveyors to try and find foundations for bridges, materials for structures and so forth; and where carriages could 'scarcely find a safe entry,' they

PLATE 37 *The unplanned viaduct at Dandry Mire with Class 9F No. 92220 'Evening Star' heading north on 13th May 1978. The dry valley below the viaduct is clearly seen. (Photo: David Eatwell.)*

laid down their iron road over 1100 feet above sea level, generally without any of the benefits of refined present-day surveying and geological techniques. To find the solid foundation rock was frequently a matter of trial and error and they had regularly to remove 20 feet or more of surface material to get a safe foundation, thus adding to the size and expense of the final structure. In some cases (e.g. Smardale and Arten Gill viaducts), the depth of foundation was nearer 50 feet. On other occasions, the heavy glacial overlay was so unconsolidated that embankments refused to bind in position—for example just north of Ais Gill:

The tipping proceeded for twelve months without the embankment advancing a yard . . . the masses of slurry rolled over one another in mighty convolutions, persisting in going anywhere and everywhere except where they wanted

F. S. WILLIAMS. *The Midland Railway*

This sort of thing was not infrequently the cause of the engineer having to change his plans. The south end of Blea Moor tunnel was planned

as cutting as has already been seen (p. 37) while the trouble at the head of Wensleydale alluded to on page 37 in respect of Dandry Mire viaduct was of similar nature, over 250,000 cubic yards of material having been swallowed up by the peat before a viaduct was decided upon.

For these reasons, therefore, it can be readily appreciated how the line's exact physical contribution to the overall scene results from a combination of economic and physical factors which interacted one upon the other. Some of the more noteworthy examples have been selected to illustrate this theme.

If one stands on the southern flanks of Blea Moor at Runscar, the natural landscape to the south is dominated by the flat topped mass of Ingleborough, but in the cultural landscape, the railway fulfils this function. In crossing the gap north of Ribblehead, it first traverses a quarter-mile of heavy embankment, then a quarter-mile viaduct and another shorter embankment before disappearing from view into Littledale. In a little

PLATE 38 *This picture, taken in 1938, shows the characteristic Midland Railway double sided distant signal which stood guard at the north end of Ribblehead viaduct for many years. LMS and BR standardisation policies were to decree that such signals were not quite proper (!) and it was subsequently removed. (Photo: Norman Wilkinson.)*

PLATES 39/40 *Class 5 4–6–0 No. 45295 approaches Ais Gill on the final stages of the southbound climb in November 1967 (above). The picture clearly shows the visual effect of the railway on the western side of the valley compared with the unmodified eastern side. The glacial shape of the valley is readily discernible even with the engine smoke partly obscuring the view. Once the line is at summit level (below), it blends much more with the surrounding landscape. This picture shows the same train a few minutes later about a mile to the south. (Photos: Peter Robinson.)*

PLATE 41 *This view of Dent Head looking north in November 1967, shows a down freight headed by a Stanier Class 8F 2–8–0. Dent Head viaduct can be clearly seen to the right. Beyond the cutting through the spur in the hillside—marked by two lines of snow fences—the line crosses Arten Gill viaduct prior to running along the hillside in the far distance (above the smoke of the engine). The train itself is passing the first site suggested for a station to serve this valley—see page 48. (Photo: John Whitley.)*

over half a mile, it divides the landscape into two parts. The explanation of this is only to be found in the height of Ais Gill summit. A purely local line up Ribblesdale would probably have kept much closer to the river and barely impinged on the landscape at all by comparison with the physical features.

Alternatively, consider the line as it traverses Mallerstang common. As at Ribblehead it dominates the man-made landscape. The B 6259 road from Kirkby Stephen to the Moorcock Inn pursues a fairly direct path parallel to the railway but keeps to the valley centre and is, by comparison, fairly inconspicuous. On the other hand, the railway, having to respond to the relief in its own fashion, cuts a huge horizontal gash in the hillside as it climbs to Ais Gill moor (Plate 39). Oddly enough, at this latter point, coming close as it does to valley floor level, it tends to blend with the landscape to a far greater extent (Plate 40).

From the north flank of Blea Moor, the line as it traverses the head of Dentdale is seen in relation to the land surface probably better than anywhere else (Plate 41). Here it is seen as a true main line with first class alignment, gentle curves and massive engineering works all dovetailed into the landscape. To the student concerned with the interplay of landscape features, it could be argued that nowhere does this interplay achieve more striking effect than here, although the fact that it is here at all can only be explained in terms of the railway politics of the 1850s and 1860s.

By way of contrast, the situation at the very beginning of the line at Settle Junction is not without interest. The presence of Ais Gill is felt even down here as the line begins its long climb. It runs immediately onto a long embankment to gain height and passes through the gap at Settle some 50 feet above river level (Plates 42 and 43). This has the effect of putting the station cheek by jowl with the town rather than in the valley proper—perhaps a good thing for traffic, but a purely incidental consideration. From the Giggleswick side the effect is equally obvious, the cultural landscape being divided and in places even obscured by the railway as it makes height.

43

PLATES 42/43 *These two photographs show the effect which Blea Moor and Ais Gill have upon the character of the line as far south as Settle. The view above, taken during the construction of the railway c. 1973, shows how the line of the railway is dominant in the view of Settle from the Giggleswick side of the river while to the left, Stanier Class 5 4–6–0 No. 44807 is seen immediately after leaving Settle station with a northbound freight in May 1962. The massive retaining wall on the right serves to support the foundations of the northbound station platform and almost obscures the water crane. (Photos: Author's collection, D. Jenkinson.)*

PLATE 44 *The landscape softens to the north of Kirkby Stephen as can be seen in the view below which shows a diverted southbound West Coast route express just after crossing Smardale viaduct on 29th April 1967. The engine is a BR Brush Type 4 and Smardale viaduct is hidden by the trees above the leading two coaches of the train. (Photo: P. Robinson)*

PLATE 45 *This view of Crosby Garrett viaduct, looking north during the construction period, demonstrates how the line, by dividing the village in two, dominates the cultural landscape. (Photo: Author's collection.)*

The alternations of viaduct, embankment, tunnel and cutting in response to the interlocking spurs of the Helm valley north of Kirkby Stephen have already been mentioned (p. 24) and, together with many others like them, provide further examples of the dominance of the railway in the landscape. From the south, the aspect of the

village of Crosby Garrett is almost totally obscured by the railway line while at Smardale, close by, the presence of the huge, 165 foot high viaduct (allegedly the tallest on the old Midland system) can hardly be ignored as a visual element.

The Eden valley below Appleby does not provide quite so many striking examples since, as has already been explained in Chapter 5, in many respects the line here is a much more 'typical' railway. Nevertheless, examples can be found where the railway has markedly changed the landscape. The river diversion at Culgaith (page 22) is one example and one can also note the effect on the appearance of the Eden gorge near Armathwaite by comparison with the largely unaltered west bank. Even Williams commented on this in 1876 when he contrasted the red sandstone, used extensively in the engineering works of the Eden valley, with the prevailing green of the surrounding area.

So far, therefore, it can be seen that the railway, but its very nature, brought in its wake a number of features which, when superimposed

PLATE 46 *This wintry view of Dent in 1947 shows the whole sweep of the line to Dent Head (extreme right). The snow fences do not seem to have been very effective on this occasion, and the view amply illustrates the severe problems which the railway can face during a bad winter. (Photo: W. Hubert Foster.)*

PLATE 47 *Garsdale, looking north from the signal box c. 1954. Note Dandry Mire viaduct in the left background.* (*Photo: Eric Treacy.*)

on a fairly virgin region as in the case under discussion, assumed a far more dominant rôle than might otherwise have been the case. This aspect is not confined to the purely engineering features occasioned by circumventing the physical environment but also expresses itself in ancillary features which owe their existence to the presence of the railway in the first place.

A characteristic example of these ancillary features can be seen near Horton-in-Ribblesdale where large parts of the landscape have been affected by the railway. The valley side is dominated by enormous quarries whose economic significance will be considered later but which in the landscape context can only be explained by the existence of the railway. This type of feature can be witnessed along the whole line at places such as Stainforth, Ribblehead, Helwith Bridge, Newbiggin, Long Meg and so forth but the Horton example is possibly the most striking.

A totally different, but just as noticeable illustration involves the whole appearance of large areas of the hillsides near Dent. At this location, the risk of snow blockage was so great that extensive sleeper built fences were erected on the hillside to prevent downward drifting of snow (Plate 46). These give to the hillside a totally different aspect to the 'norm' in this area and may even, by affording some measure of climatic protection, have saved the lives of a few sheep!

A very different feature is found at Garsdale Head where a microcosm of Swindon or Crewe has grown some 1100 feet above sea level (Plate 47). One hesitates to call Garsdale a village but, apart from the Moorcock Inn and a few isolated farmsteads and barns, almost every feature of the man-made landscape is a reflection of the railway. The line itself is dominant enough as it divides the area in two at Dandry Mire viaduct but the side effects are no less interesting.

This location was, until the branch was lifted, the junction for the Wensleydale line. Clearly, therefore, it would assume some importance. It was also the location chosen for locomotive servicing facilities for the engines employed to assist the heavier trains up the hill in either direction. There was thus the necessity to provide facilities for the railwaymen and since no settlement existed, the railway built its own. Indeed, this is one of the features of the line, condemned as it is by nature to pass well away from settlements. The railwaymen and their dependants had to be housed nearer the line and railway-built houses and cottages are numerous. Even where the line passed close to existing settlements, there were frequently no spare houses available so the railway added its own quota to the existing settlement pattern.

Other than the line itself, this addition of a considerable number of new buildings to the landscape of the Pennines was the most noticeable visible change brought by the Settle and Carlisle Railway and is considered in detail in the next chapter.

Chapter 7

Railway Landscape II
Structures and Stations

In an area not noticeably heavily built over, the railway architecture associated with the Settle and Carlisle Railway contributes a disproportionately high percentage to the sum total of man-made structures in the region. One particularly interesting aspect is that the railway structures possess little real affinity with the traditional building styles of the local areas. The 'native' architecture of the Craven district of Yorkshire, as exemplified by the farms and cottages in Ribblesdale, has little in common with that which is found in the Eden valley yet the Midland Railway erected identically styled buildings in both areas. As a result of this common house style, applied universally from Settle Junction to Scotby, it is only in the matter of building material that one can detect a relationship between local physical conditions and the finished product.

The 20th Century Briton is, of course, accustomed to seeing pretty well identically styled houses and factories from John o' Groats to Lands End, but in the 19th Century, regional differences were still strongly marked. It is, therefore, conceivable that, at first, the Derby designed 'mock gothic' of the Settle and Carlisle may have seemed like an intrusive alien element in a hitherto fairly stable scene—and yet it is at least arguable that the railway architecture acts as a unifying factor between the northern and southern sections of the line. Perhaps it is not too fanciful even to postulate that the overall unity of concept which the Settle and Carlisle architecture helps to present is, in part, responsible for some of the fascination of the line to latter day observers.

Siting the Stations

The first problem to be faced by the Midland Railway was not, however, the style of architecture but the question of location and size of the facilities to be provided and the recorded minutes on this subject tell a fascinating and revealing story of the Midland's ideas about potential local traffic on the line. The first mention of stations was on 30th September 1870 when the Settle and Carlisle Construction Committee discussed a letter from a Mr William Arkley(?)—the handwriting in the minute book is not quite legible. He had written from Settle to enquire whether the company would make a station at Helwith Bridge. A decision was held over until the sites for stations were discussed.

At this time, the company had more urgent problems to worry about than station sites. The construction work was going badly, contractors were having both monetary and labour problems and the minute book reflects a general air of pessimism and gloom. However, in September 1871, things seemed to have passed the nadir when it was ordered in committee that:

a. Messrs Allport, Crossley and Kirtley report to the committee as to the sites and sizes of the engine sheds required upon the Settle and Carlisle line.
b. Messrs Allport, Crossley and Kirtley report to the committee as to the sites of the stations on the Settle and Carlisle line.

Clearly, the Midland felt more confident.

There is no evidence given in the minute book of the basis on which the size and site of any particular station was to be decided. There were very few obvious places to locate stations and one doubts very much if the phrase 'Market Research' had ever been heard! There were a few villages near the line and, of course, the three principal market towns of Settle itself, Kirkby Stephen and Appleby but in general one gains a feeling that the company may have decided that the simplest solution, where a site was not obvious, was to locate a station every few miles and hope for the best!

The first report back to the committee was presented on 1st October 1872. Some of the expectations of traffic seem, in retrospect, to have been a little optimistic. The full report is summarised below:

Settle Junction: 'We recommend a small passenger station with requisite platform south of the junction to serve as an exchange station. Sidings to hold up trains and down trains will be required. The land for these and an approach to the station should be obtained.' The report also recommended four cottages, two each for signalmen and platelayers.

Settle Station: 'A large traffic may be expected at this station and ample siding accommodation must be provided. For the station it will be right to provide a platform 300 ft. long, goods shed for five wagons, horse/carriage way, a cattle dock with cattle pens for 12 trucks, the station buildings and station master's house. It will be needful to provide for a pumping station at the Ribble with needful tanks and engines to force water to the new station.' Six staff cottages were also recommended.

Horton-in-Ribblesdale: A small station was recommended to include station master's house, platforms, sidings for coal and goods, cattle dock for three wagons and cottages for six men.

Selside: The same arrangement and accommodation as at Horton was proposed for this location.

Hawes Junction: A small passenger exchange station was envisaged here, together with exchange sidings for goods traffic. In addition, 'For the locomotive service a steam shed to hold 24 engines with adequate water supply and for the housing of the staff, 30 cottages will be wanted.'

Hawes Station: Here, it was proposed to provide station master's house, platforms, sidings for goods and local traffic, goods shed to hold four wagons, horse and carriage dock, cattle dock to hold eight wagons, six cottages and a steam shed for two engines. Water supply was to be from the nearby tarn.

Kirkby Stephen: The proposal was for a station with two platforms, station building, station master's house, sidings for goods and coal traffic, goods shed to hold five wagons, horse and carriage dock, cattle dock for ten wagons and six cottages.

Crosby Garrett: An almost identical proposal as for Kirkby Stephen except that the goods shed was to hold three wagons and the cattle dock six.

Asby: 'A small station may be wanted for Asby and should include platforms, small station, station master's house, sidings for goods and coal, cattle dock for four wagons and six cottages.

Appleby: An identical specification to Kirkby Stephen was made with the addition that engine watering facilities were to be provided.

Long Marton: Identical to Crosby Garrett.

New Biggin: At this location, a small station was planned identical to the proposals for Horton-in-Ribblesdale except that the cattle dock should hold five wagons.

Langwathby: A station was proposed identical to Crosby Garrett and Long Marton except that the cattle dock should hold eight wagons.

Little Salkeld: The expediency of founding a station here was to be further considered.

Lazonby: As for Langwathby with the addition of an engine water supply.

Armathwaite: As for Langwathby except that the goods shed was planned to hold two wagons and the cattle dock five.

Cumwhinton: A small station was proposed to include platforms, station buildings, station master's house, sidings for goods and coal and six cottages.

Scotby: Identical to Cumwhinton.

Carlisle Petterill: Here was planned a goods shed for ten wagons, sidings for sorting, marshalling and exchange traffic, a steam shed for 24 engines at the south end of the land purchased and 40 cottages.

In addition to the above specific recommendations, the report also included a general comment that up and down lay-by sidings should generally be provided at every station and block post where crossovers should be laid. Finally, the report concluded that:

It may be found necessary to make a station for Dent dale between the north end of Blea Moor Tunnel and Dent Viaduct. There is a large dairy district adjoining, the produce whereof is now sent to Sedbergh.

Possibly the most interesting point arising from this first survey is the lavish locomotive facility originally envisaged for Hawes Junction (more recently known as Garsdale), together with the proposal to locate two further engines at Hawes itself. Of the original proposed stations, Selside was never built but Little Salkeld was. In addition, although there was never a station at Asby, one was constructed at Ormside of substantially similar nature to the version proposed.

These proposals must have been made public fairly soon for on 31st December 1872, Mr Crossley (the MR engineer) submitted to the Construction Committee a memorial from the Rev. G. W. Atkinson and other owners and occupiers of land at Culgaith and neighbourhood suggesting Culgaith as a suitable place for a station. The committee resolved that:

. . . the memorialists be informed that the question of a station at Culgaith had been previously considered and was abandoned in consequence of the extreme difficulty of finding a convenient site.

At the same meeting, an application for another station to be provided in the parish of Wetherall (in addition to Scotby and Cumwhinton) was considered. It was explained that a large plaster works was to be erected near there, traffic from which would not be less than 25,000 tons per year. The committee agreed to this suggestion and the station emerged as Cotehill although for a while it was referred to in the minutes as Duncowfold. Finally, on the same day, the committee agreed to have six further cottages erected at the Moorcock Inn near Hawes Junction. They were actually constructed immediately adjacent to the rail overbridge on the Hawes-

Sedbergh road some few hundred yards from the Moorcock.

The parishioners of Culgaith were not content with the Midland's refusal to provide a station and met to discuss the matter. In consequence of this meeting, the topic was again referred to Crossley in June 1873 to see if a satisfactory arrangement could be made. Crossley was instructed to communicate with the Reverend Atkinson but no record has been traced of the outcome (however, see below).

In September 1873, Johnson, Allport and Crossley were instructed to report on the amount of locomotive facilities required along the line as it would appear that the Midland was having second thoughts about its original plan. In February 1874 they reported:

We have considered the requirements of the locomotive department for the Settle and Carlisle district and recommend that accommodation be provided as follows: Hawes Junction—shed for 12 engines with tank to hold 36,000 gallons of water, also 20 cottages for men; Appleby—Water tank, 20,000 gallons; Lazonby—Water tank, 12,000 gallons; Carlisle—shed for 24 locomotives, complete as a locomotive station, water tank, 36,000 gallons also 25 cottages.

Tenders for the construction of the stations were received in mid-1874. On this occasion, mention was made for the first time of stations at Arten Gill and Helwith Bridge. Although tenders were approved, it was also resolved that: '. . . the site of the station for Arten Gill be held over so that details may be determined upon.' At this stage, station construction commenced but there appear to have been subsequent decisions made which were not fully minuted. For example, the proposed stations at Helwith Bridge and Selside never materialised but a station was built at Ribblehead which did not receive a mention at all until late 1875 and then only in connection with a progress report on the state of the works under construction.

In January 1875, a request was made for a station at the south end of Helm Tunnel at Breaks Hall estate. This came to nothing but the station at Ormside, like that at Ribblehead, seems to have been built without any mention in the minutes. Perhaps this was, in reality, a replacement station for Asby (see above) re-located for convenience. Also in 1875, the town of Appleby had decided to build an agricultural market near Appleby station which must have pleased the Midland—at all events, on 3rd June

1875, the company decided to build a road to the site of the market as far as the extent of the railway boundary.

Of the stations which eventually graced the line, only two remained to be settled by the time goods trains started to use the line in August 1875. These were Culgaith and Dent. Regarding the former location, certain evidence appears lacking but in October 1875, the clerk to the local highway district board wrote to Derby requesting a written guarantee from the Midland that '. . . the company would erect and keep open for traffic a passenger and goods station at Culgaith . . . in consideration of the Leith Ward Highway District Board widening and improving Scaw(?) gate road as arranged with Mr Crossley.' The Midland replied that '. . . the directors adhere to their engagement to make a passenger station at Culgaith as arranged and sidings for traffic, but not a goods station, provided proper roads are constructed to the station.'

From this exchange, one can only presume that Crossley's discussions with the local vicar in 1873 (above) had borne some fruit. At the same time, there must have been some delay in getting a decent road access because the station was not opened until 1880. Moreover, the architecture was quite unlike anything else on the Settle and Carlisle—but more of that in due course.

There is similar confusion in the committee minutes regarding the station for Dent(dale). The original proposals of 1872 envisaged the possibility of a station at Dent Head. In 1874 there was talk of a station at Arten Gill but in early October 1875, the committee resolved:

. . . that Mr Crossley and Mr Allport be requested to report to the next meeting of this committee on the site for Dent station as regards Lord Bective's offer to sell some land to the company.

Lord Bective's land would appear to have been at Dent Head for on 30th November 1875, the minutes recorded a decision to:

. . . adhere to the station being placed at Monkeybeck as arranged, the site suggested by Mr Punchard at Dent Head not being a suitable one.

This is the first positive mention in the minutes of the Monkeybeck site and, of course, the station for Dent was indeed built at this location, better known today as Cowgill.

PLATE 48 (top) This view looking south, is one of a rare pair of pictures taken at Garsdale (then Hawes Junction) in June 1905. Note, amongst other things, the immaculately groomed cattle dock, the old NER shed in the distance and the old signal box. (Photo: H. C. Casserley's collection.)

PLATE 49 (left) This second picture of 1905 vintage shows the view of Garsdale looking north. A train of MR six-wheelers is in the branch bay and the station sports a handsome complement of MR 'furniture'. Note the second signal box to the north of the down platform. In later years, the two boxes at Garsdale were replaced by the single (still extant) structure adjacent to the down station building—see Plate 50 (below). (Photo: H. C. Casserley's collection.)

PLATE 50 (below) Garsdale c. 1960. This picture, taken looking north, gives a general impression of the disposition of buildings and structures at this bleak outpost. Note that all the station buildings are basically of 'platform shelter' type. This picture presents an interesting contrast with the view at Plate 49. (Photo: Alan Robey.)

The difficulty in siting the station was road access. No matter what choice was made, the road ascent from the valley floor some 600 feet below the line would be fearsomely steep (it still is!). The Dent Head location favoured by Mr Punchard (Lord Bective's agent) may have been slightly more convenient from the construction point of view since the road through the dale passes under the line at this point. However, Dent Head is some seven or eight miles from the main village of Dent whereas the site chosen was only four miles distant!

All these delays resulted in Dent station not being opened until 1877.

At the same point in time, the Construction Committee minutes record that: 'The Hawes Junction engine establishment has been much altered and the work reduced.' In the event, all that ever appeared, other than watering facilities, was a turntable on the down side of the line and a very small engine shed on the up side which was used by the NER for its Hawes branch locomotive. Hawes itself never did get the planned shed for two engines.

By the time the line was fully opened in May 1876, only the finishing touches remained to be put to most of the stations. Shortly afterwards, on 19th June 1876, the Rev. E. H. Woodall of Settle wrote to Derby suggesting that the name of Batty Green station should be changed to Ribblehead. This was agreed and from this point onwards, the minutes are mostly concerned with tying up loose ends for the first few years of the line's life.

The Midland had planned on the grand scale for its stations and buildings on the Settle and Carlisle. Although the original 1872 proposals were slightly modified, the facilities which eventually emerged were very close to those originally planned and very impressive they were too. In fact, one of the first things that probably strikes the casual observer of the Settle and Carlisle on first acquaintance with the line is the extremely durable nature of its architecture, even where traffic must needs be rather scarce. One cannot escape the conclusion that the Midland Railway, having finally started to build the line, resolved that there were to be no half measures about it. Massive goods sheds, rows of cottages, water towers and the like were erected along the whole route and since they bid fair to become amongst the more permanent relics of this unique railway, it is, perhaps, time to study them in greater detail.

Settle/Carlisle Architecture

The railway designed buildings along the Settle and Carlisle fall into two natural categories. Firstly are the purely 'railway' structures (stations, goods sheds etc.) and secondly are the domestic dwelling houses built by the railway to house its staff.

The general style of the buildings is what might best be described as 'Derby Gothic'—a characteristic type of Midland Railway structure not confined to this area. More than many British companies, the Midland set its own stamp on the structures it built along its right of way and very similar buildings to those found on the Settle and Carlisle were erected as far afield as South West England on the route to Bath or at Wirksworth in Derbyshire. However, although very similar to that of many other MR buildings, the precise design adopted for the Settle and Carlisle structures was unique to that line.

With but one exception, Culgaith, all the stations between Settle Junction and Scotby possessed station buildings of similar type. There were three alternative designs for the principal station building and two designs of platform shelter. Most stations had one principle building and one shelter on the opposite platform but Hawes Junction (Garsdale) was entirely furnished with buildings of the 'platform shelter' type (Plate 50), while Crosby Garrett had a main building and two platform shelters. Culgaith was equipped with a totally different style of building, quite alien to the rest of the line but with a certain rustic charm somewhat reminiscent of the more exotic MR stations in the Peak District or even, surprisingly, to some of the ex-Furness Railway stations in the Lake District (Plates 51 and 52).

Turning now to the structures in detail, the main station buildings were all of a double gable type separated by a central porch through which passenger entry to the building was gained via a wood and glass screen (Plate 56). Facing away from the platforms on the other side of the buildings was a single projecting central gable. On the smallest type of building (Plates 53 and 54), there was a low roofed extension built on at the left hand end (viewed from the platform side) which contained toilets and store rooms.

PLATES 51/52 *The platform shelter (left) and the main station building of the architecturally unique Culgaith in 1963. The latter building has now (1979) been converted to a dwelling house. (Photos: D. Jenkinson.)*

PLATE 53 *Platform side view of the smallest type of standard Settle and Carlisle station building. This example is Ribblehead (taken in 1962) and shows the slight modification to the basic design caused by tile hanging on some of the walls. Note also the modified window in the left hand gable. This was the building used for many years as a venue for monthly church services.*
(Photo: D. Jenkinson.)

PLATE 54 *Hawes Joint station yard in 1963 showing a rear view of the smallest type of standard building, complete with a full set of original bargeboards. In spite of total closure, this station and goods shed have been saved from destruction to form the basis of a small museum for Upper Wensleydale.*
(Photo: D. Jenkinson.)

Front Elevation

Rear Elevation

End Elevations

PORCH ROOF

SMALL SIZED STATION BUILDING

10   5   0   10   20   30
Feet

FIG. 14 *Small sized Settle and Carlisle station building. Drawing based on photographs and field measurements taken at Hawes Joint.*

PLATE 55 *The medium sized standard Settle and Carlisle station building at Lazonby (1963). Perhaps the most characteristic of the three main types, this example is built of red sandstone and was largely unaltered at the time of photography. Note the M R station lamp. Lazonby was the last station on the line to retain a full complement of these distinctive features. (Photo: D. Jenkinson.)*

The medium sized buildings were of rather similar, but generally more massive proportions, with an extension at both ends (Plate 55). The largest buildings, confined to Settle, Kirkby Stephen and Appleby, were derived from the medium sized buildings but instead of a separately roofed extension at the left hand end, the main structure was elongated and a third, smaller, roof gable was present on the platform side (Plate 57). Line drawings of all three types of building are given at Figures 14, 15 and 16.

The building material generally reflected the local area. Thus, at the southern end of the line the buildings are of millstone grit or limestone while in the Eden valley section, red sandstone is employed. However, one or two stations were built of brick (e.g. Appleby). Considerable attention was devoted to detail work. All the stations were originally fitted at the gable ends with ornamental wooden bargeboards of which two basic styles were adopted, one for the smallest buildings and the other style for the medium

PLATE 56 *Close-up view of the station screen at Appleby (1962). (Photo: D. Jenkinson.)*

PLATE 57 *The largest type of station building was confined to three locations only. The example illustrated (Appleby) is additionally interesting in being one of the few brick built stations on the line. Comparison of this picture with plate 55 will show how the large style of building was derived from the medium sized version. (Photo: BR LMR.)*

Front Elevation

Rear Elevation

End Elevations

MEDIUM SIZED STATION BUILDING

10 5 0 10 20 30
Feet

FIG. 15 *Medium sized Settle and Carlisle station building. (Drawing based on BR official plans.)*

PLATE 58 *Rear view of the main station building at Appleby (1962). This is one of only two stations (the other is Settle) still in regular use. (Photo: BR LMR.)*

PLATE 59 (below) *End view of platform shelter at Settle—May 1962. Note the alternative bargeboard style to Appleby (below). (Photo: D. Jenkinson.)*

sized and large buildings—see pictures. A trefoil device was usually present on the upper wall of the gable ends whilst windows, especially in the smallest type of building, were often quite elaborately glazed.

The platform shelters were mostly to one basic design (Figure 16 and Plate 60). Detail differences were, however, present. For example, the bargeboards generally matched the style of those found on the main building and at Garsdale, some of the shelters were also fitted with fireplaces and chimneys. The principal exceptions to this basic style of platform shelter were at three locations in the Eden Valley (Little Salkeld, Langwathby and Newbiggin) where a wooden type of platform shelter was employed rather reminiscent of some of the structures on the London extension of the Midland Railway (Plate 61).

Apart from the passenger buildings and, of course, the inevitable signal boxes, the most commonly occurring additional structures were

PLATE 60 *The most commonly occurring type of platform shelter—this example being at Appleby. (Photo: BR LMR.)*
PLATE 61 *The much less common wooden platform shelter found at but three stations. The picture shows the shelter at Langwathby. Those at Little Salkeld and New Biggin were similar except for the detail of window design. As can be seen, this type of building was essentially a wooden version of the standard stone or brick structure. (Photo: D. Jenkinson.)*

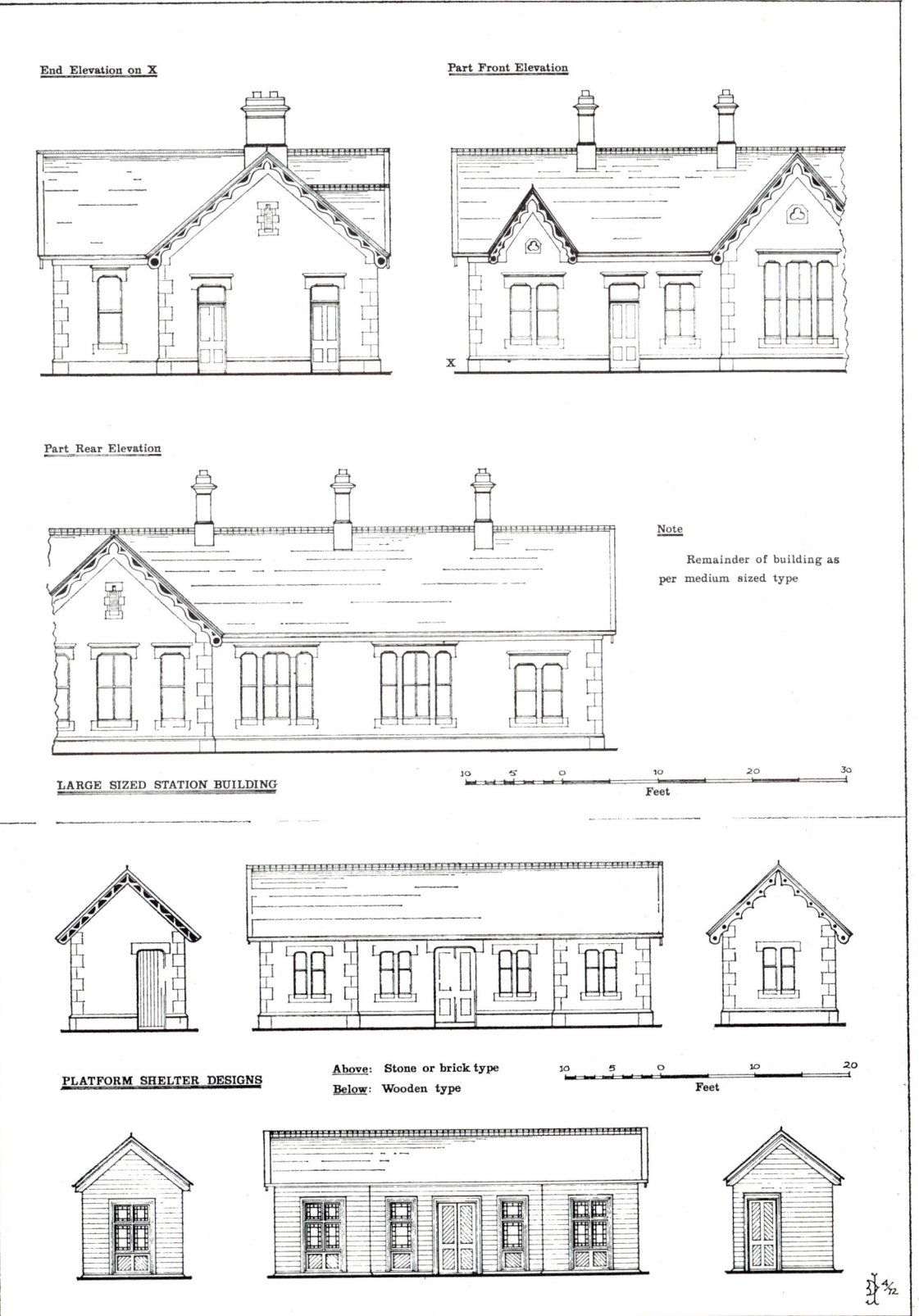

End Elevation on X

Part Front Elevation

X

Part Rear Elevation

Note

Remainder of building as per medium sized type

LARGE SIZED STATION BUILDING

10   5   0   10   20   30
Feet

PLATFORM SHELTER DESIGNS

Above: Stone or brick type
Below: Wooden type

10   5   0   10   20
Feet

FIG. 16 (*top*) *Large sized Settle and Carlisle station building.* (*Drawing based on BR official plans.*)
FIG. 16 (*bottom*) *Settle and Carlisle platform shelter designs.* (*Drawing based on BR official plans—stone/brick type; and field measurements—wooden type.*)

PLATES 62/63 *The goods sheds at Armathwaite (left) and Langwathby. All Settle and Carlisle goods sheds conformed to this pattern, variations being essentially confined to length, window design and building material. The water tank built onto the end of Langwathby shed was, however, unusual. (Photos: D. Jenkinson.)*

permanent goods sheds. These were all to one basic architectural style but varied in length according to location. They were confined to what were felt likely to be the more important stations and the original 1872 recommendations were followed almost to the letter. The main exception was at Armathwaite where a 'three wagon' shed was provided rather than the 'two wagon' shed originally envisaged (see page 48).

The goods sheds were massive (Plates 62 to 65, Figure 17) and rather reminiscent of the best ecclesiastical practice of the Nonconformist churches of the time—at least so it appears to the author who, let it be added, is of Nonconformist religious persuasion himself! Even the windows had a semi-hallowed appearance (Plate 64). In terms of building material, the goods sheds were always constructed from local stone.

Of the other, purely railway structures, the most noteworthy were the water towers. These were sited at various strategic locations along the line, generally in accordance with the plans of 1872 but with a noteworthy additional structure to serve Garsdale troughs. The style of the metal tank plates was pure Midland but the supporting structures showed some variety and, once more, reflected the local building materials (Plates 66 and 67).

Turning now to the domestic buildings, two general types of house were provided. The most imposing were the station masters' houses (Plates 69 and 70, Figure 18). These were all to a common 'L' shaped plan built either left or right-handed, but with slight detail differences between individual members. They were provided at all stations except Culgaith and Garsdale. At Culgaith, a small bungalow was built (Plate 68) and at Garsdale, the station master lived in one of the several terrace houses.

The most commonly seen dwelling houses were of two storey 'terrace' type. They were scattered along the line both at the larger stations

PLATES 64/65 *The road vehicle side of Appleby goods shed (left) and Kirkby Stephen. These were five wagon structures as is evidenced at Appleby by the more numerous windows between the loading bays compared with Langwathby and Armathwaite. This window design was repeated with but little modification at all locations except Kirkby Stephen. It is also worth mentioning that the shed at Kirkby Stephen did not have recessed wall areas on the side opposite the road vehicle access doors. There were simply seven equally spaced 'gothic' type windows of the type shown in the picture. (Photos: D. Jenkinson.)*

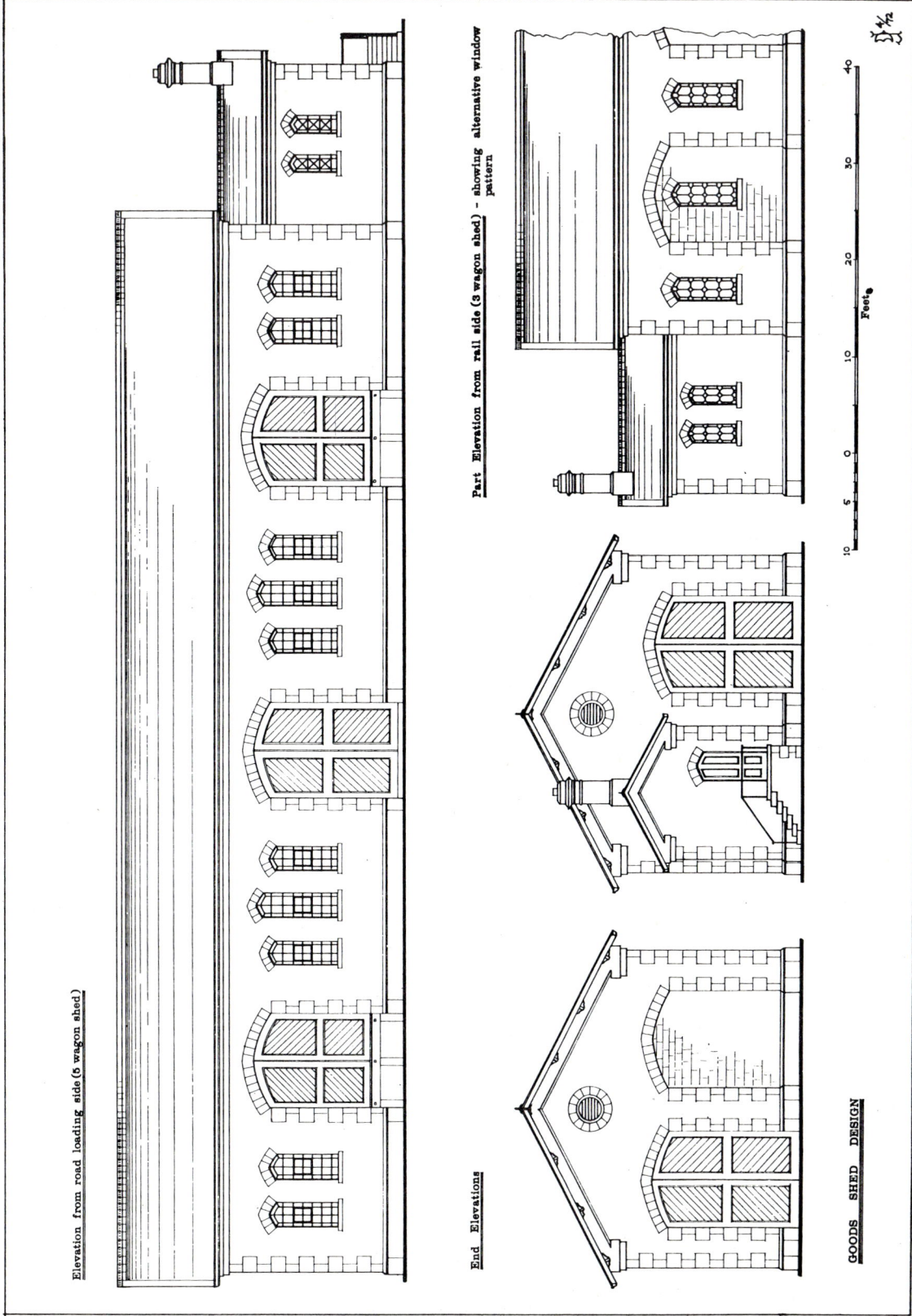

Elevation from road loading side (5 wagon shed)

Part Elevation from rail side (3 wagon shed) – showing alternative window pattern

Feet

End Elevations

GOODS SHED DESIGN

FIG. 17 *Settle and Carlisle goods shed designs. Main elevations are based on BR official plans of Settle shed but part side elevation of 3-wagon shed is based on field measurements at Armathwaite and Lazonby. Window design on this elevation is much more common than that of Settle.*

PLATES 66/67 *The two largest water tank houses on the Settle and Carlisle. Above is shown the somewhat ornate structure at Settle while below is the less ostentatious but rather more rugged structure at Garsdale—now, alas, demolished. This latter building probably achieved as much fame in its secondary function as the local village hall as it did in providing water for the railway engines! (Photos: D. Jenkinson.)*

PLATE 68 *(right) The non-standard Stationmaster's bungalow at Culgaith. (Photo: D. Jenkinson.)*

PLATES 69/70 *(below) Stationmasters' houses at Kirkby Stephen (left) and Lazonby. The two houses are opposite handed and that at Kirkby Stephen is additionally unusual in having been cement rendered and painted white. Most Stationmasters' houses conformed to one or other of these two designs—see also Fig. 18—but at one or two locations, e.g. Dent, a slightly altered version was provided. (Photos: D. Jenkinson.)*

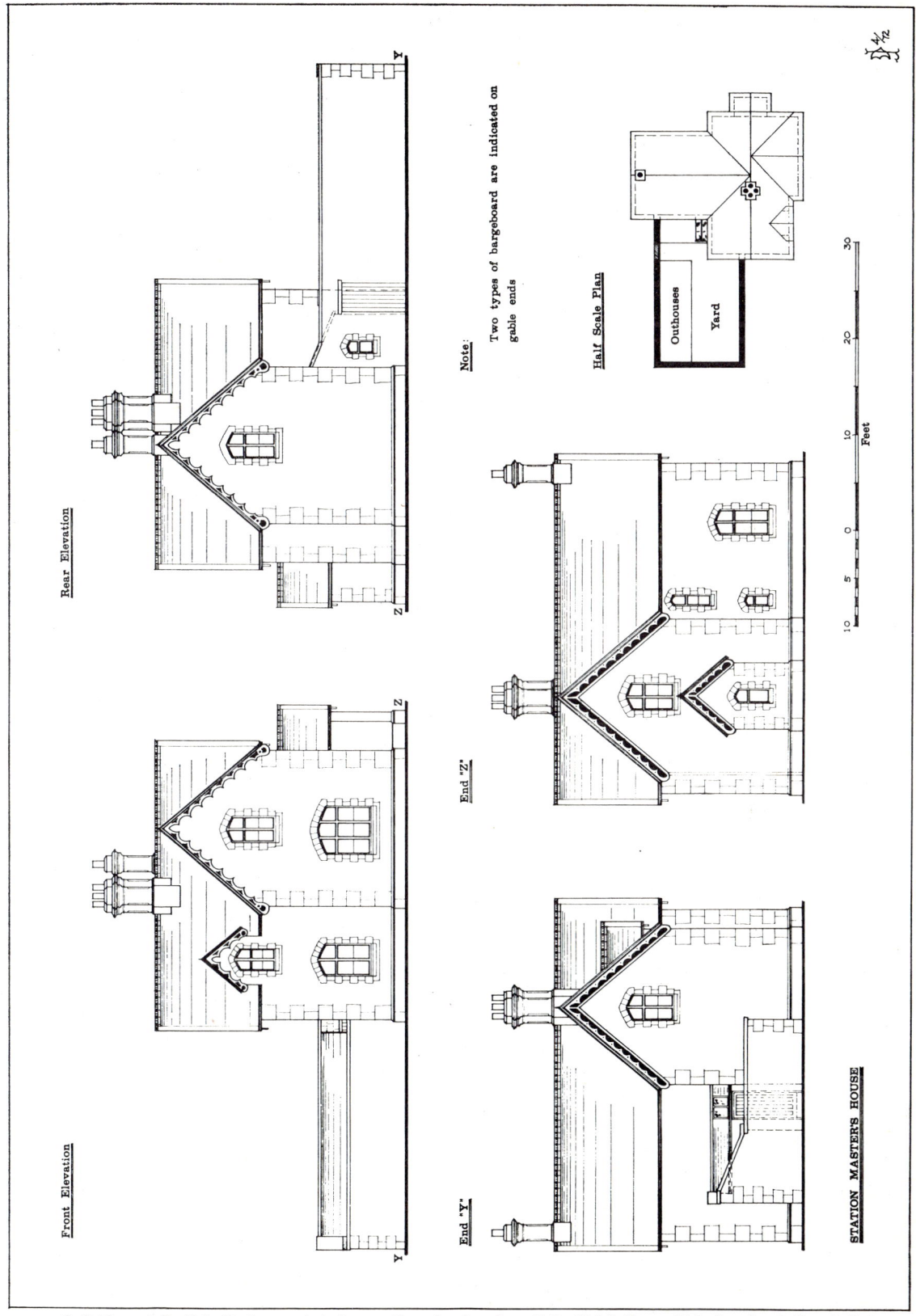

Front Elevation

Rear Elevation

End "Y"

End "Z"

Note:

Two types of bargeboard are indicated on gable ends

Half Scale Plan

Outhouses

Yard

Feet

STATION MASTER'S HOUSE

FIG. 18 *Settle and Carlisle Stationmaster's house. Drawing based on BR official plans. This drawing is 'handed' the same way as the house at Lazonby—see Plate 70.*

PLATES 71–74 *Railwaymens' houses. Above (left) is part of the terrace at Lazonby, built in red sandstone while above (right) is the similar terrace of limestone cottages at Garsdale. The stepped arrangement makes it rather attractive. Below are shown the bungalows at Kirkby Stephen (left) and details of the entry porches at Selside (right). The latter cottages—see also Plates 78/79—are representative of the alternative style of terrace with the first floor windows surmounted by gables.*
(Photos: D. Jenkinson.)

and intermediate locations, according to need, and were generally to one of two basic styles (Plates 73 and 74). In both types, entry was gained via a double sided projecting porch which served two houses. In certain locations (e.g. Kirkby Stephen), additional single storey houses were provided. Overall, the number of dwellings provided was rather less than originally envisaged by Allport, Crossley and Kirtley in 1872.

It is less easy to summarise the style of the engineering structures along the route and pictures probably afford the best method of appreciating the variety which is present. The viaducts are, of course, the dominant features but there are many other examples of massive construction in the shape of bridges, culverts, retaining walls and the like. Most engineering structures were built from local stone and frequently one can find alongside, or close to the site of the more imposing works, an abandoned quarry from whence the building materials came.

Station Layouts

A principal object of this book is to try and show how function affects the outward appearance of various aspects of the railway landscape. This is particularly true of station layouts. Firstly, however, one should define more precisely what is meant by 'station' and 'layout'. Within the context of this particular discussion, therefore, a station will be defined as any location where originating traffic, both passenger and goods, was offered to the railway and where facilities were provided to handle it. The layout of the station will be taken to embrace the disposition of both tracks and structures which were provided to enable the station to fulfil its function as defined above.

Settle and Carlisle stations were, in the main, spaciously laid out. At the same time one cannot help but feel that the company may have over-estimated the size of the facilities it was going to need. One cannot be sure, of course, but it seems highly unlikely that the majority of stations were ever seriously overtaxed in terms of accommodation space. In fact, judging by the traffic figures (see Chapter 10), it seems probable that for most of the time, even the smallest stations could have handled most of their trade with far less facilities than were, in the event, provided.

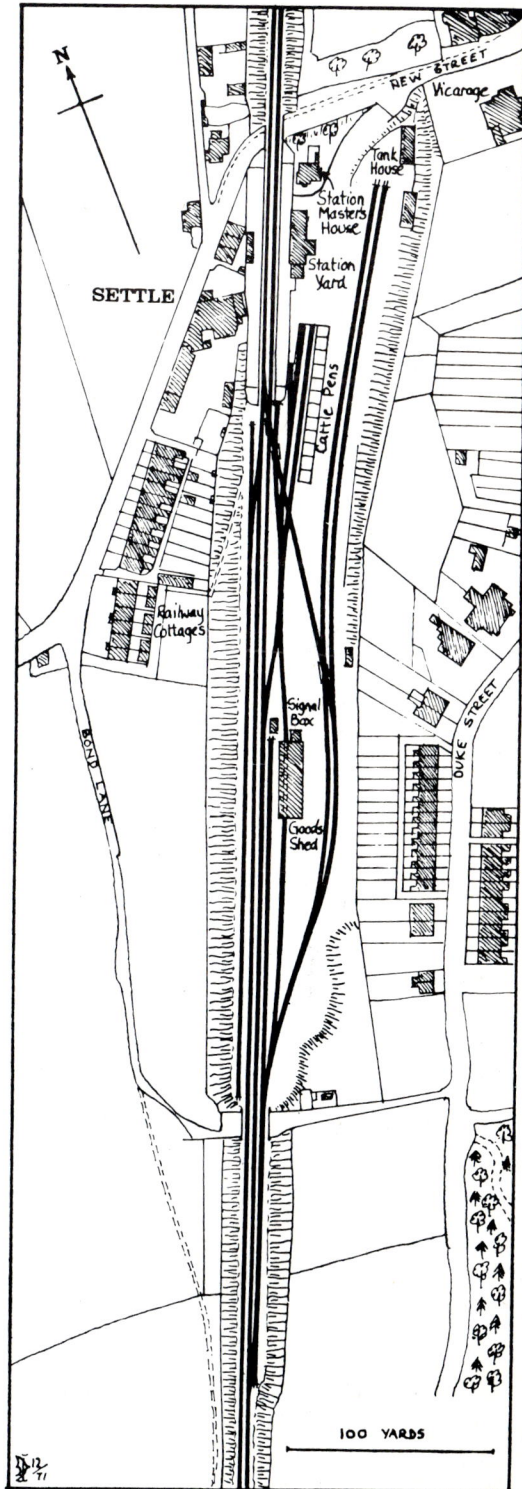

FIG. 19 *Plan of Settle Station c. 1910 (Crown Copyright Reserved.)*

It is by no means clear just why the Midland planned the stations in this way. Land was, no doubt, plentiful and probably fairly cheap but it was rarely very level. The grading of goods yard sites and the provision of cattle docks, goods sheds, platforms and so forth must have represented, in toto, a reasonably large sum of money and one might have expected rather more parsimonious facilities, bearing in mind that the line itself cost far more than was estimated. On the other hand, the Midland was not a parsimonious railway and it was entirely in character for it to establish its presence in the traditional manner.

The station layouts were designed to satisfy two considerations. First, of course, were the facilities required for local traffic but secondly, as stated in the original 1872 proposals for station sites, it was also necessary to provide lay-by facilities in order to enable slow goods trains to be shunted out of the way of faster moving traffic.

By the time the line was built, operating procedures had progressed beyond the very primitive methods adopted at the start of the railway age. Further refinement was still to come but, in general, the setting out of the tracks of a railway in the 1870s clearly reflected the 50 years of experience already gained. In particular, the inherent dangers of the facing turnout were well appreciated. It is no part of this work to go into the intricacies of railway trackwork but a brief digression on the facing point will not be out of place.

Facing turnouts are so-called because the train when running in the normal direction on the main line would approach them from the 'open' end. They thus afford a choice of path to the oncoming train; but the danger is that without adequate locking or protection, the blades might move beneath the wheels of the train thus causing derailment. To ensure that the point is locked in one position costs more than leaving the turnout as a simple pair of point blades operated by a lever or point rodding. Clearly, such locking can only be justified where main running roads diverge. In most other locations it is better to gain access to yards and the like by

PLATE 75 *In order to ensure a good run at the bank, the alignment of tracks at Settle Junction is such as to favour the northbound trains heading for Carlisle as is clearly seen in the accompanying picture of the down Leeds-Glasgow express negotiating the junction in May 1963 behind a BR Sulzer Type 4. Note how the line to Morecambe at the junction is slewed slightly to allow the Settle and Carlisle trains to negotiate the trackwork without slowing down.* (*Photo: D. Jenkinson.*)

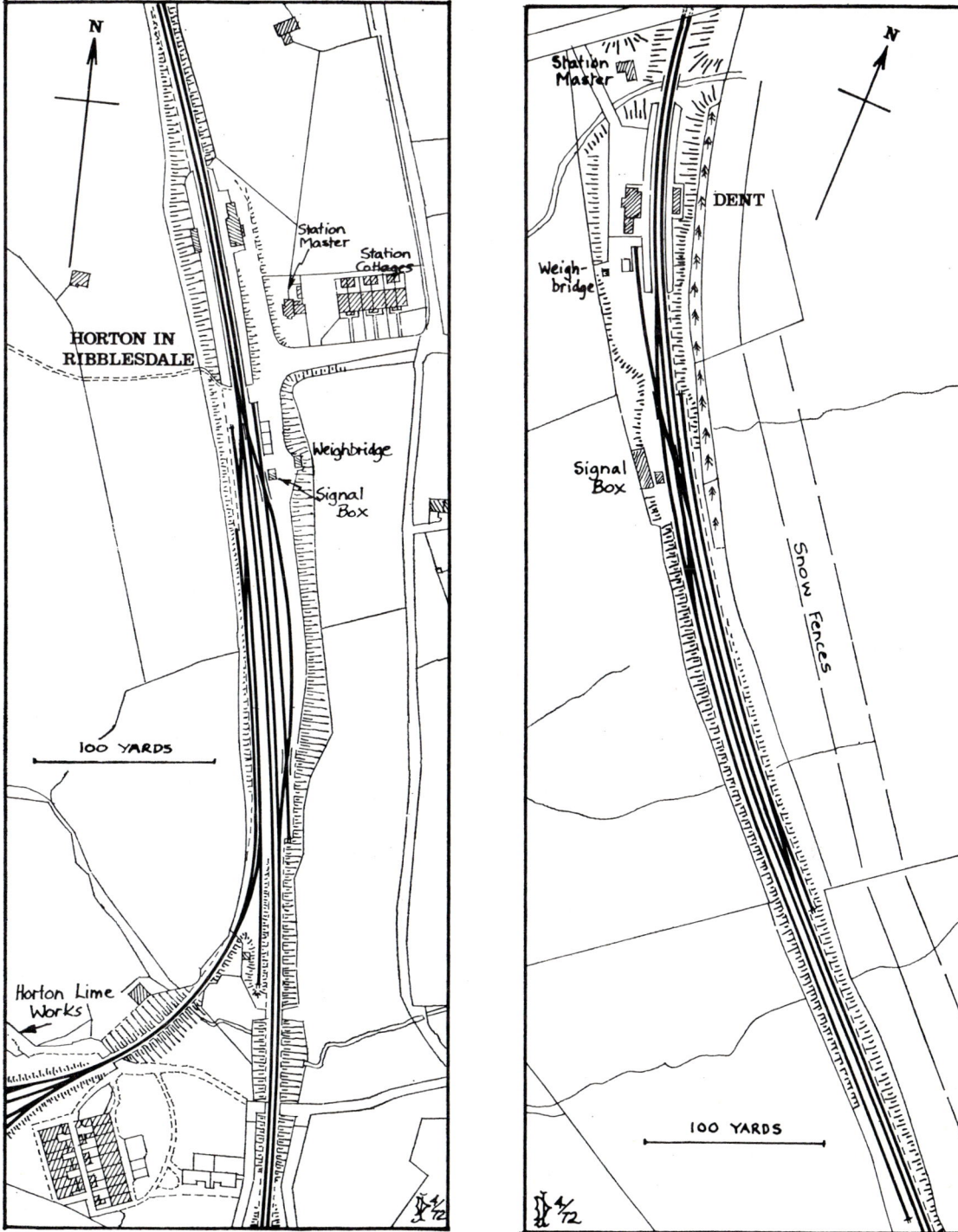

FIG. 20 (*left*) *Plan of Horton-in-Ribblesdale Station c. 1909.* (*Crown Copyright Reserved.*)
FIG. 21 (*right*) *Plan of Dent Station c. 1909.* (*Crown Copyright Reserved.*)

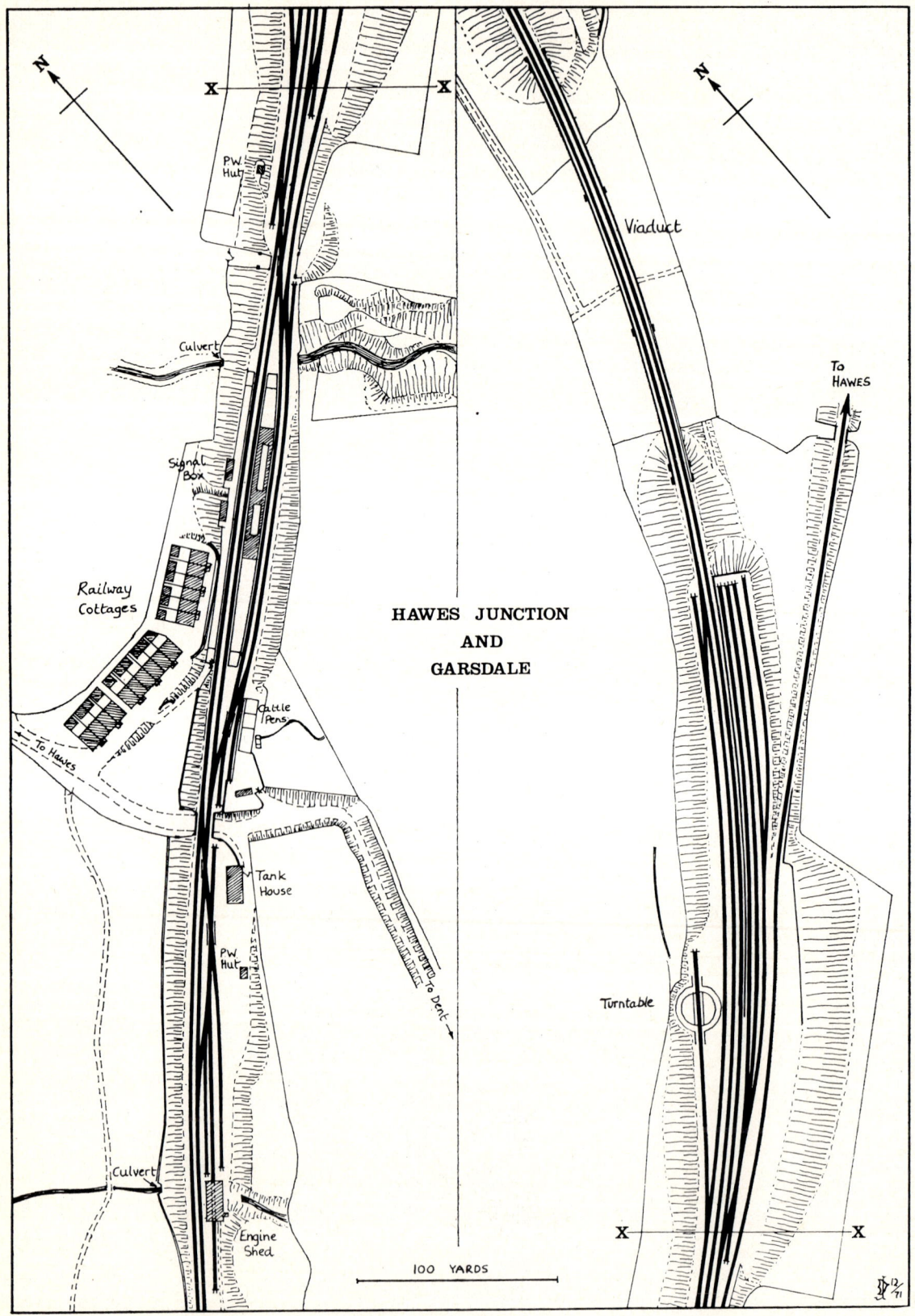

FIG. 22 *Plan of Hawes Junction and Garsdale Station c. 1930—based on BR official drawings.*

proceeding beyond the location where the yard tracks converged with the running roads and then slowly reverse into the yard, when the danger of derailment is considerably reduced by virtue of the much lower running speed. In general, only when such reversal would cause unacceptable delays to traffic is a facing turnout justified.

The Settle/Carlisle is a classic example of this philosophy applied over a considerable stretch of main line. The Midland was particularly averse to facing points and often went to more than the usual amount of trouble to avoid them. In consequence, many of its stations exhibited a quite characteristic track layout and the line under study was no exception. When originally built, there were no facing points at all in the southbound direction between Petterill Bridge and Settle Junctions and only one (immediately north of Appleby station) in the northbound direction. It was not until much later in LMS and BR days that facing crossovers were provided at Long Meg to speed up access to this very important anhydrite works (Plate 76) and genuine running loops, as opposed to lay-bys, installed at Blea Moor (Plate 31). Even at Garsdale, access to the Hawes branch could only be gained by reversal off the main line. Attention to details of this nature ensured for the Midland that its new route over the Pennines was as free as possible from possible speed and other restrictions to main line trains.

Not surprisingly, bearing in mind that the whole line was conceived and constructed as a single entity, a fairly consistent pattern of facilities was provided. The least important stations, of course, had a minimum of siding space, together with the lay-bys (fig 21); but wherever covered goods sheds were provided, the goods yards tended to be bigger, and the sheds at the main line locations were invariably located on a double ended loop off one of the goods yard sidings. At Hawes Joint, the goods shed was located on a conventional 'dead end' siding (fig 23). Regardless of the size of the station, loading banks and cattle pens were almost always placed fairly close to the station buildings which usually enabled one road access to serve for both passenger and goods traffic. Siting considerations decreed that variations did occur between individual stations but a study of

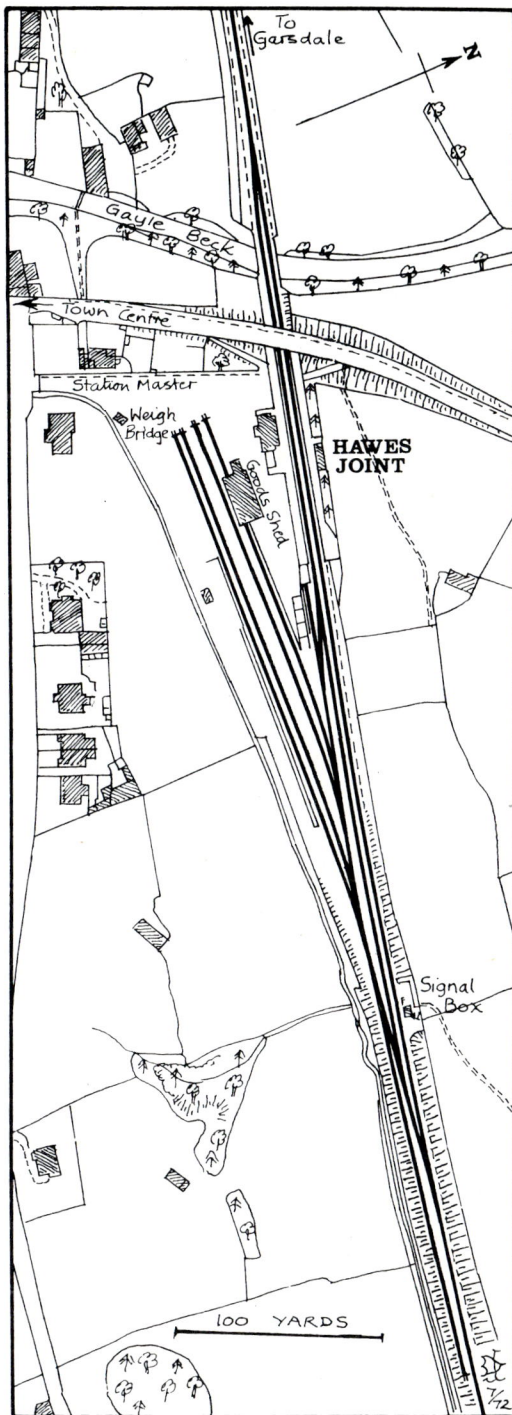

FIG. 23 *Plan of Hawes Joint Station c. 1912.* (*Crown Copyright Reserved.*)

PLATE 76 *Stanier Class 8F 2–8–0 No. 48158 heading south past Long Meg sidings with an express freight on 12th October 1965. This picture shows the engine passing over the facing turnout off the up main line which was added in fairly recent times to facilitate speedy access to the sidings. (Photo: D. Jenkinson.)*

the layouts illustrating this chapter will indicate the high degree of conformity which was achieved.

An interesting oddity about the goods yards is the side of the line on which they were built. Generally speaking, the yards were on the up side of the line south of Appleby and on the down side at and north of this town. There were exceptions and the coincidence is probably accidental but it is just conceivable that they were sited, where possible, in anticipation of a local freight movement pattern either northwards to Carlisle (in the Eden valley) or southwards to Hellifield on the remainder of the route.

Although most stations were given the basic facilities, certain locations eventually reflected particularly important local traffic. Thus, for example, Appleby and Lazonby both had large cattle yards close by the station, Ribblehead and Horton-in-Ribblesdale had provision for mineral handling, Garsdale had interchange sidings and so forth.

Completing the station 'picture' as it were, was the distribution of domestic and other buildings. These tended to be located close to the station main site and this, in turn, led to the creation of small railway 'settlements' at many places along the line. In more than one location, these settlements were the only significant signs of civilisation in the immediate vicinity of the railway (e.g. Garsdale, Kirkby Stephen). Naturally, where stations were located close to villages and towns such as Horton or Settle, the railway houses merely served to enlarge the existing settlements.

Finally, one should mention the very characteristic groups of dwelling houses totally separated from the stations. These varied from a pair of cottages to a whole terrace and were located at such places as Salt Lake, Blea Moor, Ais Gill and the like. Provided for signalmen and platelayers, these tiny communities had a character all their own and were very much part of the Settle and Carlisle scene (Plates 78 and 80).

PLATE 77 *Hawes station yard— May 1963. At this time, although the branch had been closed to passengers for many years, and closed throughout for all traffic to Garsdale, freight was still being worked eastward to Northallerton and the station was in a surprisingly good state of repair. Note the NER lamp on the cattle dock. (Photo: D. Jenkinson.)*

PLATES 78–80 *Lineside cottages at non-station locations. These pictures show (above) the front and rear views of the distinctive terraces at Selside—of which two exist at this location. A further example of these isolated mini-settlements can be seen at Ais Gill (left) where the conventional two storey house is associated with a bungalow terrace like those seen at Kirkby Stephen (see Plate 7 page 10).*
(Photos: D. Jenkinson (2); W. Hubert Foster.)

PLATE 81 *Armathwaite station in its wooded surrounds looking north in May 1964. Only a year later, the goods depot was closed and it was not to be long before this once well cared for station was to look rather neglected. (Photo: D. Jenkinson.)*

Conclusions

In this and the preceding four chapters, the writer has attempted to show some of the reasons behind the outward appearance of the Settle and Carlisle railway as a feature of the landscape of north west England. However, whether it is in the location and alignment of the route, the nature of the engineering structures or the physical and visual characteristics of its stations and buildings, the fact remains that in the last analysis, it is the sum total of all these features which is far more significant than the individual contribution of any one of them.

The whole line presents a visual unity very rare, if not unique, in the railways of Britain. This, in fair measure, is because it did not grow piecemeal like so many other main line railways; but perhaps more significantly it is also because the railway is a product of its time. When the line was built, the Victorians had mastered the techniques of the Industrial Revolution and there is in this line none of the tentative nature of many earlier railways. It was built by people who possessed supreme confidence in the technology of their age and who were not afraid to use it and show it off. Thus, the Midland's epic road to Carlisle strides magnificently on its way through the northern hills with a most remarkable sureness of foot. Built without the aid of bulldozers, earth movers and other modern impedimenta, it is, if you like, the railway equivalent of King Edward I's mighty castles in Wales. One can only hope that in the future when, perhaps, all that is left of it are the mouldering ruins amidst the barren Pennine fells, at least some of the visiting tourists will pause for a few moments to wonder at the men whose vision, persistence, sweat and lives made it all possible.

Notes 1. The following eight pages contain the remainder of the station layout plans, together with additional photographs. The main text resumes on page 79.

2. No plans have been located for Ribblehead and Scotby stations.

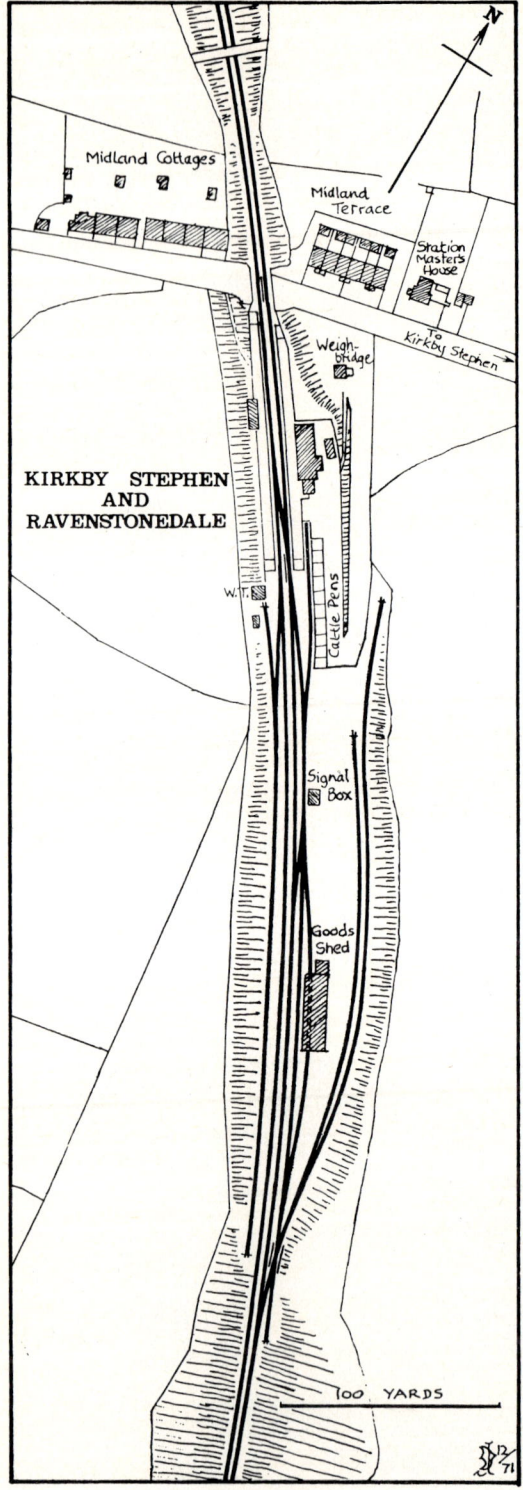

FIG. 24 *Plan of Kirkby Stephen station c. 1915.* (*Crown Copyright Reserved.*)

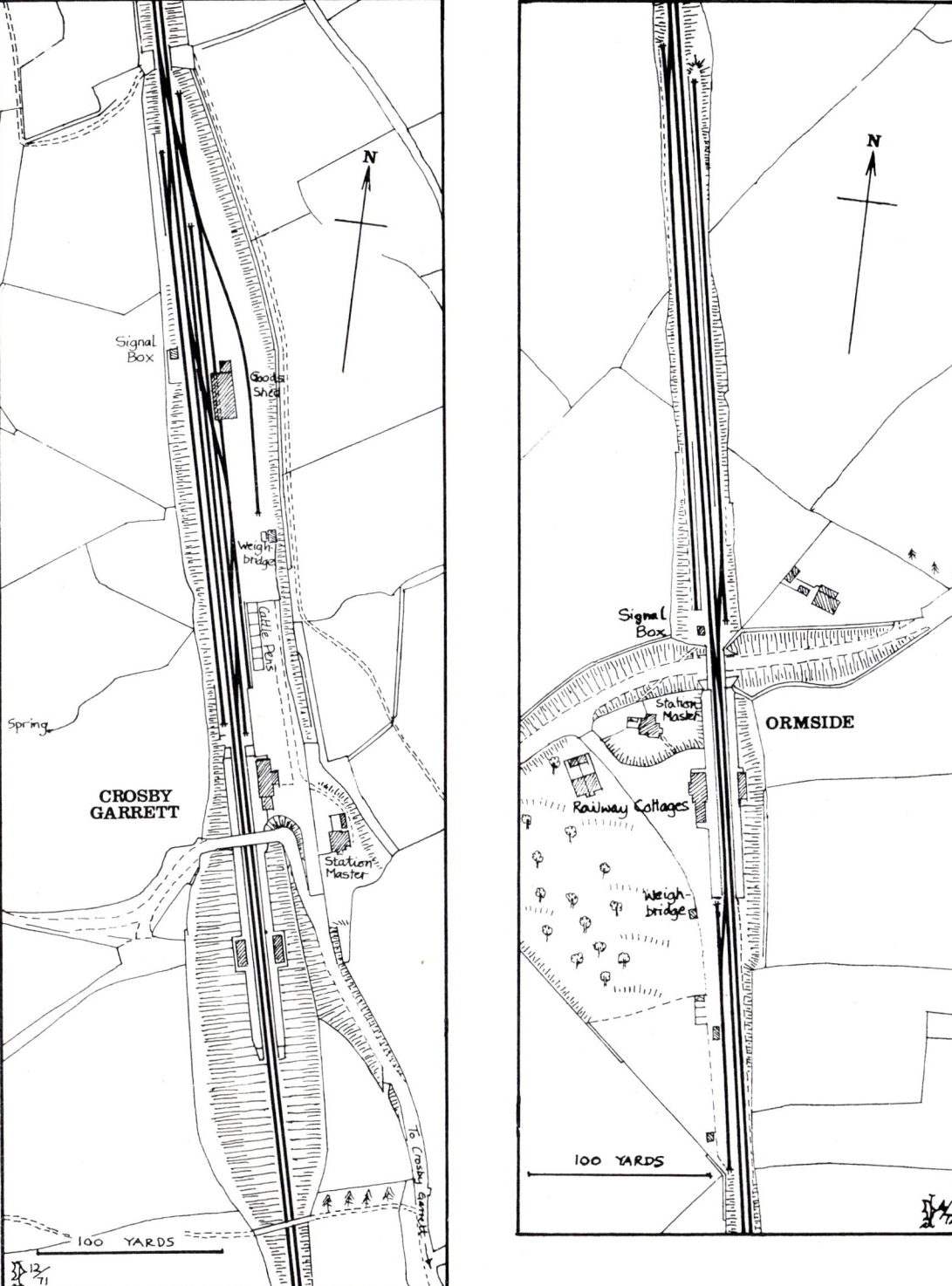

FIG. 25 (*left*) *Plan of Crosby Garrett Station c. 1915.* (*Crown Copyright Reserved.*)
FIG. 26 (*right*) *Plan of Ormside Station c. 1915.* (*Crown Copyright Reserved.*)

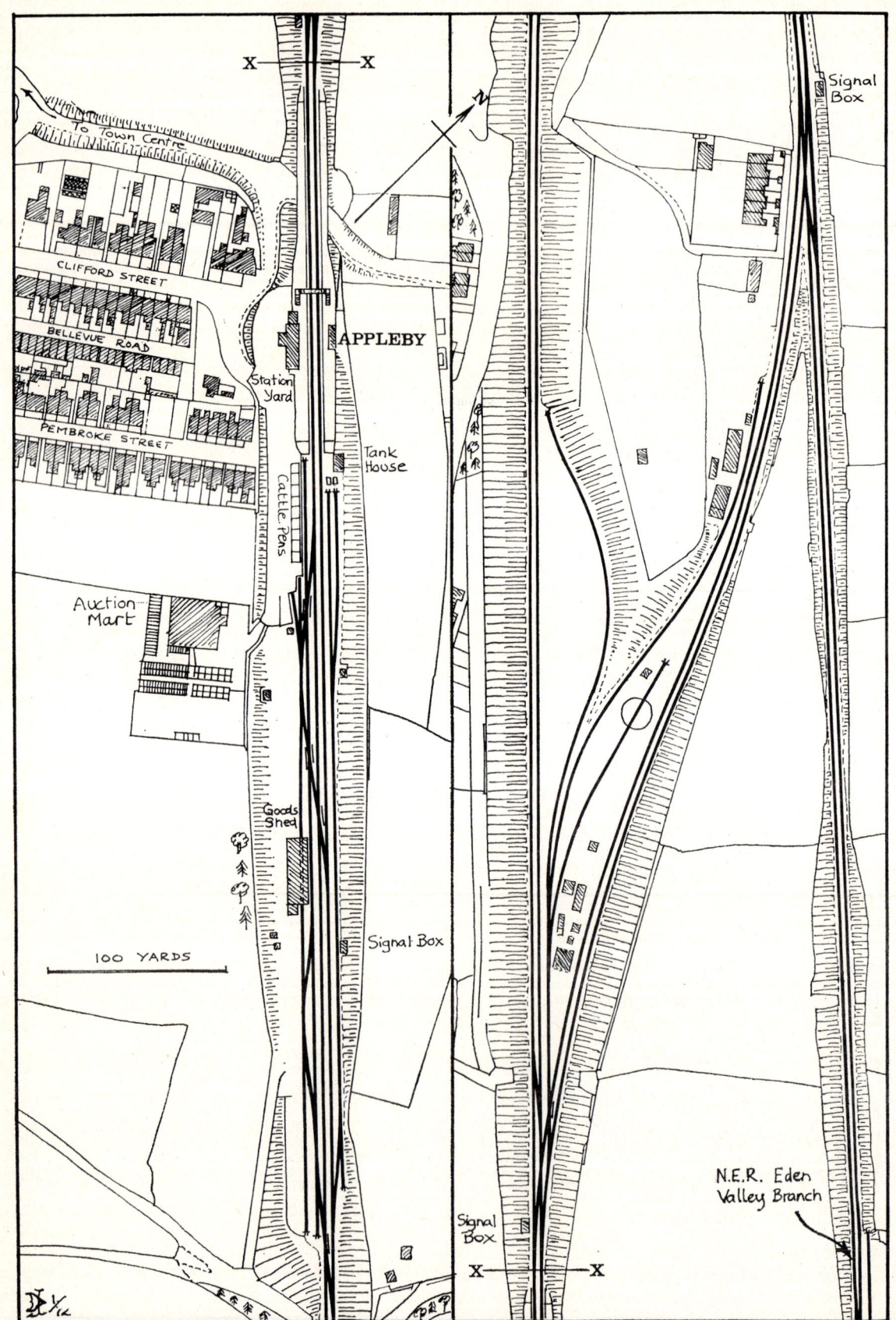

Clifford Street

Bellevue Road

Pembroke Street

To Town Centre

APPLEBY

Station Yard

Tank House

Cattle Pens

Auction Mart

Goods Shed

Signal Box

100 YARDS

Signal Box

Signal Box

N.E.R. Eden Valley Branch

X—X

X—X

FIG. 27 *Plan of Appleby Station c. 1916. (Crown Copyright Reserved.)*

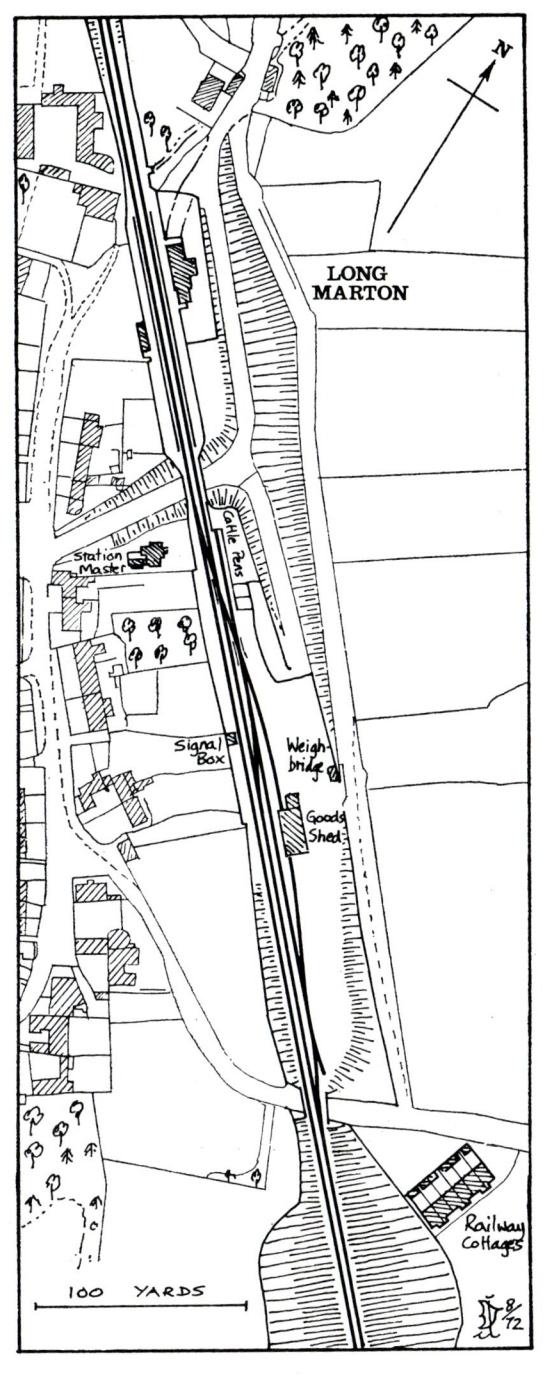

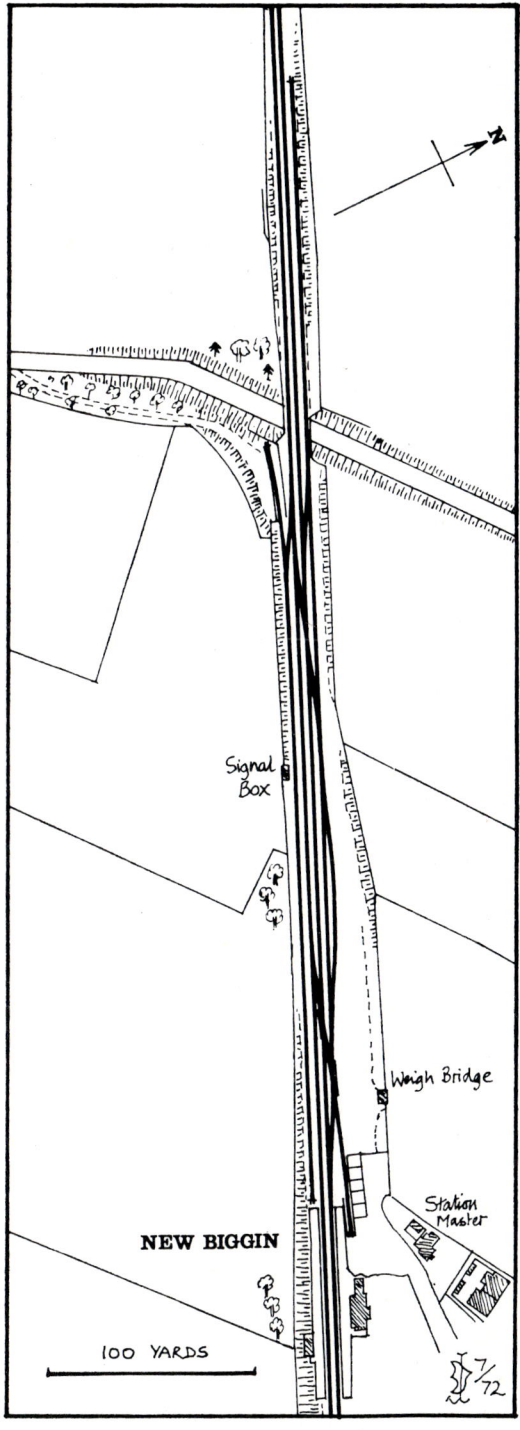

FIG. 28 (*left*) *Plan of Long Marton Station c. 1915. (Crown Copyright Reserved.)*
FIG. 29 (*right*) *Plan of New Biggin Station c. 1916. (Crown Copyright Reserved.)*

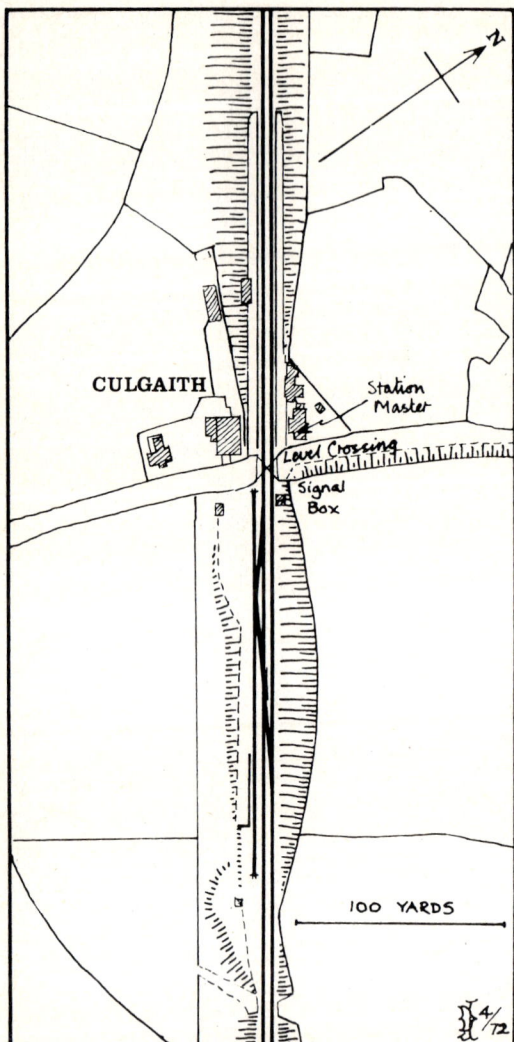

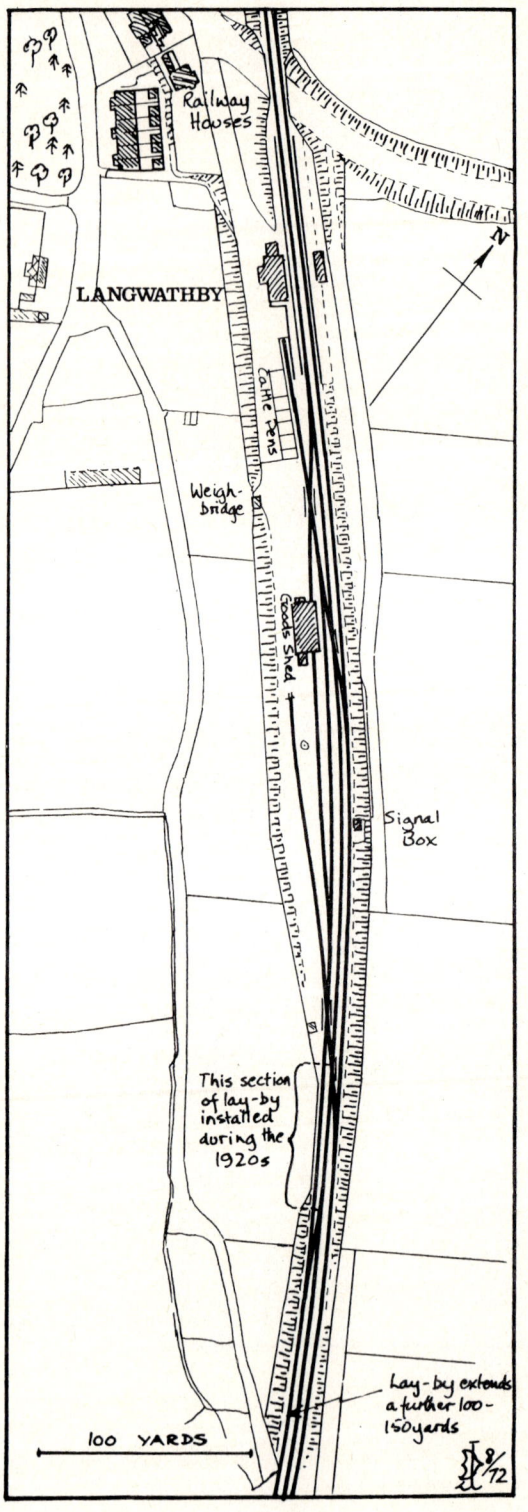

FIG. 30 (*above*) *Plan of Culgaith station c. 1925.*
(*Crown Copyright Reserved.*)

FIG. 31 (*right*) *Plan of Langwathby station c. 1925.*
(*Crown Copyright Reserved.*)

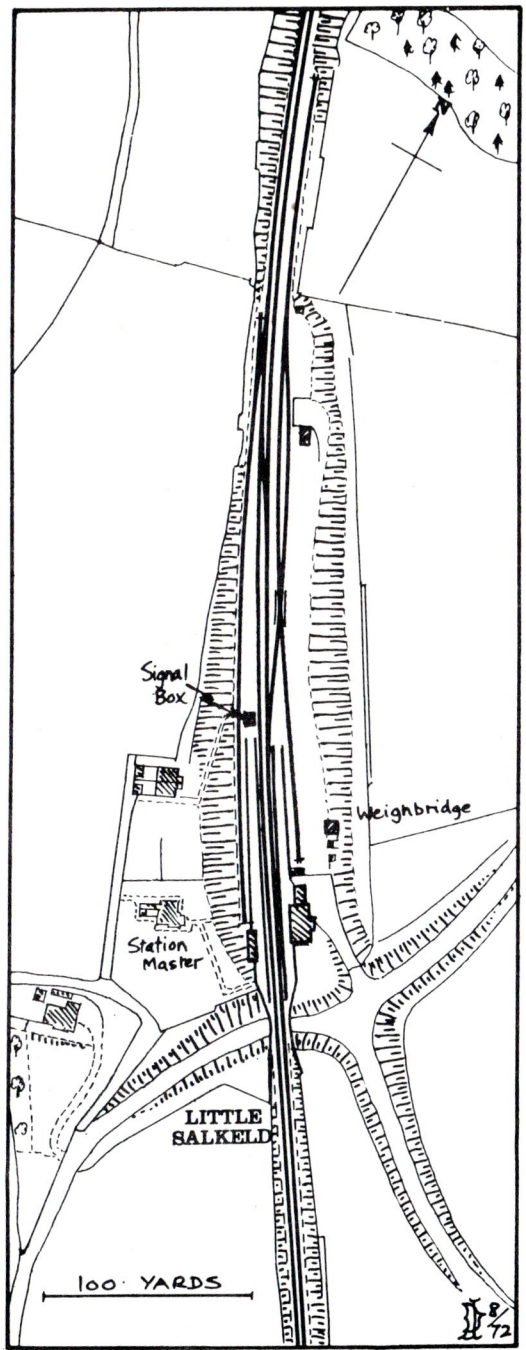

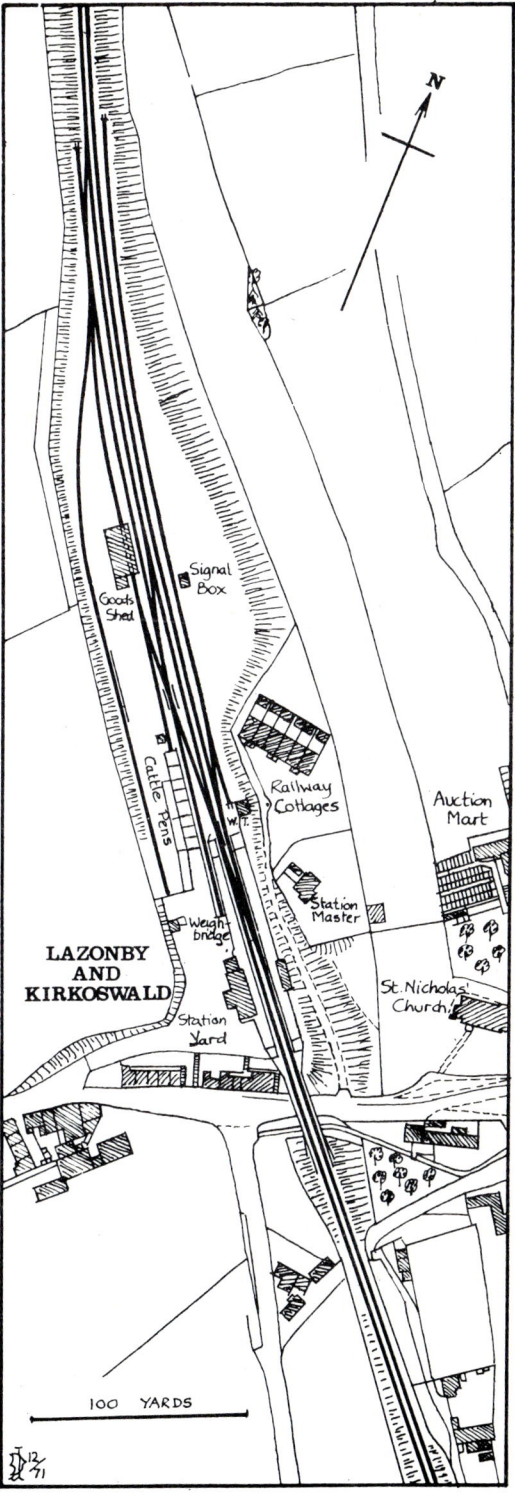

FIG. 32 (*above*) *Plan of Little Salkeld station c. 1925.*
(*Crown Copyright Reserved*).

FIG. 33 (*right*) *Plan of Lazonby Station c. 1900,*
(*Crown Copyright reserved.*)

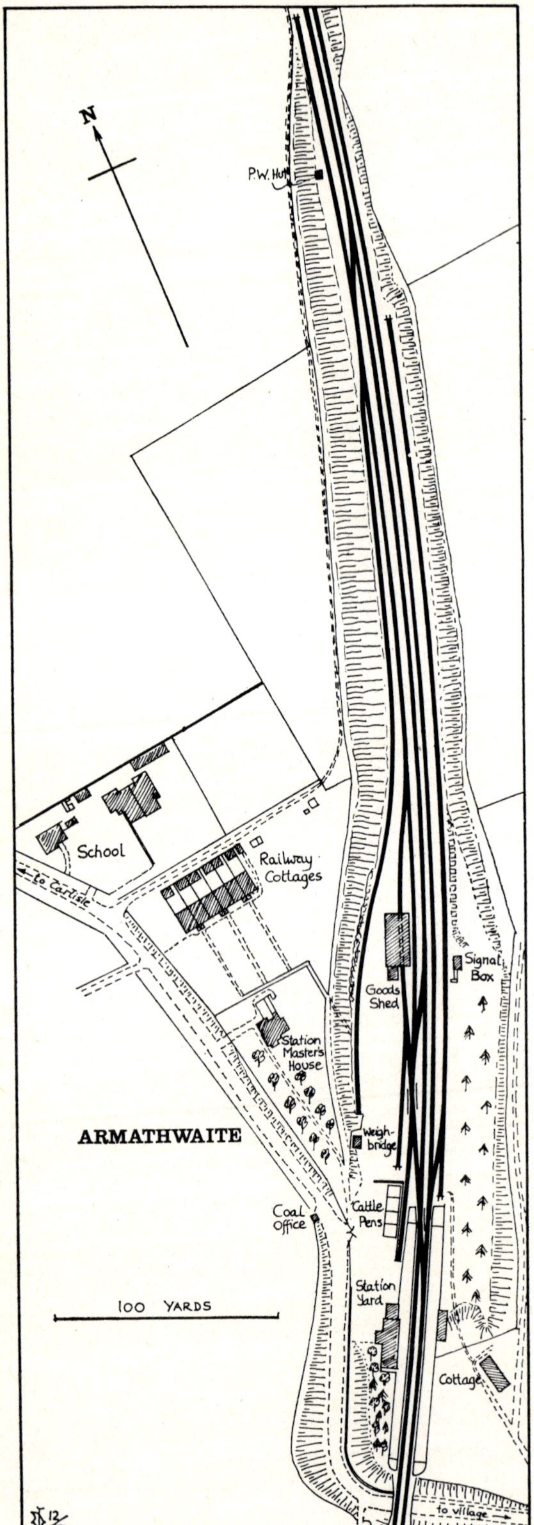
N
P.W. Hut
School
Railway Cottages
to Carlisle
Goods Shed
Signal Box
Station Master's House
ARMATHWAITE
Weigh-bridge
Cattle Pens
Coal Office
100 YARDS
Station Yard
Cottage
to village
12/71

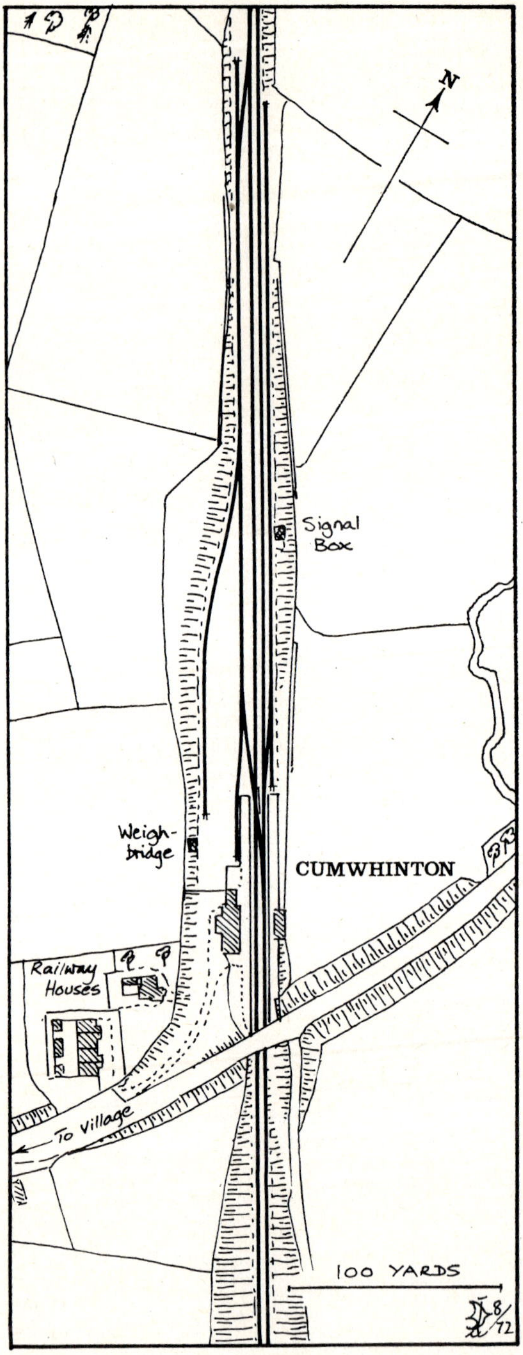
N
Signal Box
Weigh-bridge
CUMWHINTON
Railway Houses
To Village
100 YARDS
8/72

FIG. 34 (*left*) *Plan of Armathwaite station c. 1930.—based on BR official drawings.*

FIG. 35 (*above*) *Plan of Cumwhinton station c. 1925. (Crown Copyright Reserved.)*

PLATES 82–86 *Typical Settle and Carlisle station layouts. At the top of the page, the ultra simple arrangement at Dent is well represented in this view from the signalbox of a southbound freight. Above, the site of Crosby Garrett is seen in May 1964, 'X' marking the goods shed location and 'Y' that of the cattle pens. To the right, the full layout of the junction with the Hawes branch was still present at Garsdale in 1962 while \below (left) is seen a typical track arrangement at Ribblehead. The final view shows typical Midland double slips and three-way pounds at Appleby in August 1935—they were still there thirty years later! The train is the 10.20am Leeds-Glasgow headed by an as yet unnamed Stanier Class 5XP No. 5661—later 'Vernon'. (Photos: Gavin Morrison, D. Jenkinson (2), Alan Robey, Corbett Collection, courtesy National Railway Museum.)*

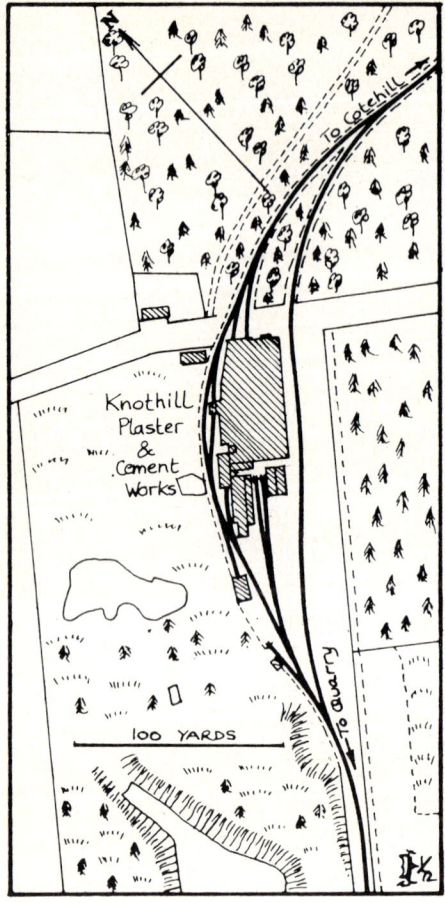

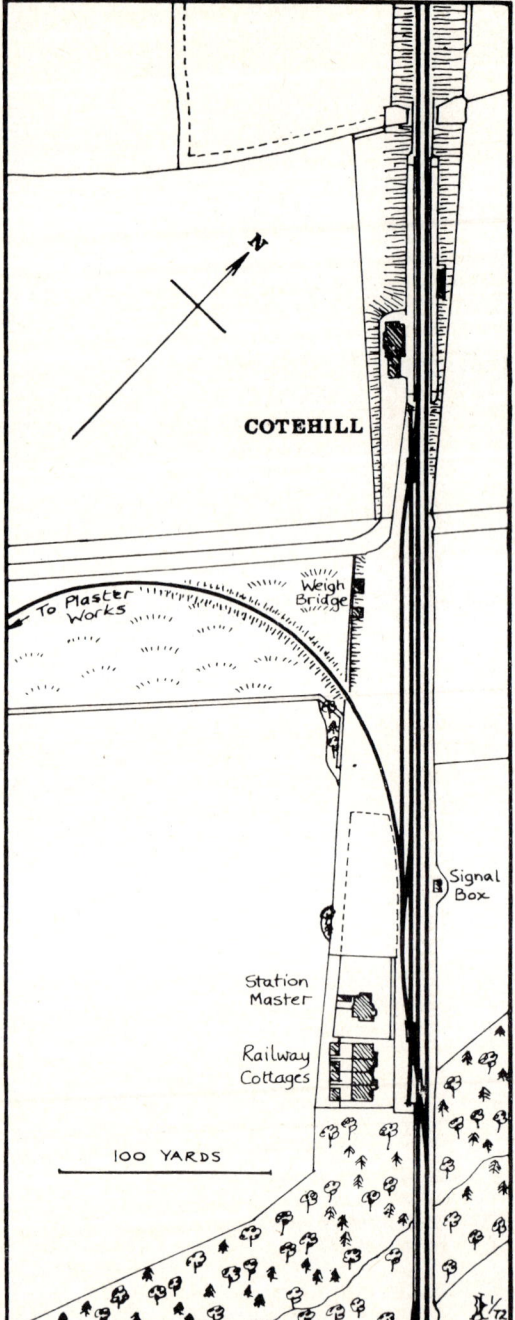

FIG. 36 *Plan of Cotehill station and Knothill Plaster and Cement works c. 1900. (Crown Copyright Reserved.)*

CLASS 5 AT KIRKBY STEPHEN

A. D. Whitehead

PART III

The Line as a Factor in Local Development

PLATES 87/88 PORTRAIT OF KIRKBY STEPHEN

Kirkby Stephen marks the point at which the region looks north to Carlisle rather than south to the West Riding; and to the traveller, it is here where he gets the first real indication that he is no longer journeying across the roof of the Pennines. Kirkby Stephen never quite lived up to the high hopes that the Midland had placed in it as a traffic centre but it always managed to present a neat and tidy appearance. The pictures on this page show the station before the post-Beeching ravages had done their worst. Above (Plate 87) the station is seen looking north in August 1906 when it must have seemed that nothing could shake the permanence of the Midland route to Scotland in these parts. From the gas lamps (actually they were illuminated by oil!) to the enamelled advertisements there is an air of confidence about the place. Even 30 years or so later in 1935 when Plate 88 (below) was taken, little had changed. Most of the MR trimmings were still intact and there is a healthy looking string of cattle wagons up by the goods shed. Who could have imagined the changes that were to take place after another 30 years? (Photos: H. C. Casserley's collection; H. C. Casserley.)

Chapter 8

What Price Statistics?

There are three kinds of lies; lies, damned lies, and statistics
MARK TWAIN
. . . the great majority of the public, whether railway users or not, remain unconvinced that the continuous cutting back of the railways is a good thing.
Lake District Herald. 16th November 1963

It is important, if we can, to divorce sentiment from reality when dealing with railway closures—a fact which is, regrettably, too often overlooked by the more vociferous opponents of change in our railway system. Intimately bound up as it was with the so called 'Industrial Revolution', the 19th Century growth of railways was in many ways the essential lubricant of that revolution. Furthermore, not only did the railway contribute to the change in society but it was itself a product of that change. We of the later 20th Century have no monopoly of change and though we may sentimentally regret the passing of parts of our railway system, we should not be too surprised by it. Only time will tell whether or not we were right as a nation to allow it to happen.

A railway is, basically, an expression in economic and engineering terms of the society which built it. It is, presumably, a reflection of a genuine economic need (as seen by its promoters) at the time of its building and, one may venture to suggest, it is designed to make a valid contribution to the society it serves. Nevertheless, it is certainly a tenable hypothesis to state that, largely because of the lack of alternative forms of modern communication, our 19th Century railway system somewhat outstripped the bounds of economic common sense and in so doing, produced more manifestations of the element of change in our country than were, perhaps, strictly necessary. This, coupled with the Victorian fear of monopoly, produced the 'Settle and Carlisles' of this world which are only now beginning to be seen for what they always were.

The fates (or, some might say, the economists) have decreed that the prime economic purpose for which the Settle and Carlisle railway was built is probably no longer relevant—indeed may no longer even exist. The line was very much a product of the *Midland* Railway, not

the LMS or BR, and the seeds were sown for its ultimate demise as far back as 1923 with the end of the MR as an independent concern. The line is taking an unconscionable time to die and there can still be advanced many cogent reasons for its continued retention as a through trunk route between the West Riding and Scotland. However, few can seriously doubt that in the present politico-economic climate, BR may wish to close it as a trunk route when the wire is complete over Shap Fell, leaving but two attenuated rumps to serve the quarries of the Eden valley and Ribblesdale. Even should this pessimistic view be unconfirmed and the line itself remain, the closure and lifting of the goods yards in the middle 1960s and the final elimination of local passenger services in 1970 (after only a six year reprieve), spelt 'finis' to any attempt to serve the local community—except via the few quarries (which would almost certainly carry on anyway); and as a provider of an ever diminishing number of jobs on the railway itself.

The objectors to closure of the Settle and Carlisle (as a *local* railway) presented their cases to the Transport Users Consultative Committees in late 1963. Although examination of contemporary local papers reveals that their evidence was largely subjective in nature, the objectors to closure seemed to have won a major victory when, in October 1964, the Minister of Transport refused closure on the grounds that undue hardship would result. It was to be but a short reprieve. Stations were reduced to unstaffed halts, diesel railcars with conductor/guards replaced locomotive hauled trains but still the local services did not pay and the final closures took place in May 1970. Students of coincidence will, no doubt, find something significant in the fact that the two dates represent almost the first and last acts of the Ministers of Transport during the term of office of the 1964–70 Labour Government.

To the writer, if the 1964 decision was correct then the 1970 decision was crazy and if the latter decision was indeed the proper one to make, why the first reprieve? Conditions in the area changed very little between the two dates. Roads did not noticeably improve—in fact one major road bridge actually collapsed at Langwathby during the period in question. The alternative bus services (always assuming they were provided) and themselves suffering severe economic pressures from the private car, took longer and were less comfortable—so who gained? The cost of maintaining the line cannot have materially changed as a result of the withdrawal of the pay trains and one cannot help feeling that the local passenger services represented but a small fraction of the total cost of the line. Surely it would have been better to keep them going until the future of the whole line could be re-assessed in the light of electrification over Shap and the ever growing appreciation of the need for long term planning of transport needs on a regional and national basis. But now we are back full circle to something suspiciously like the sentimental view!

Even so, the doubt still remains—should it have been allowed to happen?

One of the problems faced in discussing this matter is the fact that while it is not too difficult to appreciate the basic changes wrought in the fabric of our national society by the growth of railways—and, indeed, by the growth of mass, high speed communication in general—it is not always so easy to discern the effects of a railway on the more local neighbourhood. Does a railway, or more particularly *this* railway, have a catalytic effect upon changes in its immediate vicinity and if so, do such changes have to take upon themselves the magnitude of a Swindon or a Crewe to be relevant and important? This was the question to which it seemed worthwhile to try and find some sort of answer.

Perhaps the major difficulty in attempting to answer a question of this nature is the lack of objective evidence on which to base one's assessment. The railway board can provide an abundance of traffic and costing figures to show that the line is no longer a viable proposition in strictly economic terms. Indeed, for the purposes of this particular argument, the railway may conveniently choose to forget those higher minded social principles which were not infrequently invoked by the 19th Century promoters to gain approval for the line from the Parliament of the day. However, when charged by 20th Century Westminster to run a profitable system, the railway is clearly on very sound territory when it argues from the purely economic viewpoint. Small wonder that the objectors rarely win their case in the long term when, as like as not, their opposition is based on understandably subjective arguments which can rarely be bolstered by really conclusive facts. Nevertheless, however subjective the case of opponents of closure may be, it is no less real because it cannot be accurately quantified.

It does therefore seem that the only way to counter an economic argument is either to destroy it with a more cogent economic argument—conceivably impossible in the case of the Settle and Carlisle—or to introduce other factors, bolstered by reliable evidence, that economic considerations are not the only important factors. The problem is firstly that involved in obtaining reliable evidence and then defining what is and what is not relevant to the issue. The latter is the more critical since it is not entirely possible to draw accurate parameters within which to investigate the influence of a railway. There are (or were) undoubtedly other factors which also contributed to change and it is, arguably, a little dangerous to try and isolate but one of them. Nevertheless, it did seem worthwhile to attempt to investigate on a broad front over the whole line to see if any measurable trends could be detected.

It seemed to the writer that there were three fields in which the line may have had lasting influence. Firstly, the general population trend might indicate whether or not those areas served by a railway station exhibited any marked differences from those not so served. Secondly, if the ability to transport goods was important to farming, one might reasonably expect to find some changes in the overall agricultural pattern of those areas within convenient reach of a railhead. Thirdly, if the line was of importance in opening up areas for mineral extraction, a survey of quarries along the line might indicate the extent, if any, of permanent influence possessed by the railway line.

A fourth aspect has also been investigated—mainly as a result of the fortuitous circumstances

PLATES 89/90 *The Midland Railway furniture lasted well into the BR period and some still survives in 1979. In these pictures a classic swan neck water column stands sentinel at Appleby while above, a platform seat and porter's barrow are seen at New Biggin—all still in use during the 1960s. (Photos: BR LMR, D. Jenkinson.)*

which have allowed most of the records to survive. The Midland Railway from 1876 to 1922 recorded annually all the traffic originating from all its stations. This has enabled a very comprehensive pattern of passenger and freight traffic to be deduced. Unfortunately, the LMS figures for 1923–46 have been lost (believed accidentally destroyed in a fire at one of the railway record offices), but the bulk of the 1947–63 figures have survived and thus enable comparisons to be made.

The population figures for the area were extracted from the relevant ten yearly census returns and the necessary agricultural details were obtained from the annual agricultural returns held at the Public Records Office and by the Ministry of Agriculture. It so transpired that details of mineral extraction were harder to obtain and less satisfactory in terms of completeness. The evidence was somewhat inconclusive but a summary has been incorporated in Chapter 10 (page 107).

The method by which the official records are compiled caused the basis of the survey to be the parish and a group of some 86 parishes stretching from Hellifield in the south to the outskirts of Carlisle in the north were selected for analysis. These included all parishes traversed by the Settle and Carlisle together with those immediately adjacent (both east and west). It was

difficult to decide how far on either side of the line to take the sample. It was desired to have a reasonably large number of parishes without a railway line as well as the Settle and Carlisle parishes and on the east, the survey was taken to the approximate line of the main Pennine ridge. However, the western extremity was complicated by the presence of the Lancaster and Carlisle railway which, if the analysis were to be meaningful, should not be allowed to interfere since this railway too might produce its own effects on its particular parishes! The parishes traversed by the various east-west branches of the NER could not be excluded since these lines cut right across the Settle and Carlisle in several places. A map of the area surveyed is given at Figure 37.

As a basic unit of survey, the parish has several disadvantages. First and foremost is the lack of uniformity in either shape or size; and railway stations are rarely (unless one is extremely fortunate) right in the middle of the parish. Even more annoying is the fact that during the period under survey, several parishes experienced boundary changes which made exact comparisons between the present day and the 19th Century details very difficult in some cases. This was largely overcome by amalgamating parishes to produce larger recording units whose boundaries

81

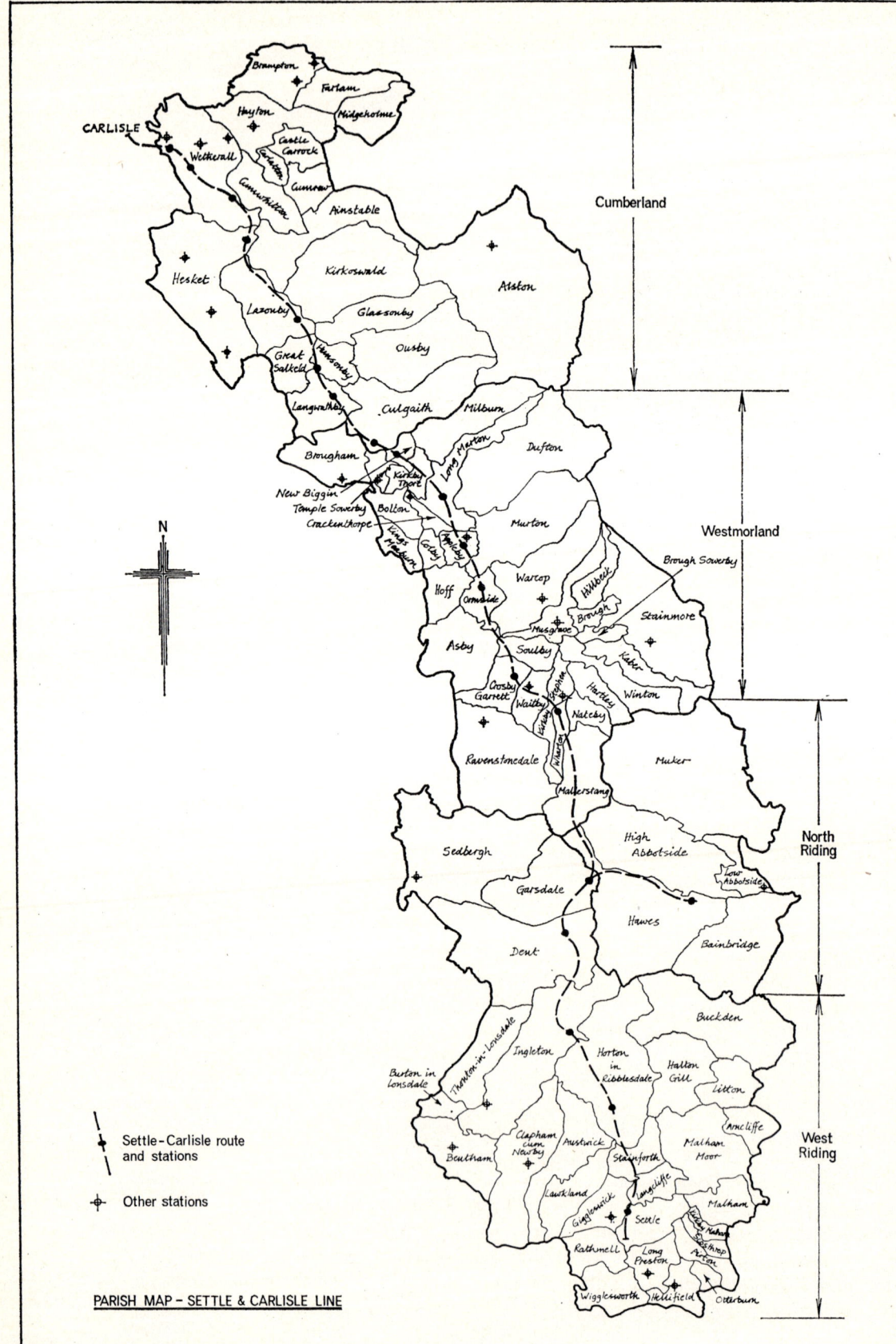

PARISH MAP — SETTLE & CARLISLE LINE

did remain the same throughout the period. Thus, to quote one example, the present day Cumberland parishes of Glassonby and Hunsonby (in which lies the Settle and Carlisle station at Little Salkeld) cover the same area which in the mid 19th Century was represented by a much larger parish called Addingham and the smaller parish of Little Salkeld itself. They have had to be counted as one parish only for this survey. There were several other similar cases and thus, although 86 parishes exist in the sample, at times they have had to be amalgamated to form rather fewer recording units. Nevertheless, no comparisons have been made in which the number of units in the sample falls below the middle 60s. However, it must be admitted that a larger sample would have been desirable.

Basically, the method adopted for the survey was to look at each of a number of features in turn (population, livestock, area of farmed land etc.) for three specific years and then compare each parish with its own performance under the same headings during the previous one or two sample periods. The changes were converted into percentage values (up or down) and tabulated. The sum totals for the whole sample group were also calculated so as to be able to derive an average trend for the whole sample.

The years finally chosen were those of the 1861, 1911 and 1961 population census returns. In the case of the annual agricultural returns, earlier figures than 1866 were not available, but fortunately, these 1866 values did precede the opening of the line. The figures for 1871 could have been chosen to represent the pre-railway situation but these were badly distorted by the presence of thousands of immigrant navvies during the building of the railway and the 1871 census report clearly states that the population

values were anomalous because of this factor. The year 1911 represents the situation just before the first world war when the line was, in traffic terms, at its zenith and the year 1961 is the final year for which full data is available before local passenger and freight services terminated. Shorter intervals of time were ruled out because it was desired to look only at broad trends rather than in great detail and it was also desired to exclude, if possible, any transient factors which may have been present as a result of the two great world wars.

When the figures were all tabulated, an attempt was made to see whether or not those parishes containing stations exhibited noticeably different trends from those which did not contain stations. In the event, it was found desirable to identify a third group of parishes—those which contained stations not on the Settle and Carlisle railway— in order to fully isolate the Settle and Carlisle itself. Of the 86 parishes surveyed, 18 contained the 20 Settle and Carlisle stations, of which four also contained eight of the non-Settle and Carlisle stations. There were in addition another 19 parishes containing 20 other stations. Thus, just less than half the sample parishes had stations in them and slightly more than one-fifth of the parishes contained stations on the Settle and Carlisle.

Clearly the analysis was going to be largely statistical (fighting fire with fire?) but in the exposition which forms the first part of the following chapter, no attempt has been made to explain the mathematics involved. However, for those who do wish to understand the basis on which some of the assertions will be made, a simplified treatment of the statistical argument is given at Appendix A. The general reader may omit this Appendix should he so wish!

FIG. 37 *Parish map of the area served by the Settle and Carlisle railway and which is analysed in detail in Chapter 9. (Crown Copyright Reserved.)*

Chapter 9

Population and Agriculture

Population

In those parishes for which full details are available for all three sample years (1861, 1911, 1961), the total population shows a steady decline from 62538 in 1861 to 50830 in 1961. The figures are summarised in Table I in which the percentage fall is also calculated. All 86 parishes are represented but only 81 recording units could be isolated to give consistent boundaries for comparison between 1861 and 1961. However, for the 1861–1911 period, only one such amalgamation had to be made.

It will be noted that this observed decline in population was against a national trend of population increase. One of the more frequent arguments against rural rail closures has been to take the view that railways helped to slow down the rate of rural depopulation and it was to test this theory that the statistics were collated. During the period in question, the fluctuations in population varied from an increase of well over 200% in one case (Hellifield) to a decrease of some 66% at the other extreme (Hillbeck in Westmorland). A cursory look at the figures made it seem possible that there might be some relationship between railway stations and rate of change of population and the summary of the results is given at Tables II, III and IV.

From the figures in these tables it is immediately obvious that the group of parishes which showed a population growth—i.e. *with* the national trend but *against* the regional trend—contain more than their 'fair share' of railway stations when taken in strict proportions. This is particularly noticeable in Tables III/IV where the 'growth'

parishes (less than 25% of the total) contain about half the stations in the area. It is not so noticeable in the 1861–1911 period where the largest group of parishes (0–24% decline) also contains the largest number of stations. However, even during this period, the 19 'growth' parishes contained more stations than the 27 parishes with a high rate of decline.

One therefore begins to suspect that there may well be a relationship between the two sets of figures. On the other hand, the distribution noted may be nothing more than a freak result of the samples taken. The figures can be tested for statistical significance and when this is done, it transpires that there is less than one chance in one hundred that the figures could have occurred by chance in Tables III/IV. However, in the case of Table II, there is a much higher probability that the figures could have occurred by chance. Nevertheless, even in this case, the figures still tend to suggest that the random element is the less likely of the two alternatives.

One cannot therefore escape the conclusion that there is (or was, since most of the stations are now closed) a very close relationship between the rate of rural depopulation and the presence or absence of a station. The significance test can be applied to either the Settle and Carlisle stations or to the non-Settle and Carlisle stations (both taken in isolation) or to all stations taken together. In Tables III/IV, a very high significance value is obtained for all three categories. However, when Table II is analysed in this way, the Settle and Carlisle stations generate a much higher significance factor than do the others,

Table I Population Figures—Area in Vicinity of Settle/Carlisle Railway

| County | 1861 | 1911 | 1961 | Percentage Changes | | |
				1861–1911	1911–1961	1861–1961
Cumberland	24250	18286	19179	−25	+5	−21
Westmorland	17158	14375	12432	−16	−13	−28
West Riding	16876	18553	16907	+10	−9	+
North Riding	4254	3075	2312	−28	−25	−46
Totals	62538	54289	50830	−13	−6	−19

Table II Population Trends: 1861–1911
Number of parishes—86; Number of recording units—81

Nature of Population Change	Number of Units Represented	Number of Stations Represented		
		Settle/Carlisle Railway	Other Railways	Total
Overall Growth	19	7	7	14
0–24% Decline	35	10	13	23
25% Decline or more	27	3	8	11
Totals	81	20	28	48

Table III Population Trends: 1911–1961
Number of parishes—86; Number of recording units—85

Nature of Population Change	Number of Units Represented	Number of Stations Represented		
		Settle/Carlisle Railway	Other Railways	Total
Overall Growth	18	10	16	26
0–24% decline	45	6	9	15
25% decline or more	22	4	3	7
Totals	85	20	28	48

Table IV Population Trends: 1861–1961
Number of parishes—86; Number of recording units—81

Nature of Population Change	Number of Units Represented	Number of Stations Represented		
		Settle/Carlisle Railway	Other Railways	Total
Overall Growth	17	10	12	22
0–24% decline	15	5	8	13
25% decline or more	49	5	8	13
Totals	81	20	28	48

even though it is not quite high enough to fall within the 95% probability level.

It is important not to read too much into such figures. All that is established is that there is a very high degree of probability of a statistical relationship betwen population change and railway stations. This is not the same as asserting that the railway stations *caused* the lower rate of population decline. It is, however, a reasonable inference from the figures that the stations may well have been a contributory cause. There were undoubtedly others. For example, it should not be forgotten that there were certain parishes containing Settle and Carlisle stations which showed a greater than 25% *decline* in population. In this respect, the five 'worst' stations for the whole period were Garsdale, Dent, Crosby Garrett, Ormside and Hawes Joint. It is interesting that the last three were amongst those stations closed well before the final closures of 1970. By contrast, the 'best' Settle and Carlisle parish was Culgaith—which may say something for the perspicacity of the Reverend Atkinson (page 49)!

A rather interesting aspect of the figures is the fact that the highest significance values for the area were generated during the 1911–1961 period (when passenger traffic was declining) rather than during the pre-1911 period when passenger traffic was increasing. If there is indeed a genuine relationship between a low rate of population decline and railway stations, it would seem that the mere presence of the station was possibly of more significance than the extent to which it was regularly used by the population as a means of transport. Could it have been, for instance, that the knowledge of the availability of public transport was sufficient to persuade some people to remain in the area, even if they did not propose to use the line regularly? If so, the wider implications are very interesting indeed! It would, for instance, suggest that we could re-examine the thesis that profitability should be the sole criterion of a public transport system. After all, many people have few occasions when they really *need* the services of a doctor but most of us do like to feel that there is one available on those occasions when need arises.

These and many other speculations could be

Table V Agricultural Details—Area in Vicinity of Settle/Carlisle Railway

Agricultural Feature	County	Livestock Numbers			Percentage Changes		
		1866	1911	1961	1866–1911	1911–1961	1866–1961
All Livestock	Cumberland	79212	150237	199436	+90	+33	+152
	Westmorland	72924	147075	203703	+102	+38	+179
	West Riding	104018	219046	298027	+110	+36	+186
	North Riding	28571	58594	67740	+105	+17	+141
	Totals	284725	574952	768906	+102	+34	+170
All Cattle	Cumberland	11966	24174	52947	+102	+119	+342
	Westmorland	13529	19521	34560	+44	+77	+155
	West Riding	20033	28769	41928	+44	+46	+109
	North Riding	3436	3849	5479	+12	+42	+59
	Totals	48964	76313	134914	+56	+77	+175
Dairy Cattle	Cumberland	4082	8215	19292	+101	+135	+372
	Westmorland	4892	7207	13368	+47	+85	+174
	West Riding	6846	12776	17293	+89	+35	+153
	North Riding	1493	1474	2221	−1	+50	+48
	Totals	17313	29672	52174	+72	+76	+202
Non-Dairy Cattle	Cumberland	7884	15959	33655	+102	+111	+329
	Westmorland	8637	12314	21192	+43	+72	+146
	West Riding	13187	15993	24635	+21	+54	+87
	North Riding	1943	2375	3258	+22	+37	+67
	Totals	31651	46641	82740	+47	+77	+162
Sheep	Cumberland	63448	123401	141564	+95	+15	+101
	Westmorland	57651	126330	168120	+119	+33	+192
	West Riding	83168	188571	254233	+104	+35	+206
	North Riding	25033	54384	62229	+117	+14	+148
	Totals	229300	492686	626146	+115	+27	+173
Pigs	Cumberland	3798	2662	4925	−30	+85	+30
	Westmorland	1744	1224	1023	−30	−16	−41
	West Riding	817	1706	1866	+109	+9	+128
	North Riding	102	361	32	+254	−91	−69
	Totals	6461	5953	7846	−8	+32	+21
		Land Acreage					
		1866	1911	1961			
Farmed Land	Cumberland	62603	80894	63491	+29	−22	+1
	Westmorland	55563	94661	91464	+70	−3	+64
	West Riding	88617	116724	71501	+32	−39	−19
	North Riding	29635	25434	12978	−14	−49	−56
	Totals	236418	317713	239434	+34	−25	+1

made from the figures quoted but they remain, none the less, only speculations and must inevitably be subjective. However, it cannot be denied that the figures themselves strongly suggest that some sort of relationship exists beyond that which one would expect to find from sampling errors.

Agriculture

Agricultural statistics have been submitted by farmers in this country for well over a century now and from these figures it is possible to detect broad trends in the change of farming pattern over the years. By adopting a similar mode of analysis to that used for the rate of change of population an attempt can also be made to detect whether or not there is a relationship between changes in farming and the presence or absence of a station in the parish. Once again a broad classification was adopted and the chosen indicators were livestock and farmed land. In the case of livestock, the changes were tabulated both on an overall basis and by livestock type. In the case of land use, 'farmed land' was defined as arable land plus permanent pasture and excluding rough grazing. It was not felt desirable to isolate arable land from pasture since many parishes had little or no arable acreage within their boundaries.

Table VI Agricultural Trends: 1861–1911
Number of Recording Units: Livestock—69; Farmed Land—63; Stations—46

Agricultural Feature	Percentage Increase	Number of Units Represented	Number of Stations Represented		
			Settle/Carlisle Railway	Other Railways	Total
All Livestock	Over 150%	18	6	**9**	**15**
	75–149%	27	5	7	12
	Below 75%	24	**9**	10	19
	Totals	69	20	26	46
All Cattle	Over 100%	14	5	**10**	**15**
	50–99%	16	5	8	13
	Below 50%	39	10	8	18
	Totals	69	20	26	46
Dairy Cattle	Over 100%	22	6	**13**	**19**
	50–99%	13	**6**	6	12
	Below 50%	34	8	7	15
	Totals	69	20	26	46
Non-Dairy Cattle	Over 100%	15	5	**10**	**15**
	50–99%	9	**6**	4	10
	Below 50%	45	9	12	21
	Totals	69	20	26	46
Sheep	Over 200%	13	4	**7**	**11**
	100–199%	28	5	7	12
	Below 100%	28	**11**	**12**	**23**
	Totals	69	20	26	46
Pigs	Increase	39	7	15	22
	0–49% decline	15	**6**	6	**12**
	50% decline or more	15	**7**	5	**12**
	Totals	69	20	26	46
Farmed Land	Over 50%	22	**11**	**13**	**24**
	0–49%	27	6	11	17
	Decrease	14	3	2	5
	Totals	63	20	26	46

Note. Bold Figures in the three right hand columns indicate at least one more than the expected number of stations in proportion to the number of recording units in that category (see also Appendix B).

The overall figures for farming activity are given at Table V and the summary of the parish surveys at Tables VI, VII and VIII. In this respect it should be noted that the 1911 statistics are not quite complete in all respects and it was also necessary to amalgamate certain parishes to obtain exact comparisons with 1861. This was particularly true in the case of farmed land where land use was recorded according to the parish in which the *farmstead* was located—not necessarily the same parish as the land itself. The 1961 figures are much more complete and less amalgamation of parishes to form homogeneous recording units was necessary. Fortunately, all the parishes containing Settle and Carlisle stations could be satisfactorily tabulated in all cases and overall, it was found possible to incorporate virtually all the parishes surveyed (either individually or by combination with adjacent areas) in some part of the survey. Nevertheless, because of the slight deficiencies in the 1911 figures, two parishes containing non-Settle and Carlisle stations (Brougham, Low Abbotside) had to be omitted from all the comparisons involving that year (Tables VI and VII).

For these reasons, the size of sample varies from 63 recording units in the lowest case (farmed land 1866–1911) to 84 in the best case (livestock 1866–1961). Essentially, the principle followed was to exclude a parish from the summary table if complete details for a particular agricultural feature were missing. The omission of certain parishes from the summary does not invalidate the mathematical accuracy of the method of analysis for reasons which are explained

Table VII Agricultural Trends: 1911–1961

Number of Recording Units: Livestock—68; Farmed Land—68; Stations—46

Agricultural Feature	Percentage Increase	Number of Units	Number of Stations Represented		
			Settle/Carlisle Railway	Other Railways	Total
All Livestock	Over 75%	9	**5**	**11**	**16**
	25–74%	33	7	11	18
	Below 25%	26	8	4	12
	Totals	68	20	26	46
All Cattle	Over 100%	19	**8**	**10**	**18**
	50–99%	26	7	8	15
	Below 50%	23	5	8	13
	Totals	68	20	26	46
Dairy Cattle	Over 100%	23	**11**	**12**	**23**
	50–99%	22	4	5	9
	Below 50%	23	5	9	14
	Totals	68	20	26	46
Non-Dairy Cattle	Over 100%	20	**9**	**11**	**20**
	50–99%	21	4	**10**	14
	Below 50%	27	7	5	12
	Totals	68	20	26	46
Sheep	Over 50%	16	2	**10**	**12**
	0–49%	38	12	13	25
	Decline	14	**6**	3	9
	Totals	68	20	26	46
Pigs	Over 100%	12	**7**	**6**	**13**
	0–99%	12	**6**	7	**13**
	Decline	44	7	13	20
	Totals	68	20	26	46
Farmed Land	Increase	7	**7**	**7**	**14**
	0–24% decline	33	5	12	17
	25% decline or more	28	8	7	15
	Totals	68	20	26	46

Note. Bold figures indicate at least one more than the expected number of stations in proportion to the number of recording units in that category.

(for those interested) at Appendix B.

At first sight, the analyses in Tables VI, VII and VIII are a little indigestible so a few words in amplification will not be out of place.

Perhaps the first thing which becomes obvious in looking at the figures is that in the great majority of cases, one observes more stations than one might expect to find associated with the group of parishes performing 'best' in each category. These have been emphasised by printing the figure for stations in bolder type. However, if one calculates the expected number of stations in strict proportion to the total number of recording units (i.e. parishes or combinations thereof) in the sample, it can be discovered that although in many cases the number of stations in each group is only one or two more than might be expected, in other cases the difference is quite large. Statistically, therefore, although some of these excesses can be attributable to the chance factor, others would seem to have statistical significance if nothing else.

From the figures themselves, the overall trends are not difficult to discern. There was a steady increase in livestock throughout the period and both cattle and sheep showed a very similar proportionate rise between 1866 and 1961 (175% and 173% respectively). Pigs did not fare anything like so well. However, dairy cattled increased in proportion rather more sharply than did non-dairy cattle and when tested for significance, there is a very strong statistical relationship between the increase in dairy cattle and the presence of a station. This relationship is less well marked for non-dairy cattle and one could therefore reasonably

Table VIII Agricultural Trends: 1866–1961

Number of Recording Units: Livestock—84; Farmed Land—77; Stations—48

Agricultural Feature	Percentage Increase	Number of Units	Number of Stations Represented		
			Settle/Carlisle Railway	Other Railways	Totals
All Livestock	Over 200%	25	**7**	**13**	20
	100–199%	38	9	9	18
	Below 100%	21	4	6	10
	Totals	84	20	28	48
All Cattle	Over 200%	27	**11**	**16**	27
	100–199%	28	3	5	8
	Below 100%	29	6	7	13
	Totals	84	20	28	48
Dairy Cattle	Over 300%	19	**9**	**14**	23
	100–299%	37	7	7	14
	Below 100%	28	4	7	11
	Totals	84	20	28	48
Non-Dairy Cattle	Over 200%	27	**10**	**15**	25
	100–199%	25	5	7	12
	Below 100%	32	5	6	11
	Totals	84	20	28	48
Sheep	Over 200%	37	9	**14**	23
	100–199%	24	5	9	14
	Below 100%	23	6	5	11
	Totals	84	20	28	48
Pigs	Increase	32	**11**	12	23
	Decrease	52	9	**16**	25
	Totals	84	20	28	48
Farmed Land	Over 50%	12	**8**	**11**	19
	0–49%	18	3	7	10
	Decrease	47	9	10	19
	Totals	77	20	28	48

Note. Bold figures indicate at least one more than the expected number of stations in proportion to the number of recording units in that category.

postulate that the observed increase in emphasis on dairy cattle was, in part, related to the existence of railway facilities. It should, however, be noted that the Settle and Carlisle stations generate a less significant figure on this score than do the other stations.

The increase in sheep seems virtually unrelated to the presence of a railway station as, taken overall, does the much smaller increase in pig population. However, the figures tend to suggest that there was a more than average decline in pig keeping during 1866–1911 near the vicinity of the Settle/Carlisle stations! By contrast, the 1911–1961 increase in pig keeping also seems statistically related to the Settle and Carlisle line. Bearing in mind that the absolute number of pigs in any parish was quite small, a change of but a few head of livestock would cause the percentages to alter quite sharply. For this

reason, the figures for pig keeping are felt to be somewhat inconclusive since no really strong trend seems to have taken place.

Turning to farmed land, there is a strong suggestion of a relationship between rate of increase and railway stations (taken as a whole) during the 1866–1911 period and for the overall period 1866–1961. Even so, taken in isolation, the Settle/Carlisle stations seem less important than the other stations in the area and it is only when one considers all stations together that a strong statistical correlation can be observed. The figures seem less significant—even unrelated —for the 1911–1961 period although the 'best' group of parishes still contains more than its proportionate share of stations.

An attempt to sum up the whole picture is given at Table IX. In order to compile this table, the performance of each parish was considered

Table IX All Line Comparisons: 1866–1961
Number of Recording Units—78; Stations—48

Times above average	Number of recording units	Number of Stations Represented		
		Settle/Carlisle Railway	Other Railways	Total
19–24	6	7	8	15
13–18	20	3	9	12
7–12	35	7	8	15
0–6	17	3	3	6
Totals	78	20	28	48

under each of the seven agricultural headings and also under the population heading for each of the three comparison periods. This gave 24 observations for each parish which were then compared with the corresponding whole line averages. In theory, the best parish could exceed the average 24 times and the worst parish be below average 24 times. In fact, the best parish (Hesket, Cumberland) exceeded the average 23 times out of 24 and the worst (Crosby Garrett, Brough Sowerby and Muker) were each below average 23 times. Low Abbotside did, in fact, give exclusively below average figures but some data was missing (see page 87). Interestingly,

both Hesket and Crosby Garrett contained Settle and Carlisle stations but Hesket also contained three stations on the Lancaster and Carlisle main line while Low Abbotside contained a non-Settle and Carlisle station on the Wensleydale branch of the NER.

It is interesting to note that, except for Appleby, all the parishes in the top group in Table IX were in Cumberland and quite near to Carlisle (Wetherall, Hesket, Glassonby/Hunsonby, Hayton, Culgaith). This at least might suggest that the presence of the large urban settlement should not be ignored when assessing the figures.

It will also be seen that only one-third of the

PLATE 91 *This picture of the stretch of line between Stainforth and Helwith Bridge is typical of the Dales country at the southern end of the line. This was the only region traversed by the railway where taken overall the population did not suffer a decline during the 1861–1961 period. The train is the down 'Thames-Cylde Express' on 19th May 1964 headed by BR Sulzer Type 4 diesel No. D135. (Photo: Gavin Morrison.)*

Table X Significance Values

Indicator	Period	Settle/Carlisle Stations	Other Stations	All Stations
Population	1861–1911	*	NR	NR
	1911–1961	**	**	**
	1861–1961	**	**	**
All Livestock	1866–1911	NR	NR	NR
	1911–1961	NR	**	**
	1866–1961	NR	*	NR
All Cattle	1866–1911	NR	**	**
	1911–1961	NR	NR	NR
	1866–1961	*	**	**
Dairy Cattle	1866–1911	NR	**	**
	1911–1961	*	NR	**
	1866–1961	*	**	**
Non-Dairy Cattle	1866–1911	*	**	**
	1911–1961	NR	*	*
	1866–1961	NR	**	**
Pigs	1866–1911	*†	NR	NR
	1911–1961	**	NR	**
	1866–1961	NR	NR	NR
Sheep	1866–1911	NR	NR	*
	1911–1961	NR	*	NR
	1866–1961	NR	NR	NR
Farmed Land	1866–1911	*	*	**
	1911–1961	NR	NR	NR
	1866–1961	NR	**	**
All Line Comparisons	1866–1961	NR	**	**

Key ** Higher than 95% probability of a statistical relationship
 * Approaching 95% probability
 NR No statistically significant relationship
 † This value is approaching 95% *negative* correlation

78 recording units could be classified in the overall sense as being 'above average' and these contained 27 out of the 48 stations in the sample. The chances of such an unbalanced distribution of stations appearing at random are less than one in one hundred so there is an extremely strong probability that a relationship of some sort exists between railway stations and parish 'performance'. However, when taken in isolation, the Settle and Carlisle does not show up as well as the other lines, having but half its stations in the above average group. Nevertheless, this is still more than one would expect to find on a strictly proportionate basis.

Taken overall, therefore, the figures tend to suggest that if the presence of a railway station has indeed had a measurable effect upon activities within parishes over the last century, this effect was less marked along the Settle and Carlisle route than elsewhere in the region. To illustrate this idea, Table X has been compiled. In this case, attention has been particularly drawn to those instances where the statistical relationship between the chosen indicators and the railway stations can be calculated to be within the 95% probability zone.

A quick perusal of Table X will reveal that only on three occasions did the Settle and Carlisle stations (taken on their own) generate a higher than 95% probability figure by contrast with 11 occasions for non-Settle and Carlisle stations and 14 occasions for all stations. However, against this fact it must also be noted that there were many other instances in which the relationship of the Settle/Carlisle stations to the chosen indicator was approaching the 95% probability level. Neither must it be overlooked that even where no statistical significance could be calculated for the figures observed, there were more than the expected number of Settle and Carlisle

PLATE 92 *The wild moorland environment just south of Dent station is illustrated in this picture. It was districts of this nature which showed the sharpest decline in population during the period surveyed in this chapter although the traditional livestock farming managed to keep going and indeed increase. The train is a northbound express in 1947, headed by LMS Class 5 No. 5081.* (*Photo: W. Hubert Foster.*)

stations in the above average parishes no fewer than 22 times out of 25 sets of observations and one of the other three (pigs, 1866–1911) was approaching the significantly *small* level.

Conclusions

Trying to bring all these observations together to form a reasonably objective conclusion is not very easy—trying to establish facts on a purely statistical basis rarely is. It could, for instance, be argued that the parishes may well have performed in identical fashion had there been no railways present, but this cannot be proved. It could also be argued that, by their very nature (altitude, climate, fertility etc.), certain parishes would inevitably support less activity than others. In absolute terms (e.g. livestock per acre) this is certainly true but the author has some doubts as to its truth in a *relative* sense. For instance, one can easily establish that a parish composed mainly of rough moorland cannot support as many people or animals per square mile as a lowland parish with lush meadows and rich soil but it does not follow that when looking at rates of *change* (e.g. percentage increase in livestock over a given period), the same argument holds good. It seems just as reasonable a hypothesis to suggest that the availability of transport may well have had some effect on the rate of growth if not the absolute growth; and it is *rate* of growth (or decline) which has been considered in this chapter.

PLATE 93 *The rich woodlands and pasture country of the Eden Valley are a notable feature of the northern part of the Settle and Carlisle line. This view taken a mile or so to the south of Armathwaite clearly shows the nature of this part of the route. The train is the first southbound 'Return to Steam' special on Easter Monday 1978. The locomotive is the preserved LNER Class V2 2–6–2 'Green Arrow' based at the National Railway Museum and it is believed that this was the first occasion on which it had worked on this line. (Photo: J. A. Coiley.)*

On this basis there is a very high probability of a statistical relationship during the past century between the presence of railway stations and a slower than normal rate of decline of population, a higher than normal rate of increase in cattle (particularly dairy cattle) and a higher than usual rate of increase in farmed land. These figures come well within the 95% probability level for all stations and for the non-Settle/Carlisle stations. However, for the Settle and Carlisle stations taken in isolation, although the figures still tend towards the high probability side, only in the case of population do they come within the 95% level.

Bearing in mind that these are only statistical relationships—not cause and effect—the implications are less easy to discern. However, a particularly interesting fact is that some of the stronger relationships are to be found during the period when railway traffic began to decline—a fact which has already been remarked upon (page 85). What it could possibly indicate is that prior to the motor age the railway was beginning to have some influence on retaining activities in rural areas against the national trend towards urbanisation. If so, this would give a breathing space to some of the threatened rural communities during the later 19th and early 20th Centuries. Once motor vehicles began to take over many of the traditional railway functions they would tend to magnify any trend which the railway had begun to establish, even though the railway's share of the traffic would *fall*. This explanation would, at least, fit the facts of the case in this area. It would also tend to encourage the view that while the railway may well have played a significant role in helping to retain activities in rural areas during the pre-motor age, its major purpose was fulfilled when car ownership approached the present day universality. For instance, the fall in passenger traffic on the Settle and Carlisle railway during 1911–1961 was proportionally far more rapid than the rate of decline of population as the next chapter will show.

Similar arguments can also be advanced in

respect of agriculture. The railway may well have stimulated dairy farming during the pre-motor age but the far greater flexibility of the motor vehicle may well have held even greater attraction to those farmers who had been only too willing to use the railway when it was the sole means of widespread distribution for their products. This being so, those areas which performed best (relatively speaking) during the railway age would probably do even better with the addition of motor vehicles to their assets during the last 50 years. Again this would generally accord with the statistics.

If, however, these arguments are reasonable, then two contradictory conclusions emerge. The first, which tends to support present BR philosophy, is that modern circumstances have tended to render local railway lines redundant in the face of competition from the much more flexible motor vehicle—in spite of the fact that the *pattern* of activity which the motor vehicle consolidates is one which may well have been partly established by the railway.

The second conclusion—and the author ventures to suggest that if one accepts the first then in logic one cannot reject the second—is that the statistical evidence also strongly suggests that *where no alternative exists* (e.g. 1866–1911), then the presence of a rural railway may well play a vital role in the development (or at least the lack of decline) of the district. And here lies the rub. No matter how many motor vehicles appear, there will always be a section of the community which either does not or cannot possess its own personalised alternative transport. In the days when very few people could be self-sufficient in this respect it did not make much difference; rich and poor alike were both dependent on public transport. Nowadays, it is generally only the poorer folk who are wholly dependent on public transport and, thankfully, this category of person is annually getting less in proportion to the more affluent. However, no transport operator can run profitably while serving an ever diminishing section of the community.

Unfortunately, there will always be a poorer section of the community and one can envisage the lack of public transport giving rise to a new population migration of these people to areas still served by such facilities. Only future, as yet unrecorded statistics can establish the fact

beyond doubt but it does seem to the writer that there is a real risk that the rich may well 'inherit the earth' in the rural areas—unless a deliberate social decision is taken.

The chairman of British Railways (Mr Richard Marsh) said in a TV broadcast in October 1971 that it was the task of Governments to solve the social problems—his remit was to run a profitable railway system. In logic he cannot be faulted and unless the Settle and Carlisle line can play a profitable role in BR's overall policy then there is no real argument, in present day railway terms, against its closure.

However, if social considerations matter—and this author is in no doubt that they do—then the figures analysed for the purposes of this chapter strongly suggest that, taking all matters into consideration, the case for rural rail closures is, at the very least 'not proven' on the passenger front. It may not matter too much for goods traffic in the light of the evolution of road traffic.

This being so, the author ventures to suggest that we may well live to regret the day we ruthlessly closed our rural railways on the grounds of pure economics. Others have said this before and there is nothing original about the thought. However, the argument has always been subjective and this analysis has tried to be a little more objective in its approach.

The Settle and Carlisle Railway was built with very little *genuine* thought for the local community—in spite of what some of the more public protestations from the Midland Railway might imply—and yet the evidence presented in this chapter indicates that there is at least a possibility (in some cases a strong probability) that its mere presence may have had a beneficial effect on the local area and that the long term effects of closure may be adverse. If this is true of the Settle and Carlisle, how much more true might it be of those other lines (built more specifically to serve the local community than this one) which are also in danger? One thinks of the Kyle of Lochalsh and Central Wales—to name but two—or are we all doomed to exist on a pre-stressed concrete altar to the all-conquering motor car?

The extent to which the Settle and Carlisle railway really *did* provide a local service will be considered in the next chapter.

Chapter 10

Local Traffic Patterns

From 1876 to 1922, the Midland Railway maintained precise records of traffic at all its stations and by fortunate coincidence, this period exactly corresponds to that during which the Settle and Carlisle railway was in operation before the grouping. The LMS and BR continued this practice but, regrettably, the 1923–1946 records could not be traced (they are thought to have been accidentally destroyed). The 1947–1953 figures are only part complete so it is not until 1954 that full details are again available. This is particularly irksome since the figures for the missing period could almost certainly shed light onto the dramatic fall in local activity during the LMS period. They might also indicate reasons why certain stations were closed well before the Beeching era.

It should, therefore, be made clear from the outset that this survey of local traffic can do little more than speculate about the missing period. However, sufficient data has survived for the overall patterns of activity to be discerned and it is with these patterns that this chapter is principally concerned.

In order to make the data manageable, the figures have not been studied on a year by year basis but have been averaged out over rather longer periods. This tends to mask any odd freak years but at the same time does not obliterate the basic trends. The first four periods selected are the successive 10 year cycles from 1876 to 1915. The fifth period (1916–22) covers the first world war and the years immediately following (up to the railway grouping), while the sixth period covers the last ten years for which full data is available (1954–63). This period has been subdivided into two five year cycles in order to highlight the basic trend of the 1954–63 records.

PASSENGER TRAFFIC

The figures available give the number of passengers booking tickets at the stations in question, together with the total amounts of the fares collected. These two sets of data have been converted into visual form and are presented as histograms at Figures 38 and 39.

From these diagrams, the dominance of certain stations along the line becomes very clear. Settle and Appleby stand out on both counts as, to a lesser extent, does Lazonby. However, for other stations there are considerable differences between the two sets of figures. For example, Cumwhinton (when open) generated a very high number of passengers but a relatively low level of overall takings whereas at Dent, there is a tendency towards the opposite situation. One concludes, therefore, that the far fewer passengers from Dent were paying more per person (and therefore travelling further) than the many more passengers at Cumwhinton. Unfortunately, the official figures do not record the destinations of the various passengers but it is quite possible to calculate the average fare paid by each passenger at each station during the period in question. This has been done and the results are given in visual form at Figure 40.

Since the fares paid were an accurate reflection of the distances travelled, it seemed reasonable to plot them along a base line where the stations, instead of being equally spaced, were spaced according to their distances apart. On doing this, a very clear pattern emerges. The line can now be seen to reflect the presence of three important centres, namely Settle, Appleby and Carlisle. With but few exceptions, the further away stations were from these focal points, the higher became the average fare paid per passenger. Thus, fares tended to approach a maximum at the approximate half-way points between the three primary locations.

FIG. 38 (overleaf page 96) Settle-Carlisle Railway— Average Passenger Bookings by Stations, key to columns as follows:

a. 1876–85   e. 1916–22
b. 1886–95   f. 1923–53: data missing in whole or part
c. 1896–1905   g. 1954–58
d. 1906–15   h. 1959–63

FIG. 39 (overleaf page 97) Settle-Carlisle Railway— Average Annual Passenger Takings by Stations for the same periods as in Fig. 38.

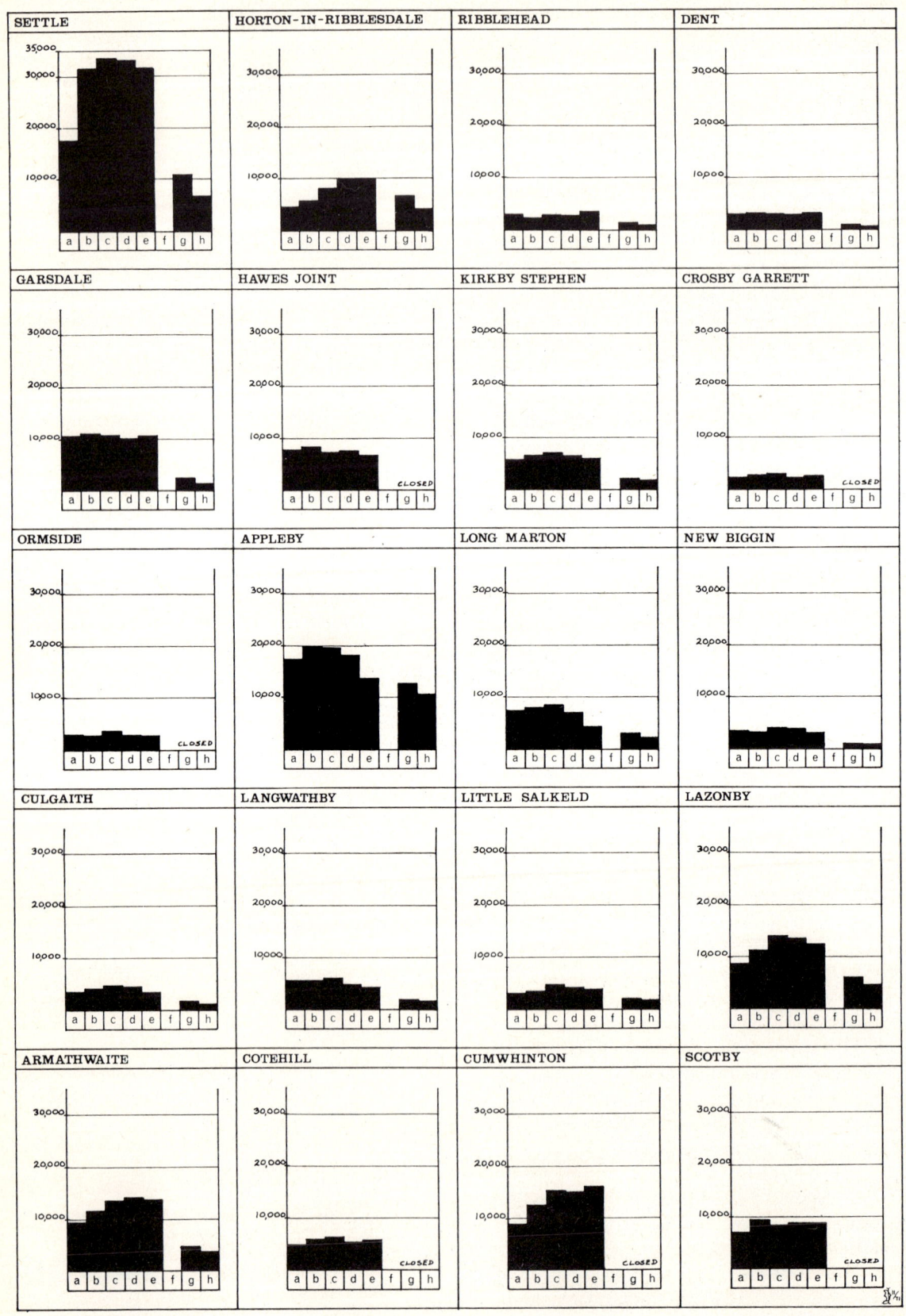

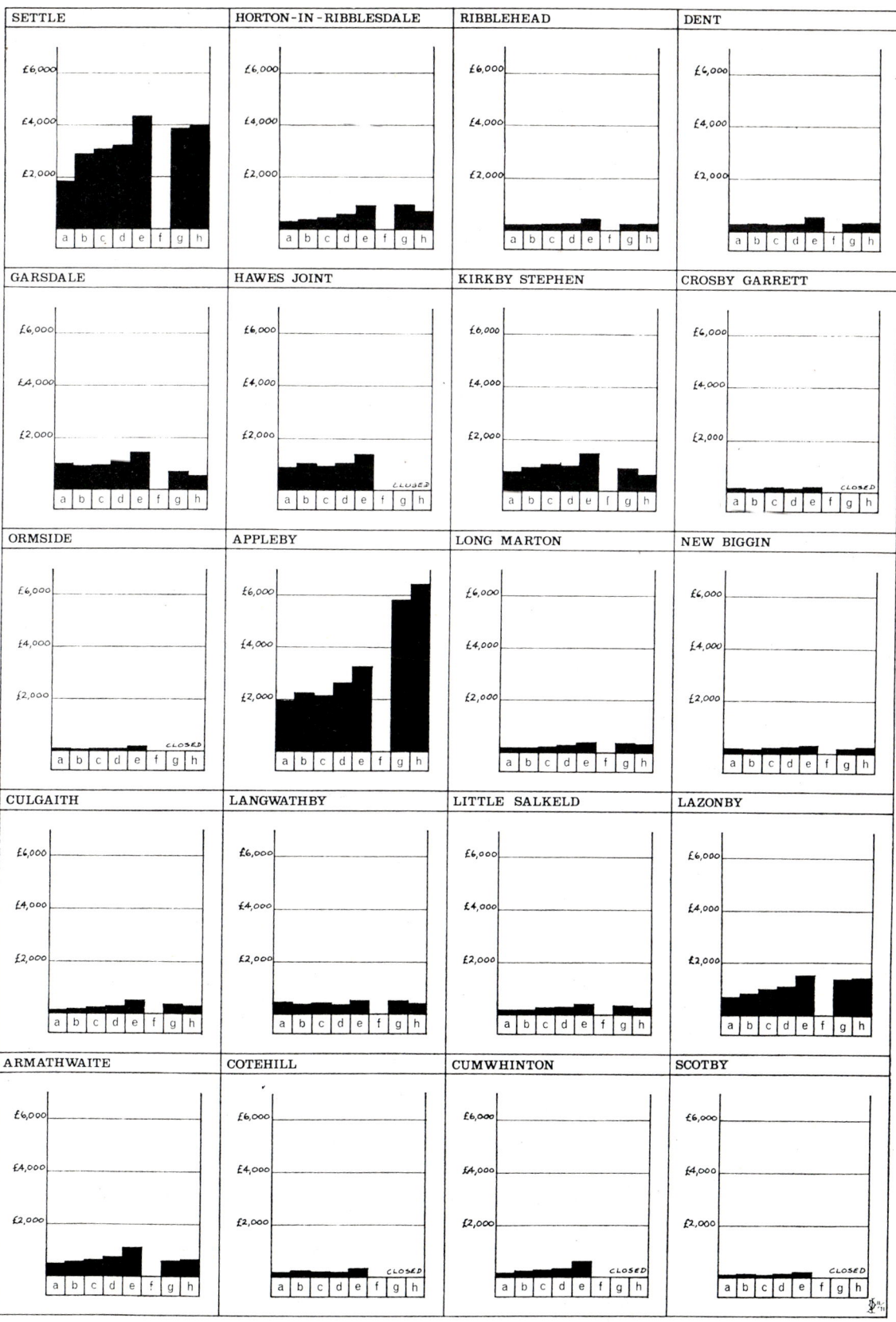

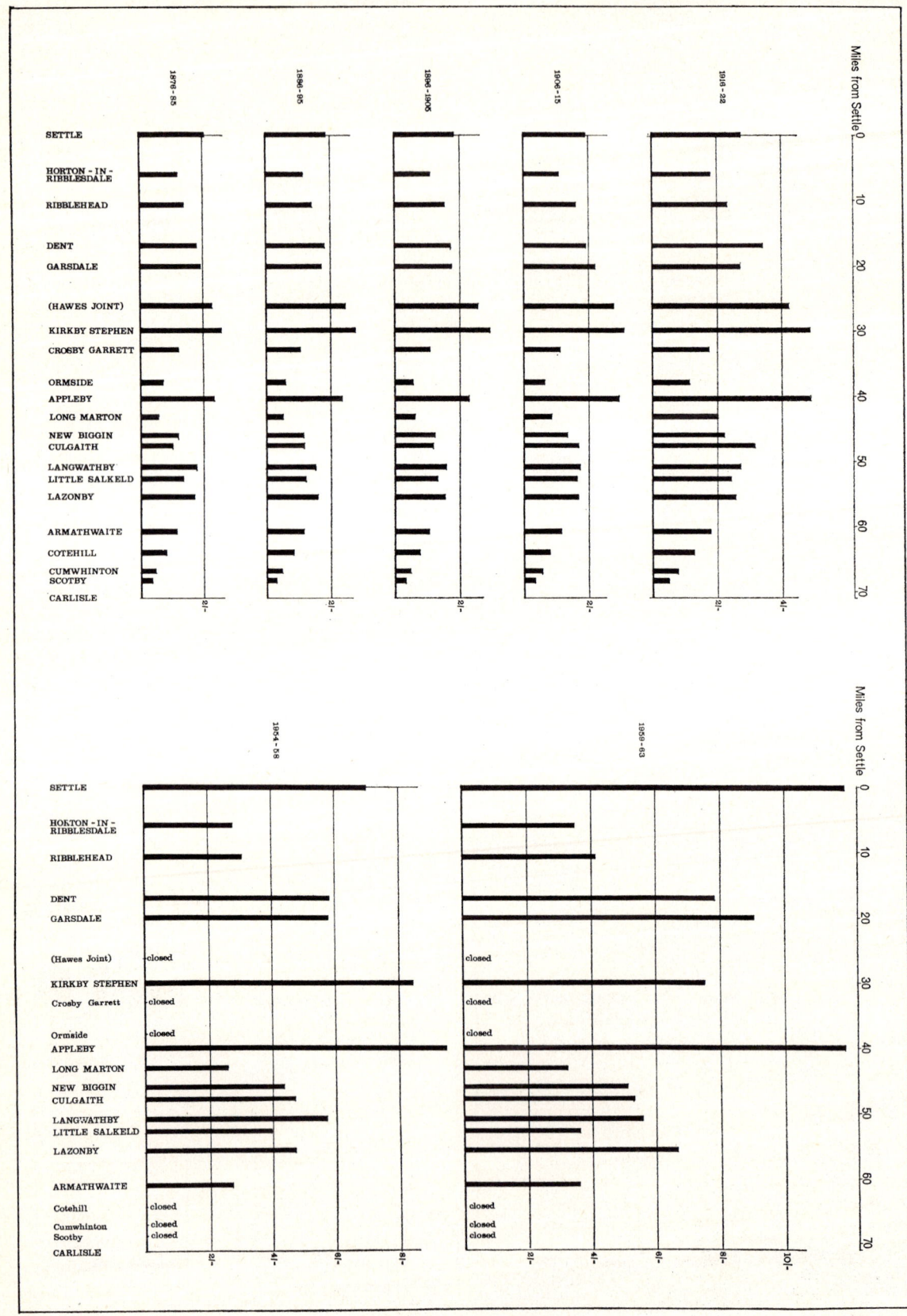

At first glance, the values for Appleby and Settle themselves, together with Kirkby Stephen and Hawes, seem not to fit this pattern. However, it should be born in mind that these four locations were the only places along the route which would qualify as important centres in their own right. It is somewhat unlikely that travellers from these centres would feel much need to travel but a few stations down the line. It is much more likely that when travellers from these towns used the railway it was usually in order to go to another major centre for facilities not available in their own town. Viewed in this light, the pattern becomes consistent again.

For instance, the figures for Appleby and Kirkby Stephen suggest that the average traveller from these locations was not journeying much further than the extremities of the line (probably mostly to Carlisle in the case of Appleby). The values for Hawes Joint turn out to be consistent with this town's distance from Settle (or Appleby) while the average fare at Settle itself again suggests that most travellers were not going too far afield. In fact, many passengers were probably using Settle in preference to Giggleswick on the 'Little' North Western Line. After the building of the Settle and Carlisle line, the new station at Settle was much more centrally located than its predecessor on the Gigglewick side had been.

It is, however, worth noting that the average fares at the Settle end of the line (e.g. Horton, Ribblehead, Dent) were rather more than those at similar distances from the Carlisle end of the line. From this one can conclude that a greater proportion of passengers were travelling beyond Settle than travelled beyond Carlisle. This is not really surprising. Carlisle is a well marked and dominant regional capital and focal point. Settle, although an important market town, cannot really be regarded as a major regional centre and it is more than likely that quite a number of people at the southern end of the line were using the railway to gain access to larger centres such as Skipton.

FIG. 40 (*opposite*) *Settle-Carlisle Railway—Average Fares by Stations. Note: Since in Britain, fares are generally calculated on a mileage basis, the lengths of the columns for the various stations give a visual indication of the comparative distances travelled by passengers. The gradual increase in column from period to period is a measure of the steady financial inflation since the time of the first world war.*

Overall, however, the inescapable conclusion is that the bulk of the passengers originating their journeys at the Settle-Carlisle local stations were using the railway to reach one of the focal points along the route, or just off it, and that very few passengers were using the line to travel further afield. In other words, the line was being used almost exclusively as a local amenity rather than as a means of leaving the area.

The pattern shows surprisingly little change for the first 40 years, either in shape or fares paid, and the first noteable change did not come until the final pre-group period (1916–22) when the level of fares increased significantly after some 40 years of relative stability. This inflation undoubtedly reflected the first world war but it is interesting to note that even during this more turbulent period, the actual pattern of travel is virtually unchanged from that of the late Victorian and Edwardian age.

The story is resumed in 1954–63 after six of the stations had closed and when further inflation had caused fares to rise considerably. Even so, the basic shape of the diagram still reflects the dominance of Carlisle, Appleby and the major centres at the southern end of the line. Right to the very end, the pattern of travel on the local services bore striking similarities to that established in the 1870s. However, from the data depicted in Figures 38 and 39, it is clear that although the pattern remained consistent, it was established by considerably fewer travellers than in the pre-1923 period. By the end of passenger services, the average number of people annually booking tickets at Settle and Carlisle stations had fallen from a high point of almost 150,000 per year (1896–1905) to as few as 35,000 per year (1959–63). Some of the decline may have started during the final pre-group years but the bulk of it almost certainly took place during the inter-war and World War II period. Such passenger traffic figures as have survived for the 1947–53 period (not given in this chapter) suggest that the major decline had already been witnessed at the time of nationalisation. In fact, there is some evidence that the 1954–58 figures, poor though they were by comparison with the pre-1923 values, were a slight improvement on the 1947–53 situation.

One cannot be too certain of the precise reasons for the closure of six stations long before the more widespread slaughter of 1970. In terms of passengers booked, the Eden valley stations nearer to Carlisle were quite high up the list. However, the revenue collected from them was very small and this may have been the vital factor. Moreover, the 1923–53 figures are missing which, if present, might indicate whether there was an excessive decline during the LMS period. Ormside and Crosby Garrett neither generated much traffic nor received much revenue so their demise was understandable; while Hawes was probably more a victim of the pre-Beeching assault on branch lines than anything else. Part of the reason for early closures may be attributable to freight traffic so this matter will be reconsidered later in the chapter.

Closer analysis of the available passenger traffic figures indicates that in its heyday, the Settle-Carlisle line undoubtedly generated a small proportion of commuter traffic—especially at the northern end. The stations in the Eden Valley all produced a goodly number of passenger bookings and even Scotby sold more tickets than Kirkby Stephen. This assertion is reinforced when one looks at the distribution of season tickets during the period—Table XI.

Although the yearly average is small, these figures are additional to the totals depicted in Figure 38. When one realises that one season ticket was probably equivalent to some 250 or so normal passenger bookings per year, it can be seen that even the few season ticket holders

in the Eden valley represented quite a high proportion of the total journeys made (probably approaching 15–20% in the case of such places as Lazonby and Cumwhinton).

However, this analysis merely serves to emphasise what has always been true of the Settle and Carlisle—the small number of local passengers in absolute terms. Even at its peak with 150,000 passengers per year this only amounted to some 500 per day and these were spread over six or seven trains and some 20 stations. Thus, even at maximum, the average number of passengers offering themselves for each local train at any one station was less than five! When one considers that the average 'all line' local fare for this period was probably about 1/4d, the line hardly represented a goldmine for the Midland Railway!

At its worst, the situation became farcical. By 1959–63, the average annual passenger bookings at Dent had fallen to 790 per year— scarcely two per day. Since six trains per day served the station, only one in three received a customer. Even at the best station during this period (Appleby with an average of 10,000 passengers per year), the average number of passengers per train was less than six. In any case, Appleby remained open after the widespread closures of 1970.

One therefore wonders whether the local passenger services can ever have paid their way

Table XI Settle-Carlisle Railway—Passenger Season Tickets 1876–1922

Station	Number of Season Tickets issued					Total	Yearly Average
	1876–85	1886–95	1896–1905	1906–15	1916–22		
Settle	7	519	758	868	659	2811	60
Horton-in-R.	—	—	8	47	63	118	2.5
Ribblehead	—	2	2	—	9	13	.28
Dent	—	—	—	—	1	1	—
Garsdale	—	55	35	7	19	116	2.5
Hawes Joint	—	1	1	2	11	15	.32
Kirkby Stephen	2	13	6	—	8	29	.62
Crosby Garrett	11	41	35	20	20	127	2.7
Ormside	—	4	22	2	3	31	.66
Appleby	2	42	35	38	24	141	3.0
Long Marton	—	2	4	9	14	19	.4
New Biggin	2	14	20	22	8	66	1.4
Culgaith	3	4	58	28	11	104	2.2
Langwathby	—	8	12	11	16	47	1.0
Little Salkeld	1	5	46	30	15	97	2.0
Lazonby	5	100	121	134	98	458	9.75
Armathwaite	1	33	84	99	154	371	6.8
Cotehill	7	35	51	23	47	163	3.5
Cumwhinton	17	49	86	132	214	498	10.5
Scotby	—	2	15	29	52	100	2.1

PLATE 94 *This view of a local train near Barons Wood dates from 1910. The train is quite a lightweight (compare Plate 118) and, somewhat unusually, is hauled by a '999' Class locomotive (995). These engines were usually confined to the heavier expresses on the route. (Photo: BR LMR.)*

on the Settle-Carlisle railway. The peak period for receipts was during the 1916–22 cycle. During this time the average 'all line' annual receipts were almost exactly £20,000 of which some £7,500 came from Settle and Appleby alone. The other 18 stations contributed scarcely more than an average of £700 each to the receipts. Even bearing in mind that salaries and wages were low and that maintenance costs were well below present values, it is hard to see these sort of figures making shareholders very enthusiastic.

The missing LMS figures cannot even be estimated but one suspects from the final BR returns that the inter-war picture was not, in any essentials, different from the pre-1923 situation. It was certainly no better and it almost begins to look as though for the whole of its lifespan, local passenger services on the Settle and Carlisle were more of a philanthropic gesture by the various railway managements than viable commercial operations. This being so, one can hardly blame BR, when asked to look at matters in purely economic terms, for taking the view that enough was enough. The wonder is that the local services survived for as long as they did.

Sufficient has been said in this and the last chapter to demonstrate that in spite of the minimal nature of the traffic, the line did serve as a valuable amenity to those local people who used it. Nor can the evidence suggesting a slower rate of population decline and the clearly marked pattern of local traffic be ignored when making a final assessment. The trouble is that such truths as they may reveal affect such a small number of people in absolute terms. Nevertheless, they do serve to highlight a fundamental dilemma of public transport—namely the extent to which it should provide a service rather than make

a profit and, if a service, then for how few (or many) people. Most, if not all suburban commuter lines show a steady loss—even with thousands of passengers daily—but their prime usefulness is not seriously questioned. Why, therefore, should not similar arguments be applicable to more rural rail services? What possible reason can there be for assuming that a handful of citizens and schoolchildren in Armathwaite are less important than the thousands who flock into Waterloo from Woking, Surbiton and all parts adjacent? Could it be that, collectively, the inhabitants of rural Britain wield less voting power than the clamorous hordes of suburbia?

The writer is well aware that his findings in respect of the Settle and Carlisle may not, in themselves, be particularly startling. But it does seem rather odd that our privately owned railways, where the profit motive was implicit in the structure of their orgainsation, seemed better able to provide marginal social services than can their nationalised successor in our present, supposedly more enlightened age.

This should not be construed as an attack on British Rail but rather on the system which allows it to happen. And for this situation, the politicians (of all political colours) must take a major portion of the blame. Over the last 20 years or so, BR management has had to work within a framework set up by the politicians containing so many contradictory guidelines that it beggars the imagination. It has more than once been suggested that while Dr Beeching and his successors may have provided the right answers, they were probably asked the wrong questions in the first place! The evidence afforded by the Settle and Carlisle would strongly support this view.

PLATE 95 *The final pattern of locomotive hauled local train is depicted in this picture of BR Class 6 4-6-2 No. 72008—formerly 'Clan MacLeod'—leaving Carlisle with the 4.37 p.m. to Bradford on 28th March 1966. The coaches are of corridor type with a Stanier LMS brake leading and an early BR coach bringing up the rear. The BR 'Clan' Class 4-6-2s were somewhat rare visitors to the line compared with other locomotive types. (Photo: Peter Robinson.)*

PLATE 96 *The final local services were operated by DMUs with conductor/guards. Here the 4.37 p.m. from Carlisle is seen passing Low House crossing near Armathwaite during the last few months of local services in 1970. (Photo: Peter Robinson.)*

Almost as far back as records go, the tradition of service has been implicit in the activities of most British railway companies. That they were able to provide it and still make a profit was probably as much a product of their 19th Century monopoly position as of anything else. However, it resulted in successive generations of citizens growing up in the belief that service to the public was a vital aspect of railway operation. The public can hardly be blamed for continuing to hold this view. In the long term, they may still be proved correct.

FREIGHT TRAFFIC

Freight traffic was classified for recording purposes into four main categories, viz: Livestock; General Merchandise; Coal, Coke, Lime and Limestone; Other Minerals. The wide variations between the highest and lowest figures recorded under these categories make it impossible to devise a suitable scale by which the majority can be presented in visual form, other than as a table of values. However, general merchandise can be presented by means of a visual diagram and this has been done. There is little apparent inter-relationship between the categories of freight traffic so each will be treated separately.

Livestock

The difficulty with the livestock figures given at Table XII is twofold. Firstly, the quantities are given either in truckloads (1876–1922) or tonnage (1947–63), neither of which indicates how many head of livestock were concerned. (Note. For the purposes of compiling Table XIII, page 108, one truckload of livestock was arbitrarily equated to four tons.) The second difficulty is that the figures do not indicate the type of livestock carried—cattle or sheep. A trainload

Table XII Settle-Carlisle Railway—Livestock Traffic

Station	1876–85	1886–95	1896–1905	1906–15	1916–22		1947–53	1954–58	1959–63
Settle	1838	1681	1394	1695	1583		?	56	1
Horton-in-R.	97	123	163	231	281		?	41	nil
Ribblehead	68	131	117	120	114		?	66	20
Dent	64	76	89	122	182		2	19	19
Garsdale	418	481	435	436	479		51	20	211
Hawes Joint	464	595	748	708	1068		?	closed	closed
Kirkby Stephen	317	622	671	687	821		638	125	17
Crosby Garrett	41	51	86	72	88		?	closed	closed
Ormside	nil	nil	nil	nil	nil	Data Missing	?	closed	closed
Appleby	725	837	831	1223	1387		2116	535	180
Long Marton	69	71	113	93	55		26	2	nil
New Biggin	193	271	456	616	449		15	1	1
Culgaith	nil	nil	nil	nil	nil		nil	nil	nil
Langwathby	572	641	554	406	298		114	33	6
Little Salkeld	nil	nil	nil	nil	nil		nil	nil	nil
Lazonby	736	920	1296	1969	2435		884	414	169
Armathwaite	261	512	570	565	441		69	2	1
Cotehill	nil	nil	nil	nil	nil		?	closed	closed
Cumwhinton	nil	nil	nil	nil	nil		?	closed	closed
Scotby	2	39	52	38	19		closed	closed	closed
Totals	5865	7031	7575	8981	9700		?	1312	625

Note. Figures for 1876–1922 quoted in average annual number of truckloads.
Figures for 1947–63 quoted in average annual tonnage.

of sheep would represent considerably more head of livestock than a similar trainload of cattle.

Although conclusive evidence is lacking, it is felt most probable that the farming patterns of the area would tend to make the traffic in livestock somewhat seasonal. In the case of the larger centres (Settle, Appleby), weekly stock auctions would probably generate at least some traffic on most market days but it is felt that the livestock figures recorded by the railway were probably compounded of a relatively small number of actual movements of traffic, each of which involved a sizeable number of animals.

However one looks at it, the use made by farmers of the Settle and Carlisle line in its prime was considerable. Even 100 trucks of livestock represent a sizeable number of cattle and a very much larger number of sheep. Furthermore, it should be remembered that livestock 'passengers' were making one journey only— not commuting along the line every day! Thus, to take the 1906–15 period, every year saw an average of almost 9000 wagonloads of livestock traffic in the area served by the line. At a very conservative estimate, this must represent some 25–30,000 head of livestock which, if reference is made to Table V in Chapter 9, can be seen to be equivalent to the total dairy cattle population of all the parishes included in the survey for 1911.

PLATE 97 (*left*) *Redundant Cattle Pens at Horton-in-Ribblesdale—May 1962. (Photo: D. Jenkinson.)*
PLATE 98 (*right*) *Most of the local trains on the Hawes branch were worked by the North Eastern Railway and its successors, the LNER and BR(NER). This view shows a local from Northallerton entering Garsdale on 30th May 1951 behind ex-LNER Class D20 4-4-0 No. 62391. (Photo: H. C. Casserley.)*

PLATES 99/100 *Prosperous days at Lazonby in 1913. Above is seen the well-filled goods yard with a string of cattle wagons indicative of the importance of this type of traffic; while below, a Midland Railway and an LNWR van await loading in the shed.* (*Photos: Roy Anderson's collection.*)

That this new facility for moving livestock in large numbers must have affected farming seems obvious. Alone of the various statistics quoted in this chapter, livestock traffic for the line as a whole showed a *steady* rise from an average of just under 6000 truckloads per year (1876–85) to almost 10,000 per year during 1916–22. This represents a 65% increase in traffic which accords very well with the rate of increase in livestock during the 1866–1911 period (see Table V, page 86).

No doubt all types of livestock were handled at one time or another but one suspects that a principal usage of the line was for transporting fairly young animals to the more rich pastures of the lowlands for fattening purposes at the onset of winter. One of the problems of the hill farmer (or any farmer with a proportion of rough moorland grazing) is that his farm cannot, as a rule, carry as much stock in winter (when the hilly areas are impossible to graze) as it can during the summer months when he can utilise all his acreage. The ability to cut down the size of his flocks and herds in autumn is, therefore, very important.

By contrast, many lowland farmers, especially in the eastern parts of the country, need their land for crops during the spring and summer period but can run larger herds during the post-harvest period. The presence of good communications between the two areas can materially assist the integration of the two types of farming enterprise and one cannot but conclude that the Settle and Carlisle must have been used for this purpose.

Livestock traffic on the line dropped startlingly during the 1923–47 period—coincident with the growth of road traffic. Here one feels that it was simply a question of road traffic gradually becoming more attractive to the farmer than rail. It was more flexible in that animals could be loaded at the farmstead rather than the railhead and the transit time was probably shorter also. Here is a classic example of a case where a suitable alternative to the railway did present itself and proved in time to be a totally acceptable substitute. The 1959–63 averages are low enough in themselves but by the time the last set of figures was collated for 1963, livestock traffic had all but ceased along the railway. There could be and was no reason for its retention.

However, it should not be forgotten that for some 50 years the Settle and Carlisle provided a facility which would otherwise have gone by default. It is probably not too fanciful to assert that many present day farmers in the North West Pennines may have had no farm to operate had not the Settle and Carlisle provided the essential communication facilities for their fathers and grandfathers.

The main livestock centres on the line included, as might be expected, all the main market towns (Settle, Appleby, Kirkby Stephen and also Hawes on the branch line), but perhaps the most striking case of increase came at Lazonby which more than trebled its livestock traffic during 1876–1922, finally accounting for the largest single proportion (25%) of the traffic handled in the pre-grouping period. It is difficult to see why it should have achieved this dominance— Lazonby was by no means the fastest growing livestock parish—but its situation at one of the few bridging points in the Eden gorge area would have enabled it to act as a gathering centre for parishes on both sides of the river. There is also the point that the Midland had a monopoly at Lazonby whereas it had to face competition from the NER at both Appleby and Kirkby Stephen.

It is also interesting to note that livestock traffic was one of the few instances (the other being passenger traffic receipts) where Kirkby Stephen achieved a reasonably high position amongst the Settle and Carlisle stations. In general, Kirkby Stephen did not generate anything like the amount of Settle-Carlisle traffic which one might have expected for its size. This aspect is analysed later in the chapter.

General Merchandise

Other than livestock and mineral traffic (see page 107), all other freight was categorised as general merchandise and recorded in the traffic returns by tonnage. The figures are presented in diagram form at Figure 41. As with livestock, the details recorded do not enable the precise nature of the traffic to be determined.

The pattern of activity is fairly clear from the diagram and little needs be said in amplification. Perhaps the most noteworthy feature is the dominance of three relatively small stations in the Eden valley, namely Cotehill and Cumwhinton during the 1876–1922 period and New Biggin in the 1954–63 cycle. While it is not possible to be dogmatic, one suspects that this particular traffic may have been connected with the brick and plaster works in the north of the Eden gorge and the latter day operations of British Gypsum in the New Biggin area. Any freight traffic connected with these operations which was not in the form of loaded wagons of mineral produce would be classed as general merchandise.

As might be expected, the volume of general freight generally reflected the size of the associated settlements with Settle, Appleby and Lazonby

PLATE 101 *This view of Hawes Joint Station was taken in the 1920s and shows a local freight departing for Garsdale behind ex-MR Kirtley 0–6–0 goods engine No. 2716. (Photo: The late W. O. Steel's collection—courtesy R. J. Essery.)*

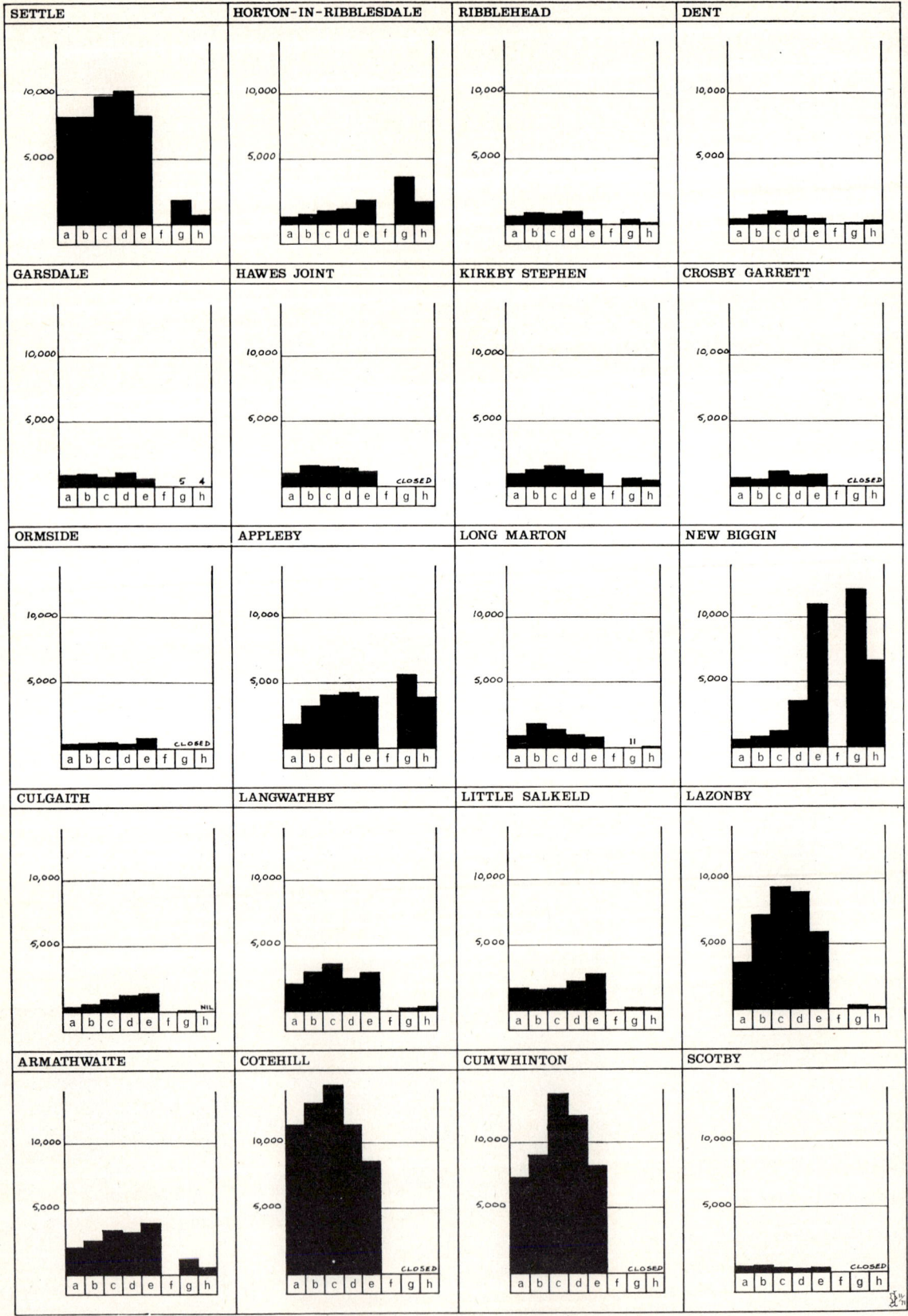

showing up well. It is, however, worth noting that Kirkby Stephen, one of the largest settlements en route, was well down the list in terms of volume of freight traffic. The station was, of course, some two miles from the town and the NER (later the LNER) had an important station at Kirkby Stephen which was much more centrally placed for local trade. One feels from the figures that the Settle-Carlisle traffic at Kirkby Stephen suffered considerably from the fact that the station's location reflected the presence of Ais Gill rather more than it reflected the town itself.

In general it seems true to remark that more general freight originated from the area north of Appleby than from the mountain section of the line. Again this is not too surprising. The settlements in the Eden valley are generally larger and, as has already been explained in Chapter 5, the stations were less remote from them.

As with livestock, the utilisation of the line during the pre-1923 period was quite high. The peak period was from 1896–1915 when the annual average tonnage handled amounted to 70,000 or more. This may not seem very much—just over 200 tons per day. However, when considering general merchandise, it must be remembered that although the goods wagons themselves were rated to carry six, eight or ten tons of freight, it was rare that a full load tared anything like this amount. General merchandise was

FIG. 41 *(opposite) Settle-Carlisle Railway—Average Annual tonnage of General Merchandise by Stations, key to columns as follows:*

a. 1876–85   e. 1916–22
b. 1886–95   f. 1923–53: *data missing in whole or part*
c. 1896–1905 g. 1954–58
d. 1906–15   h. 1959–63

frequently light but bulky and 200 tons of freight probably represented anything between 50 and 150 wagonloads—a not inconsiderable daily total for such a sparsely populated region. Even at the least important stations such as Scotby, Ribblehead or Ormside, generally averaging only 3–400 tons per year, this would, on average, amount to a daily wagon or two.

As with most other traffic, general merchandise declined rapidly during the inter-war period and by 1959–63, the average annual tonnage had fallen to some 15,000 of which over 10,500 tons were accounted for by Appleby and New Biggin. Even at these latter locations, this represented a considerable fall away from the 1954–58 situation. Clearly, the motor vehicle had taken over and during the middle 1960s, most of the local goods depots were closed. As with livestock, one feels that no great local hardship can have resulted.

Mineral Traffic

One has only to look at the figures given at Tables XIII to XV to realise that mineral traffic represented a very high proportion of the total freight tonnage connected with the Settle and Carlisle railway. This dominance is depicted visually at Figure 42.

Mineral traffic was recorded in two groups, namely the coal classification (which included lime and limestone) and 'Other Minerals'. In the case of the Settle-Carlisle, this latter category would include such materials as Gypsum, Anhydrite, brick clay and the various non-limestone rock types (frequently and quite erroneously referred to as 'granite') quarried in

Table XIII Settle-Carlisle Railway—Total Freight Tonnage

Station	1876–85	1886–95	1896–1905	1906–15	1916–22	Data Missing	1947–53	1954–58	1959–63
Settle	68032	71077	91812	110978	115971		?	58255	2384
Horton-in-R.	20670	74754	123841	141931	131506		?	218352	151355
Ribblehead	10455	12378	7240	2662	1484		?	3146	9222
Dent	2528	2392	2725	2382	2169		1105	1012	988
Garsdale	2996	5271	3430	4303	3226		522	320	215
Hawes Joint	9011	15710	10173	8307	7385		?	closed	closed
Kirkby Stephen	4175	5984	5746	5929	4739		2084	3335	2807
Crosby Garrett	1726	1582	2234	1830	1708		?	closed	closed
Ormside	1383	1042	1101	1052	1505		?	closed	closed
Appleby	8801	10350	12031	14192	14657		13155	17107	12193
Long Marton	2786	3394	3438	2852	2361		9597	7146	7981
New Biggin	3225	5171	7016	9895	18085		75158	118463	116709
Culgaith	2328	2367	2354	2634	2688		1139	113	nil
Langwathby	5938	7567	7545	5422	5403		1196	1578	1571
Little Salkeld	3857	3391	3626	4359	5067		2502	2035	1120
Lazonby	13998	17755	22888	26616	21610		35431	248745	296393
Armathwaite	5549	6463	7289	7888	7275		1249	1798	1001
Cotehill	15080	16939	19026	17067	18834		?	closed	closed
Cumwhinton	14113	19352	24491	21098	19285		?	closed	closed
Scotby	828	1120	1274	865	757		closed	closed	closed
Totals	202379	284359	359280	392262	385715		?	681405	613939

Note. These figures are computed on the basis that one loaded livestock truck (method of recording before 1923) is approximately equivalent to four tons of livestock traffic (1947–63 method of recording). The figures quoted are the *average annual tonnage* for the period in question. No data is available for the period 1923–47 and is only partially complete for 1947–53.

Table XIV Settle-Carlisle Railway—Coal, Coke, Lime and Limestone Traffic

Station	1876–85	1886–95	1896–1905	1906–15	1916–22	Data Missing	1947–53	1954–58	1959–63
Settle	46899	53416	45942	43320	41247		?	10727	1279
Horton-in-R.	16977	44058	70941	50606	36716		?	23704	22263
Ribblehead	6769	3493	2021	626	306		?	nil	nil
Dent	1308	1225	1180	1075	949		1090	911	740
Garsdale	958	580	575	888	643		428	285	nil
Hawes Joint	1995	1903	1657	1725	855		?	closed	closed
Kirkby Stephen	1629	2106	1306	1773	446		777	91	15
Crosby Garrett	795	719	624	620	346		?	closed	closed
Ormside	643	527	521	494	443		?	closed	closed
Appleby	3561	2964	3539	3655	4174		3782	5637	4272
Long Marton	1336	1165	1269	1120	1047		726	505	51
New Biggin	1670	1232	777	1077	1311		14	nil	nil
Culgaith	1390	1270	1004	905	889		4	nil	nil
Langwathby	1423	1206	1012	1038	914		nil	815	781
Little Salkeld	1933	1660	1715	1852	1857		2046	1735	932
Lazonby	3170	3686	3935	5110	2472		3560	3533	3000
Armathwaite	1713	1516	1248	1225	1002		90	82	34
Cotehill	2771	3328	3199	3000	2371		?	closed	closed
Cumwhinton	3463	4732	5397	4378	2635		?	closed	closed
Scotby	247	305	405	272	103		closed	closed	closed
Totals	100650	121090	148268	124758	100619		?	48025	33367

Note. Figures are average annual tonnages for the period in question.

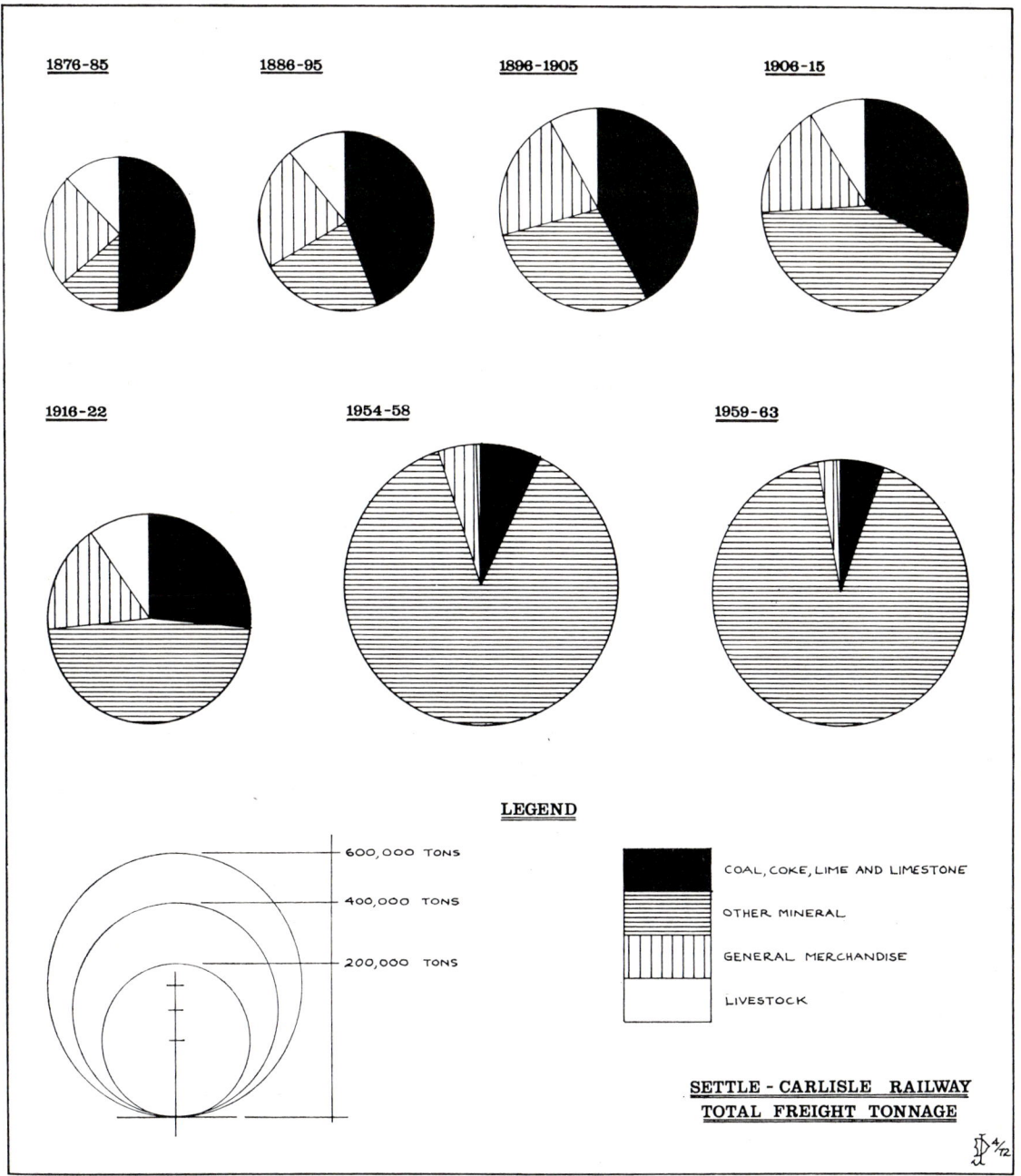

FIG. 42 *Settle-Carlisle Railway—Total Freight Tonnage. Note the overwhelming preponderance of mineral traffic in more recent years.*

the Ribblesdale area, especially at Horton-in-Ribblesdale and Helwith Bridge.

Perusal of the tables indicates that with the exception of the major centres (Settle, Horton, New Biggin and Lazonby), mineral traffic was spread fairly evenly along the line. The natural presumption is that in the case of most stations it mostly reflected local demand for domestic coal, lime for farm use and so forth. No really

startling figures emerge on this basis but once again, it appears that the line was quite well used for local traffic in its heyday. Clearly, the coal classification was usually more dominant in local terms than 'other minerals' and even quite small stations were handling between 500 and 1000 tons per annum. In the case of this type of traffic this would amount to 60 or more wagonloads per year, depending on the size of

Table XV Settle-Carlisle Railway—Other Mineral Traffic

Station	Recording Period								
	1876–85	1886–95	1896–1905	1906–15	1915–22		1947–53	1954–58	1959–63
Settle	5111	1902	29235	48801	58757		?	44741	nil
Horton-in-R.	2756	29455	51214	89258	91782		?	191069	127367
Ribblehead	2790	7446	3888	615	409		?	2749	9106
Dent	539	124	191	185	61		nil	nil	nil
Garsdale	323	1773	338	559	146		nil	nil	nil
Hawes Joint	4144	9766	3897	2367	1014		?	closed	closed
Kirkby Stephen	340	118	217	142	53		443	2512	2318
Crosby Garrett	110	135	102	87	123		?	closed	closed
Ormside	355	101	134	170	203		?	closed	closed
Appleby	360	531	926	1161	840	Data Missing	2565	5157	3770
Long Marton	203	331	231	298	216		8770	6628	7860
New Biggin	113	1940	3116	2779	3951		53989	106336	110056
Culgaith	500	472	373	425	400		945	69	nil
Langwathby	85	770	620	217	309		388	521	423
Little Salkeld	163	124	204	204	318		145	105	19
Lazonby	4207	3111	4304	4594	3441		30300	244504	293051
Armathwaite	630	185	355	1147	520		365	500	450
Cotehill	811	501	1332	2600	7847		?	closed	closed
Cumwhinton	3265	5571	5420	4678	8393		?	closed	closed
Scotby	61	231	237	81	192		closed	closed	closed
Totals	26839	64589	106334	160368	178831		?	604891	554420

Note. Figures quoted are average annual tonnages for the period in question.

the wagons which generally carried some 8–10 tons of mineral at that time.

In the case of purely local mineral traffic, the same inter-war period decline was seen as with the other freight classifications. Several stations had ceased to handle mineral traffic at all by the 1950s and at others, it had dropped to ridiculously small proportions compared with the peak years at the turn of the century. Not surprisingly, when the freight depots were closed in the 1960s, local mineral traffic also ceased to be handled. Only the major locations (Horton, New Biggin and Lazonby—the centre for the Long Meg quarries) remained in business and one is naturally tempted to wonder whether the railway has had any significant influence on developments at these places.

There are insufficient areas of mineral extraction along the Settle and Carlisle railway to enable a parish by parish survey to be made in the same way as for population and agriculture in Chapter 9. It was therefore resolved to make direct enquiries of the quarries concerned to determine the effect of the railway. The writer would like to acknowledge the help given to him by the various quarry owners in answering a whole battery of questions. He will respect their confidences by cloaking his conclusions in anonymity!

Basically, there are only a few areas where mineral extraction is carried out on a large scale in quarries which are rail connected. These are the gypsum and anhydrite quarries in the Eden Valley (at places like Long Meg and New Biggin) and the limestone and other quarries in Ribblesdale—mainly at Helwith Bridge, Horton and Ribblehead. All these quarries are of quite large extent—particularly at Horton—and most of them have been in operation for a considerable time. At the present time, the bulk of activity as far as the railway is concerned seems to be concentrated in the Eden Valley area which uses the railway line proportionately rather more than do the quarries in Ribblesdale. In this latter area, an increasing proportion of the material extracted goes by road. It should also be mentioned that one of the largest and oldest quarries along the line (at Stainforth), although dating back to the period of the line's construction, is now closed. The mineral traffic figures given for Settle during 1876–1922 and from 1954–58 reflect its presence.

It is clearly obvious that the mere possession of rail connections affords strong evidence that the railway was of influence in locating the quarry in the first place. What this does not necessarily imply is that the railway continues to be a vital factor. In most cases, the amount

PLATES 103–105 *Mineral traffic on the Settle-Carlisle. One of the staple traffics for many years originated from the Long Meg sidings (now closed). Above left can be seen a Class 5 4-6-0 departing northbound in 1965 while above right, a diesel hauled southbound train en route from Long Meg to Widnes crosses Dent Head viaduct in Spring 1971 behind an English Electric Type 4 diesel. The third picture shows British Gypsum's 0-4-0ST 'Jane Derbyshire' shunting at Howe & Co's sidings near Cotehill in 1969. This engine is now preserved at Carnforth. (Photos: D. Jenkinson (2), Peter Robinson.)*

of minerals consigned by rail has been diminishing for some time now and in one case, the only mineral traffic consigned by rail is material for the railway itself (i.e. track ballast)! Several owners admit that rail is the preferred method of transport in many cases but in almost every case, the owners also give the impression that the mineral is of sufficient value to merit extraction anyway. In other words, the railway is used because it is there not because there is no alternative. Only one of the quarry owners contacted by the author lodged formal objection to the proposed passenger closures in 1963 which would seem to indicate that in those circumstances, the quarry owners did not even regard the line as essential for getting their workpeople to the site.

The figures given in Tables XIV and XV give indication of how the mineral traffic is concentrated on certain stations only and it seems clear that the sheer bulk of the traffic makes it profitable for the railway. One imagines that it will continue to be so for some time to come. Indeed, there is no suggestion by BR that mineral traffic will cease. Even should the Settle and Carlisle be totally abandoned along the mountain section between Ribblesdale and Appleby, it seems as near certain as can be that the two ends of the route will be retained for the mineral traffic—including that from the former NER Eden Valley line between Appleby and Kirkby Stephen.

In all, therefore, the only significant conclusion that one can reasonably make about the influence of the Settle and Carlisle upon mineral extraction is that it may well have had some effect upon the initial siting of the quarries during the 19th and early 20th Centuries. As far as the present day is concerned, the railway is regarded as one of the possible methods of transport and must be judged entirely in terms of its competitive value. It seems reasonably certain that should BR ever reach the position where it cannot compete for mineral traffic, the quarry owners

Table XVI Settle-Carlisle Railway—Order of Importance of Stations for Local Traffic

Stations

Commodity	Period	Settle	Horton-in-R.	Ribblehead	Dent	Garsdale	Hawes Joint	Kirkby Stephen	Crosby Garrett	Ormside	Appleby	Long Marton	New Biggin	Culgaith	Langwathby	Little Salkeld	Lazonby	Armathwaite	Cotehill	Cumwhinton	Scotby
Livestock	1876–85	1	10	12	13	6	5	7	14	N	3	11	9	N	4	N	2	8	N	N	15
	1886–95	1	11	10	12	8	6	5	14	N	3	13	9	N	4	N	2	7	N	N	15
	1896–1905	1	10	11	13	9	4	5	14	N	3	12	8	N	7	N	2	6	N	N	15
	1906–15	2	10	12	11	8	4	5	14	N	3	13	6	N	9	N	1	7	N	N	15
	1916–22	2	10	12	11	6	4	5	13	N	3	14	7	N	9	N	1	8	N	N	15
	1954–58	5	6	4	9	8	C	3	C	C	1	11	12	N	7	N	2	10	C	C	C
	1959–63	8	11	4	5	1	C	6	C	C	2	12	10	N	7	N	3	9	C	C	C
General	1876–85	2	16	15	19	11	9	12	14	20	7	10	13	18	6	8	4	5	1	3	17
Merchandise	1886–95	3	15	13	16	12	10	11	19	20	5	8	14	17	6	9	4	7	1	2	18
	1896–1905	3	14	17	15	18	10	9	13	19	5	11	12	16	6	8	4	7	1	2	20
	1906–15	3	13	16	18	14	10	12	17	19	5	15	6	11	8	9	4	7	2	1	20
	1916–22	3	10	20	18	17	12	13	14	16	6	15	1	11	8	9	5	7	2	4	19
	1954–58	4	3	7	11	14	C	6	C	C	2	13	1	12	9	10	8	5	C	C	C
	1959–63	4	3	11	8	13	C	6	C	C	2	12	1	N	7	10	9	5	C	C	C
Coal, Coke	1876–85	1	2	3	16	17	8	12	18	19	4	15	11	14	13	9	6	10	7	5	20
Lime and	1886–95	1	2	5	14	18	9	8	17	19	7	16	13	12	15	10	4	11	6	3	20
Limestone	1896–1905	2	1	7	13	18	9	10	17	19	5	11	16	15	14	8	4	12	6	3	20
	1906–15	2	1	17	13	16	9	8	18	19	5	11	12	15	14	7	3	10	6	4	20
	1916–22	1	2	19	11	15	14	16	18	17	3	9	8	13	12	7	5	10	6	4	20
	1954–58	2	1	N	6	9	C	10	C	C	3	8	N	N	7	5	4	11	C	C	C
	1959–63	4	1	N	7	11	C	10	C	C	2	8	N	N	6	5	3	9	C	C	C
Other	1876–85	1	6	5	9	14	3	13	18	12	11	15	17	10	19	16	2	8	7	4	20
Mineral	1886–95	7	1	3	18	8	2	19	16	20	10	13	6	12	9	17	5	15	11	4	14
	1896–1905	2	1	6	18	13	5	16	20	19	9	15	7	11	10	17	4	12	8	3	14
	1906–15	2	1	10	16	11	7	18	19	17	8	13	5	12	14	15	4	9	6	3	20
	1916–22	2	1	10	19	17	7	20	18	15	8	14	5	11	13	12	6	9	4	3	16
	1954–58	4	2	7	N	N	C	8	C	C	6	5	3	12	9	11	1	10	C	C	C
	1959–63	N	2	4	N	N	C	7	C	C	6	5	3	N	9	10	1	8	C	C	C
Passenger	1876–85	1	13	19	18	3	7	10	20	17	2	8	14	15	11	16	6	4	12	5	9
Bookings	1886–95	1	11	20	17	6	8	10	19	18	2	9	16	14	13	15	5	4	12	3	7
	1896–1905	1	9	20	19	6	10	11	18	17	2	7	16	15	13	14	4	5	12	3	8
	1906–15	1	7	19	18	6	9	11	20	17	2	10	16	15	13	14	5	4	12	3	8
	1916–22	1	7	15	18	6	9	10	20	17	3	12	19	16	13	14	5	4	11	2	8
	1954–58	2	3	12	14	7	C	8	C	C	1	6	13	11	10	9	4	5	C	C	C
	1959–63	2	4	12	14	10	C	7	C	C	1	6	13	11	9	8	3	5	C	C	C
Passenger	1876–85	2	9	14	10	3	4	5	18	20	1	13	12	17	8	11	6	7	16	15	19
Takings	1886–95	1	9	15	10	4	3	5	18	20	2	16	17	13	8	14	6	7	12	11	19
	1896–1905	1	9	17	13	6	5	4	18	20	2	14	15	12	8	11	3	7	16	10	19
	1906–15	1	8	16	14	4	5	6	19	20	2	13	15	11	9	12	3	7	17	10	18
	1916–22	1	8	15	12	5	6	4	18	20	2	14	17	11	10	13	3	7	16	9	19
	1954–58	2	4	14	12	6	C	5	C	C	1	9	13	10	8	11	3	7	C	C	C
	1959–63	2	4	14	11	7	C	5	C	C	1	9	13	10	8	12	3	6	C	C	C

Note. This table, based on the Midland Railway and BR traffic returns for the periods in question, gives, for each station, its order of importance during each of the seven selected recording periods in terms of the volume of local traffic handled.

N No Traffic under this category.

C Station Closed.

Table XVII Settle-Carlisle Railway—Frequency Table for Order of Importance of Stations for Local Traffic

Station	Order of Importance																				nil	closed
	1	2	3	4	5	6	7	8	9	10	11	12	13	14	15	16	17	18	19	20		
Settle	16	14	4	4	1		1	1													1	
Horton-in-Ribblesdale	8	5	3	3		2	2	2	4	5	3		2	1	1	1						
Ribblehead			2	3	2	1	3			3	2	5	1	3	4	2	3		3	3	2	
Dent				1	1	1	1	2	2	5	3	5	4	1	3	1	7	3			2	
Garsdale	1		2	2	1	8	2	4	2	1	3	1	2	3	1	1	3	3			2	
Hawes Joint		1	2	4	4	2	3	2	6	4		1		1				•				12
Kirkby Stephen		1	2	8	4	3	4	1	6	3	3	2			2		1	1	1			
Crosby Garrett												2	6		1	3	10	4	4			12
Ormside												1			1	1	6	1	7	8	5	12
Appleby	6	12	8	1	5	3	2	2	1	1	1											
Long Marton				2	2	1	4	4	2	5	4	7	4	5	2							
New Biggin	3		2		2	3	2	2	2	1	1	4·	6	2	2	4	3		1		2	
Culgaith											3	8	6	2	2	5	2	2	1		11	
Langwathby				2		4	5	7	8	3	1	1	6	3	1			1				
Little Salkeld				2		2	4	5	4	4	3	1	4	2	2	2					7	
Lazonby	4	5	9	11	6	5		1	1													
Armathwaite				4	6	2	12	4	4	5	2	2			1							
Cotehill	3	2	1		5	2	1			2	5					3	1				5	12
Cumwhinton	1	3	9	5	2			1	2	1				1							5	12
Scotby						1	3	1					2	5	1	1	2	5	9			12

Note. This table, based on the data given in Table XVI, gives the number of times that each Settle-Carlisle station held the position, in order of importance, listed at the head of the columns concerned.

will, in the main, be quite capable of transferring to alternative forms of transport rather than go out of business.

The social consequences of closure of the railway to mineral traffic would probably be unpleasant. The thought of a vast increase of heavy lorries carrying thousands of tons of minerals along totally unsuitable rural roads is not pleasant to contemplate. But once again, as with local passenger traffic, it is not part of BR's present day terms of reference to provide social services at a loss unless given a subsidy to do so. We must hope that in the case of the Settle and Carlisle quarries, the situation will never arise—it is bad enough avoiding the lorries in Ribblesdale already!

THE OVERALL PICTURE

It is interesting to attempt a general classification of stations on the Settle and Carlisle route to see whether, taking all local traffic into consideration, any sort of pattern emerges and if so, what its implications might be. To this end, Table XVI has been compiled. In this table, the stations have been placed in order of importance for each type of traffic during each of the periods for which full data is available. The number of times each station occupied a given position in the hierarchy is summarised at Table XVII.

From these tables it can be seen that certain stations performed consistently well under all categories and others performed consistently badly! For example, Settle was either first or second in importance on 30 occasions out of 42 and Lazonby was only out of the top six stations on two occasions. By contrast, Ormside only once managed to achieve a position higher than 15th out of 20.

To be absolutely accurate, the figures for 1923–53 should also be included but if one accepts the limitations caused by the absence of this data, it is still possible to arrive at an approximate 'pecking order' for the stations which gives a fairly accurate picture of their relative importance. The missing figures might have caused one or two slight changes in position but the basic distribution would not change too much.

The method adopted was simply to total the values arrived at for each station under all categories and then find its arithmetic mean. Where no traffic was handled, the stations were ranked 'equal last' but where stations were closed, the mean values were taken only for those years when the stations were in use. It will be obvious that a low mean value arrived

Table XVIII Settle-Carlisle Railway—Overall Classification of Local Stations

Station	'Mean' Order of Importance	Main Building Type (see Chapter 7, p. 51)	Goods Shed Type
Settle	2.48	Large type	5 Wagon shed
Appleby	3.84	Large type	5 Wagon shed
Lazonby	3.84	Medium type	3 Wagon shed
Horton-in-Ribblesdale	6.45	Small type	No goods shed
*Cumwhinton	6.97	Medium type	3 Wagon shed
*Hawes Joint	7.10	Small type	4 Wagon shed
Armathwaite	7.65	Medium type	3 Wagon shed
Kirkby Stephen	9.08	Large type	5 Wagon shed
Langwathby	9.58	Medium type	3 Wagon shed
Garsdale	9.95	Non-standard	No goods shed
*Cotehill	10.00	Small type	No goods shed
New Biggin	10.70	Small type	No goods shed
Long Marton	11.28	Medium type	3 Wagon shed
Ribblehead	12.10	Small type	No goods shed
Little Salkeld	12.20	Small type	No goods shed
Dent	13.44	Small type	No goods shed
Culgaith	13.80	Non-standard	No goods shed
*Scotby	16.25	Medium type	No goods shed
*Crosby Garrett	17.10	Medium type	3 Wagon shed
*Ormside	18.20	Small type	No goods shed

* Station closed before 1970.

Note. This table, based on the data given at Tables XVI and XVII, represents an attempt to give classification for the local stations (taking all traffic into consideration) in order of their importance to local traffic.

at in this way will reflect a high position in the overall hierarchy so the stations were then placed in their 'order of merit' as revealed by these mean scores. This analysis is presented at Table XVIII, along with the basic details of the traffic handling facilities provided at each station.

Although this is basically a mathematical exercise, several rather interesting facts emerge. Firstly, it is remarkable how accurately the Midland's original estimate of facilities needed (see page 48) actually predicted the use made of the line, particularly in terms of freight traffic. Only nine stations were provided with covered goods sheds and seven of them are found in the first nine positions. Even Long Marton is not too far down when one considers that the high positions of Horton and New Biggin almost entirely reflect the massive mineral traffic at these locations. Garsdale is rather higher than might have been expected and the position of Cotehill and Cumwhinton may be inflated by the absence of the 1923–53 figures. However, the only major miscalculation by the Midland seems to have been in the facilities provided for Crosby Garrett and it is not too difficult to see why this station, along with Ormside and Scotby were amongst the first to close.

In spite of the fact that the missing 1923–53 data may have caused the final position of Cotehill and Cumwhinton to be a little high, it is still not easy to see why they were closed at an earlier stage than the bulk of the stations. Both generated high numbers of passengers (albeit with low receipts) and during the pre-1923 period they were at the top of the general freight category. One can only conclude that a dramatic drop in passenger traffic may have taken place during the LMS period. Freight traffic recorded at these locations was probably, in the main, originated from such establishments as Howe and Co's sidings, Lonsdale's Brickworks etc., all of which had private rail access and whose traffic could just as readily be recorded elsewhere.

One feels too that the traffic at Hawes, had it not been on the branch line, would have probably kept the station open until the end. However, any hidden subsidy that the main line stations may have received would not, of course, be available at the branch line centre.

The only other serious miscalculation appears to have been at Kirkby Stephen. The facilities provided here were substantially identical to those at Settle and Appleby but the use made of them was, for the most part, well below expectation.

PLATE 106 *Shows the rarely photographed Ormside station in late LMS days. The train is a southbound local headed by one of Holbeck's last two surviving Johnson Belpaire Class 3P 4-4-os No. 720. This is a particularly interesting picture since these engines were very rare visitors to the line during later LMS days and the station itself was to close only a few years later. (Photo: W. Hubert Foster.)*

It seems reasonable to conclude that Kirkby Stephen suffered considerably from the overall concept of the line. To reach Ais Gill, the railway had to by-pass Kirkby Stephen at a much higher level (see page 10). Therefore, not only was the station two miles from the town but also at the top of a rather steep hill. The NER had its station much closer to the centre of the town at a much lower level. Moreover, Kirkby Stephen was a junction on the NER system and the general facilities provided by the NER at the town were lavish. In consequence, one feels that the Settle and Carlisle was not in too strong a competitive position at this location.

A somewhat similar situation probably existed at Appleby. On the face of things, it is surprising that this station only ranks equal with Lazonby— one would, perhaps, have expected it to be closer to Settle in potential. However, the figures for Lazonby are strongly influenced by the massive mineral traffic from Long Meg and by the large amount of livestock traffic. Appleby, on the other hand, was cheek by jowl with the NER establishment and, doubtless, had to share its trade whereas Lazonby had a virtual monopoly of all that was going.

Appleby, of course, was eventually to develop a considerable milk traffic—particularly between the wars with the establishment of the Express Dairy with its own private sidings for the loading of milk tanks. Statistics for this traffic are hard to find and do not appear in the summaries given elsewhere in this chapter. However, the limited

PLATE 107 *The Express Dairy milk sidings at Appleby in 1947. These are now closed. (Photo: W. Hubert Foster.)*

PLATE 108 *Stopping passenger train, 1935 style, at Kirkby Stephen. The engine is ex-MR Johnson 'Belpaire' No. 739 and backwards from the tender is the following assortment of vehicles: Milk tank, LNWR six-wheel brake, two LMS corridors, GSWR six-wheel brake, LNWR corridor, two more milk tanks . . . what an inspiration for modelmakers!*
(Photo: Corbett Collection, courtesy National Railway Museum.)

data which has survived for 1947–63 indicates that during this period, the average annual receipts for milk traffic were in excess of £125,000 and at the peak period (1954–58) were running at some £250,000—a considerable sum of money indeed. For this reason it seems quite logical to place Appleby ahead of Lazonby in order of importance. Indeed, were the 1923–47 figures available, it is possible that Appleby might, overall, have proved to be more important than Settle.

In general, only at Appleby and Kirkby Stephen were the local stations of the Settle and Carlisle route in direct competition with those belonging to other railways. Although there were other stations close to the line—particularly those of the NER and the LNWR in Cumberland and Westmorland—it is not possible to determine the effect, if any, they may have had on Settle-Carlisle traffic. The Settle-Carlisle was the last railway to appear in the area so, in a sense, some of the traffic it gained could be considered to be at the expense of the NER and LNWR, rather than the other way round.

CONCLUSION

Bearing in mind the generally low level of population and economic activity in the surrounding region, it seems clear beyond all reasonable doubt that the Settle and Carlisle railway made a valid and substantial contribution to local activity in the area during the first 50 years or so of its existence. The degree to which this extended into the post-1922 period cannot be ascertained but it is obvious from the figures that in many areas, quite spectacular downward trends must have appeared during the 1923–47 years. Any possible revival of fortune during World War II was clearly short lived if the post-war statistics are any guide.

From the details quoted in the previous chapter, agricultural activity and population changes generally followed similar trends in the post-1911 period to those established in the earlier years; so one can presume that transport needs remained substantially similar. They may even have increased. It is therefore quite clear that the railway's former customers must have increasingly turned to alternative forms of transport during the inter-war years. In the case of freight traffic (except for mineral extraction), this changeover was all but complete by the middle 1960s and one feels that withdrawal of most local freight facilities and the closure of all but one or two goods depots was of no great concern in real terms.

However, one cannot be so sanguine about passenger traffic. It is true that in absolute terms the number of passengers declined over the years but even at the end, a fair number of people (in relation to the area) were still making use of the line and producing a traffic pattern clearly reflecting the local nature of the journeys they made. There is no real evidence that a wholly acceptable substitute has yet been made available for these people.

STOCKADED TURNTABLE AT GARSDALE

A. D. Whitehead

PART IV

The Line
and its Trains

PLATES 109/110 BLEA MOOR
A handful of cottages, a
lonely signalbox and
numerous sheep in the fields
by the lineside are the trade
marks of Blea Moor, the last
staging post in the main
northbound ascent, and by the
time Blea Moor signal box
and its attendant cottages
were passed, the tunnel was in
sight and firemen could think
about the slightly easier task
ahead. The train in this
picture is the down 'Thames-
Clyde Express' c. 1957 headed
by a somewhat unusual
locomotive for this period—
Compound 4-4-0 No. 1068
and an unidentified Class 5
4-6-0. The characteristic
profile of Ingleborough forms
an unmistakeable backdrop to
the scene. In the picture
below, taken in 1947, the
Stanier look on the Settle-
Carlisle is exemplified in the
shape of Rebuilt Scot No.
6190 'Royal Engineer' with a
southbound express overtaking
Class 8F No. 8177 which has
been put into the loop. Both
engines are from Holbeck
Depot. (Photos: Alan Robey,
W. Hubert Foster.)

Chapter 11

Coaching Stock

When the construction of the Settle-Carlisle railway began in 1869, the MR was a 'Four Wheel' line in terms of coaching stock and its almost flat roofed, box like vehicles were typical of the frugal accommodation provided throughout Britain at that time. However, James Allport was soon to change all this and during the next 50 years or so, the evolution of coaching stock at Derby was to make the name 'Midland' synonymous with rail passenger comfort.

In 1874/5, new eight wheel bogie stock was introduced on the northern main line out of St Pancras and in 1876 some sumptuous clerestory twelve-wheelers were built for the Scottish services. Ordinary stock became standardised on a six-wheel chassis but in all coaches, third class compartments were upholstered throughout and the dividing partitions were taken up to the ceiling—not much by modern standards but considerably superior to anything seen on other lines in Britain at that time. To these changes should be added those occasioned by the Midland's pioneering of American style Pullman bogie coaches in 1874. The first of these vehicles were built in America and assembled at Derby works. By the standards of the day they represented an almost revolutionary improvement in travel with their spacious open saloons, revolving armchairs, foldaway sleeping berths and all. So well made were they that one or two bodies survive as lineside huts until the present time.

The carriage superintendent at Derby during those momentous years was Thomas Clayton who, after 1877, omitted the clerestory from his designs. He reintroduced the feature in 1892, almost contemporaneously with the first of the soon to be famous Midland Dining Carriages. At first, Clayton's re-instated clerestory was very similar to his original design of the 1870s but in 1897, he changed its profile to that which has traditionally been referred to as the 'Midland' clerestory. The roof now formed a deep semi-ellipse out of which the clerestory seemed to grow naturally rather than be added on as an afterthought. For twenty years, this distinctive roof shape was to be the hallmark of the Midland company until more modern ideas rendered it obsolete.

In 1902, David Bain replaced Clayton and for a while retained most of the Clayton design features—most noticeable of which (apart from the clerestory) was the square cornered exterior body panelling which had also appeared with the new roof shape. However, by about 1905, round cornered windows and panelling re-appeared. Although Bain's suburban stock usually sported a low elliptical roof, the classic clerestory profile was retained on main line coaches and was not superceded by the full elliptical roof until the last few years of the independent Midland company, after Reid had become carriage superintendent.

PLATES 111/112 *Typical of the style of coaches being built for the first services over the Settle and Carlisle are the vehicles shown here. Left is a four wheel luggage van (MSJS No. 7) built in 1879 while right is a six wheel third class (MSJS No. 8) built in 1883 by the Glasgow and South Western Railway to a pure Midland design. The general style of body detail shown on these two coaches was also used on the original bogie coaches (both 8 and 12 wheel) built for the Scottish services. Some of the early bogie coaches had clerestories of a very similar style to that shown on the dining car at Plate 126. (Photos: BR LMR.)*

PLATES 113–115 (*left*) *The later evolution of Midland Railway coach styling is represented by the three vehicles shown in the accompanying pictures. Above is a 54ft sleeping composite (first class sleeping, third class ordinary) No. 02770 dating from the turn of the century. The coach is shown in the first LMS livery which, apart from company markings, was identical to the final MR style. Note the typical square cornered panelling and the characteristic Midland clerestory profile. The vehicle is shown on GSWR territory behind a Manson 4-4-0. The centre illustration shows No. 2951, another lavatory brake composite; this time a 54ft coach of David Bain design c. 1905. The classic MR clerestory is retained but the panelling has reverted to round cornered style. Although a later design than the previous illustration, this picture shows the earlier style of MR livery. The final picture in this group depicts elliptical roof lavatory composite No. 3330. This roof style was introduced during the first world war and remained the MR standard until grouping. Although the LMS did not build any coaches of this precise design, most of the styling features were adopted for LMS standard stock until 1930. The picture shows the final style of MR livery with large figures on the doors. (Photos: Author's collection, BR LMR (2).)*

Although Bain's carriages can, with justice, be regarded as the finest flowering of the Midland period, those built by Reid can be regarded as the true harbingers of the LMS standard coach; for Reid was appointed carriage superintendent to the newly formed LMS in 1923. Not surprisingly, early LMS designs had a distinctly Midland 'look'—some were, in fact, identical to the final MR designs. Coupled with the fact that the LMS also adopted the fully lined Midland Lake locomotive and coach liveries and it will be appreciated that as far as the Settle and Carlisle was concerned, little seemed to have changed for quite a few years after the grouping.

Ernest Lemon succeeded Reid and began to establish a somewhat more specifically 'LMS' style in new coachbuilding from 1929 onwards. The corridor vehicles were low waisted and had large 'picture' windows, thus affording to the passenger a much less restricted view of the passing scenery. Handsome and popular though these new coaches were, not many were built before the onset of the Stanier régime in 1933. During the stewardship of Ernest Lemon, exterior wood panelling had finally been eliminated and Stanier took the process to its logical conclusion by introducing the fully flush sided, steel panelled coach which was to continue,

PLATES 116/117 *These two pictures show 54 ft corridor coaches. Above is No. 3421, a Bain clerestory composite of 1907 vintage and below is shown a Reid elliptical roofed brake composite (No. 2845) of late pre-group period. The clerestory design was one of the commonest of MR types and similar vehicles were built both for M & GSW and M & NB joint stock. The later coach shows the larger corridor side windows introduced c. 1909 on the later clerestory designs and perpetuated during final MR and early LMS days. The coach is also interesting in having steel end panels. (Photos: BR LMR.)*

virtually unchanged, as the LMS standard until it too was superceded by BR designs during the 1950s. The Stanier period was also notable for the first departure from the traditional, fully lined and ornate Midland coach livery. The lake colour was retained but the lining became very much simpler and austere.

Little further change took place until a year or so after nationalisation when the coaches, including the new BR designs, were given either a crimson and cream livery (corridor stock) or a plain red finish of quite bright hue (non-corridor stock). The red shade was somewhat lighter than the MR/LMS colour and the two tone coach scheme was sometimes irreverently referred to as 'blood and custard'!

The first BR coaches were superficially similar to their LMS counterparts (although some six or seven feet longer) and many of them ran on well into the 1970s. Their initial two-tone livery was not long-lived for in 1956/7 there was a welcome return of something very much akin to the old Midland/LMS shade and this colour remained standard until the close of the steam hauled period. As an aside, expert opinion at Derby works assured the author a few years ago that BR Maroon, as this colour was called, was intended to be as close as modern paint techno-

PLATE 118 (*above*) *This southbound local train near Cotehill in 1910, headed by MR Class 2 4–4–0 No. 367, exhibits a fascinating assemblage of Midland carriage designs. At the front are two fairly modern horseboxes, followed by a Bain 54 ft corridor clerestory of 1905/6 vintage. The rest of the train is a mixture of Clayton stock, both clerestory and low roofed. The considerable length of the train is remarkable for a stopping passenger service on this line even at this period in history. The engine is a first stage Deeley rebuild of an earlier Johnson design. (Photo: BR LMR.)*

PLATE 119 (*below*) *The afternoon local train from Hawes to Hellifield was, for generations known as 'Boniface'. This picture shows it c. 1947 at Hawes, headed by an ex-MR Class 2 4–4–0 No. 470 in the final superheated form as rebuilt by Fowler. The first and third coaches are typical LMS standard non-corridor vehicles of the period and the centre vehicle is an ex-LNWR composite of substantially similar type but dating from c. 1920. (Photo: W. Hubert Foster.)*

PLATE 120 (above) *Ex-MR Compound 4–4–0 No. 1018 is seen heading a southbound train at Lunds viaduct c. 1946. The train is an interesting assortment of LMS standard corridor stock.* (*Photo: W. Hubert Foster.*)

PLATES 121/122 (right) *These pictures indicate the high standard reached by the Midland Railway in coach interior design. Above is shown the interior of a third class compartment of an elliptical roof corridor third No. 1348 while below is one of the first class compartments from brake composite No. 2845 (Plate 117).* (*Photos: BR LMR.*)

logy could get to the old Midland Lake shade. It was called maroon to avoid giving offence to other regions of BR! Finally, in the middle 1960s, the red colour began to disappear from the trains as the new BR Corporate Image colours made their bow.

So much for externals but what about the types of carriage provided?

Essentially, the Settle and Carlisle has mainly been a bogie coach line, although it is quite true that six-wheelers were used during early years, especially on local trains. However, passenger traffic has always been predominantly of the long distance type and since bogie coaches were adopted in quantity by the Midland for this class of traffic from the earliest days of the line, it is not too surprising that most Settle-Carlisle trains have been generally composed of the more modern vehicles of the period.

PLATES 123 (a) & (b) *Although the quality of these pictures is not of the best, they are of considerable historic interest in showing contemporary trains of the 1930s. At the top, an LMS built compound 4–4–0 heads north at Kirkby Stephen on 6th July 1935 with the 'Thames-Clyde Express' while the lower picture, taken at much the same period in history shows the lunchtime Glasgow-St. Pancras express (with through LNER coaches from Edinburgh) southbound at Ribblehead with a Stanier Jubilee in charge. The train formations (except for the leading brake composite on the 'Thames-Clyde'— probably added at Leeds) are almost exactly the same as those quoted on Page 151 for the 1938 season.* (*Photos: Corbett Collection, courtesy National Railway Museum.*)

The first Anglo-Scottish services mostly utilised the low roofed Clayton bogie coaches—both eight and twelve-wheeled varieties—although some of the early clerestories and six-wheelers would be in evidence. By modern standards, the absence of a continuous corridor was probably the most noteworthy feature. Indeed, the Midland was somewhat late amongst the British companies to introduce this feature, not adopting the idea until 1898. Prior to this date, only limited corridor facilities were available (e.g. between the vehicles of a dining car set or the centre gangway running the full length of one of the American Pullmans).

The American Pullmans were, in part, procured by the Midland for its Scottish services but although their lineaments continued to be found in sleeping cars for quite some time, in general they proved less popular than expected. It was rare to find more than one or two in a train in spite of the fact that their riding qualities were extremely high.

The onset of the classic gangwayed Midland clerestory coaches also saw the widespread adoption of that typically British institution, the side corridor coach with individual separate compartments seating four, six or eight people, depending on the class of vehicle. This is a somewhat extravagant design in terms of coach weight per passenger (especially when, in later LMS days, the thirds were generally reduced from eight to six per compartment).

Over the years, the side corridor style of vehicle provided the bulk of accommodation on the Settle-Carlisle expresses and its length gradually evolved from the earliest 50 feet MR specimens to the final BR 64 feet coaches. However, it is only in relatively recent years that it has given way in any quantity to the open saloon coach with its larger seating capacity per vehicle. Until well into LMS days, open saloon seating was confined principally to dining cars.

At the present time, only the first class passenger can expect to find side corridor accommodation as of right. Its provision in second class vehicles (the modern day equivalent of the MR and LMS third class) seems largely to be an accident of carriage marshalling as BR scrap more and more of their side corridor seconds.

Changes to the more specialised type of vehicle used on the line have been mostly confined to externals. However there was a fundamental change in concept when the Pullman type sleeping cars gave way to the Midland design of vehicle. The original Pullmans and some early MR cars were fitted with longitudinal berths (one upper and one lower per seating bay on either side of the centre gangway), whereas the later Midland designs from about the turn of the century saw the introduction of transverse sleeping berths of a kind very similar to those still in use today.

Dining Cars have been synonymous with the Settle and Carlisle since first they were adopted by the MR. There has been the inevitable transformation of exterior appearance and interior styling over the years but at all times since the introduction of dining cars, it has been possible to partake of a full three or four course meal on at least some services on the line—in fact the 'Thames-Clyde Express' did at one stage rate a mention in one of the more famous guides to good eating! The modern BR buffet car is the only real innovation in dining facilities on the route but this type of vehicle has never found widespread use on the line.

Local passenger services saw considerable changes before their final demise. The earliest Midland trains may well have been composed of six-wheelers but these probably gave way to bogie coaches quite early in the day. For many

PLATES 124/125 *The Pullman sleeping cars operated by the MR have been well publicised and illustrated. Perhaps less well known were the true Midland sleeping cars of Bain design of which 12-wheel carriage No. 2778 is illustrated here, both exterior and interior. Although fashions in interior design have changed radically since this coach was built, a present day traveller would find the interior layout of this car surprisingly similar to that of a modern BR sleeping car. (Photos: BR LMR.)*

PLATE 126 (*above*) *MSWJS first class dining carriage No. 1. When Clayton reintroduced the clerestory in the 1890s, it was of very similar style to that which had been used in the early days of the Settle and Carlisle. This dining car was an early example of the revival.* (*Photo: BR LMR.*)

PLATE 127 (*below*) *M & GSW first class dining carriage (No. 208) of square panelled Clayton clerestory style. These cars were 65 ft long and ran paired with an identically styled third class carriage. The kitchen was contained in the first class coach. Note the two windows per seating bay compared with the previous picture.* (*Photo: BR LMR.*)

PLATE 128 (*above*) *David Bain 59 ft clerestory dining carriage No. 2793, built in 1908. These vehicles also ran paired with matching third class carriages and were the most numerous of the many different types of MR dining cars.* (*Photo: BR LMR.*)

PLATE 129 (*below*) *Reid design M & GSW first class dining car No. 216, built in 1917. These were the final pre-group dining cars and contained many design detail features subsequently adopted by the LMS as standard for general service stock.* (*Photo: BR LMR.*)

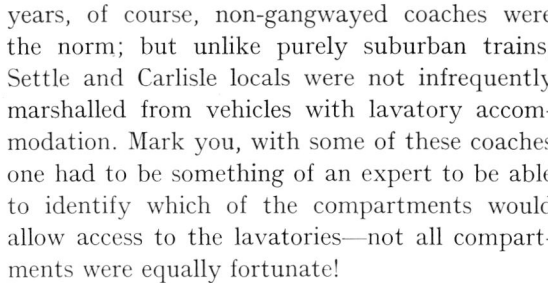

years, of course, non-gangwayed coaches were the norm; but unlike purely suburban trains, Settle and Carlisle locals were not infrequently marshalled from vehicles with lavatory accommodation. Mark you, with some of these coaches one had to be something of an expert to be able to identify which of the compartments would allow access to the lavatories—not all compartments were equally fortunate!

From about the close of the LMS period, passenger services increasingly made use of gangwayed stock which, towards the end of the locomotive hauled period gave a somewhat spurious air of importance to these poorly patronised trains. Indeed, during the early 1960s the locals became quite impressive. It was nothing unusual to see rebuilt 'Scots', 'Britannia' pacifics or even the odd Brush Type 4 making their way majestically up to Blea Moor with the three or four coaches of the lunchtime Hellifield-Carlisle service. Since this not infrequently represented a customer ratio of one passenger per coach, it could hardly have endeared itself as an economic exercise to the post-Beeching management!

The final change in local passenger services came with the introduction of Diesel multiple units and the reduction of most stations to unstaffed halts in a final attempt to make things pay. On these trains one paid one's fare to the guard. Railway enthusiasts quickly discovered the virtue of these trains for sightseeing and for a few years it was possible for the ordinary fare paying passenger to obtain what amounted to a driver's eye view of this famous route. In fact, a very rewarding Saturday day excursion could be made from Skipton in the late 1960s by going out to Carlisle on the morning Birmingham-Glasgow express (usually steam hauled until 1967) and then returning on the afternoon DMU. However, such pleasures were to be short-lived

PLATES 130–132 *Midland dining carriage interiors were always very luxurious and three examples are shown here. Above left is shown the interior of a* third *class carriage of 1894 period! These were the matching coaches to the first class carriage shown at Plate 126. Above right is the interior of Bain 12-wheel first class carriage No. 2509 built in 1906 while below is shown the interior of one of the final Reid first class cars of 1917, probably carriage No. 216—Plate 129. (Photos: BR LMR.)*

and the DMUs were withdrawn in May 1970.

In the early 1970s, most of the passenger services on the Settle and Carlisle seemed to be diverted West Coast expresses travelling via Ais Gill during the pre-electrification work on Shap. These diversions have continued on many weekends since electrification and have brought the latest BR Mark II and Mark III stock to the line. However the few remaining 'native' trains continued to be formed of rather older vehicles until the late 1970s.

Chapter 12

Motive Power

It is hard enough trying to condense the story of Settle-Carlisle coaching stock into the confines of one chapter but when it comes to locomotives, the task is well nigh impossible. While there were many types of coach which did not find their way onto the Carlisle line, the same cannot really be said of railway engines. Virtually all types of Midland Railway and most types of LMS standard main line classes have been seen on the line not to mention the many BR designs which have made their appearance over recent years. Add to this the drafting to the line of certain classes of non-LMS or MR origin during the steam years and the complete story of Settle and Carlisle motive power could fill a book in its own right.

Fortunately, however, most railway enthusiasts over the years have been far more interested in locomotive matters than anything else and this has led to a great deal of literature on the subject, of which the Settle-Carlisle and its working forms a not insignificant proportion. It is, therefore, quite possible for the reader who would know more about the subject than can be contained within these pages, to turn for supplementary information to most of the references contained in the bibliography at page 154.

This narrative, therefore, does not profess to be a detailed history of the subject. It can more properly be regarded as a general review of a century of traction and its more noteworthy trends together with an illustrated survey of some of the engines not depicted in illustrations elsewhere in the book.

The first point to make clear in the story is that motive power along the route has always reflected the main purpose for which the line was built—the operation of main line through trains. The Settle-Carlisle has never been a locomotive backwater and even the local trains have, as often as not, been powered by more up to date prime movers than their counterparts in many other parts of the country. The vision of quaint antiquated locomotives trundling peacefully through the English countryside with a train of superannuated vehicles has never really been appropriate to the Settle and Carlisle. Older engines have, of course, put in their appearances, but in general, the main services on the line have usually been entrusted to some of the more modern engines available.

This trend started from the beginning of services on the line. That grand old man Matthew Kirtley, although very much involved with Crossley and Allport in the planning of the route, had died before it was completed and by the time the line opened for all traffic in 1876, the Midland Railway was already two or three years into the Johnson era of locomotive affairs. Thus, early engine working was very much a reflection of late Kirtley/early Johnson ideas. In general, the more up to date machines were drafted to the line and in many cases, whole batches of engines were supplied new to work the route. Thus, the Kirtley outside framed engines together with the early Johnson equivalents were the first classes to see widespread use.

In general, the first few years saw 0–6–0s on freight trains and 2–4–0s on passenger workings. As far as the Midland was concerned, the 0–6–0 remained a universal standard for freight traffic and the only variation as far as the first 50 years of the Carlisle road was concerned was the gradual transition from the outside framed Kirtley 0–6–0s of the 1870s, via the small and larger boilered Johnson engines of the late Victorian period, to the Deeley Class 3 and Fowler Class 4 0–6–0s of the first quarter of the 20th Century. In fact, it was not until several years into the LMS period that anything other than 0–6–0s worked the Settle-Carlisle freight.

However, things were not quite so simple on the passenger side. Passenger trains are more prestigious to the railway and their motive power is more in the public eye; so it was not too surprising that as new classes came along, members of them soon found their way onto the Midland's Anglo-Scottish trains. Furthermore, train weights increased considerably during the later part of the 19th and the early part of the 20th Century as companies vied with each other to add more and more amenities to their services. As a result, it became necessary to design ever more powerful engines—frequently to handle trains containing very few additional passengers than had travelled in the older lighter coaches.

On the Midland Railway, this resulted in a gradual transition from the old Kirtley 2–4–0s (of which the '800' class was, perhaps, most strongly associated with the Carlisle line) to larger and more modern engines. Virtually all the Johnson passenger types were seen on the route with, as far as is known, the solitary exception of the beautiful and famous 4–2–2 bogie 'singles'. They would have looked superb against the mountain setting but adequate visual compensation was probably provided by the equally graceful lines of the Johnson 2–4–0s and early 4–4–0s, most versions of which saw service over Ais Gill almost as soon as anywhere on the Midland.

The two final Johnson 4–4–0 designs were particularly significant. The earliest were his Class 3 'Belpaire' engines and the working of the Settle-Carlisle trains was undoubtedly a major consideration in their design. The first five members of the class were sent to Holbeck in 1900. Large though these engines were for the time, and 80 were eventually built for the whole Midland system, it was only some two or three years later that the first of the even more powerful and celebrated Class 4 Compounds appeared on the line. Although the name of Deeley is inescapably bound up with the story of the Midland Compounds, the first five of these engines were actually built by Johnson. Deeley added 40 more to the list, also rebuilding the Johnson machines to the same standard, and the LMS built no fewer than 195 further examples in the

PLATES 133/4 (above) *Samuel Johnson caused 0–6–0 goods engines to be built by the hundred—many for the Carlisle line. The upper view shows No. 3352 in LMS condition at Skipton in 1946—hardly altered in any significant respects from when built in 1891. Below is shown No. 3078 near Keighley. This engine dated from 1881 but had been rebuilt by the MR with belpaire boiler and new cab. No. 3352 was scrapped in 1946 but 3078 ran on into BR days as 58212—a very old engine indeed! (Photos: W. Hubert Foster; Eric Treacy.)*

PLATE 135 (below) *This picture was taken in May 1940 in the Baron's Wood area. It shows ex-MR Class 3F 0–6–0 No. 3231 on a southbound freight. (Photo: Norman Wilkinson.)*

PLATES 136/137 *The earliest MR express locomotives to work the Carlisle route were the 2–4–0s of Kirtley design. Perhaps the most famous of these were the outside framed 800 Class of which an example (No. 50) is seen in the picture above piloting a southbound express at Armathwaite c. 1910. The engine is carrying its 1907 series number; it was formerly No. 817. The train engine, unidentified, is a first stage Deeley rebuild of a Johnson 4–4–0 while the train itself is mostly composed of square panelled clerestory stock. Note the distinctive 'clipper' profile of the dining car—the fourth vehicle in the train. To the left are two more first stage rebuilds of Johnson 4–4–0s (444, 430) also at Armathwaite. Both these engines were rebuilt yet again in a similar style to that shown at Plate 119 and in this form lasted until the 1950s. (Photos: BR LMR.)*

early post-grouping years. For some 20 years or more, the Settle and Carlisle resounded to the distinctive three-cylinder beat of the 'Crimson Ramblers' on most principal trains and even when later designs had relegated them to lesser workings, they remained a familiar sight until well into BR days.

For comparison with the compounds, Deeley also built a batch of ten simple expansion 4–4–0s of the same power class and these engines became particularly associated with the Carlisle route. They were usually referred to as the '999' Class (their running numbers ran from 990–9) and they spent virtually all their working life north of Leeds. Few instances (other than trips to Derby for maintenance) have been recorded of their being seen anywhere else. Fine machines though they were, they suffered in LMS days from being 'non-standard' and all had gone by 1928.

Apart from his Class 4 engines, Deeley did not introduce any other new express engines onto Midland metals. However, he was responsible for a major rebuilding programme on the majority of the early Johnson 4–4–0s which were now somewhat less powerful than was necessary to haul even the lesser expresses. The original Johnson 4–4–0s were placed in Midland Railway power class 1 but after the Deeley rebuilding they became the first of what was to eventually total a considerable number of Class 2 4–4–0s. The graceful Johnson lines were sacrificed in the rebuilding and the resulting engines exhibited quite a variety of different appearances depending on the precise nature of the changes effected to them. Eventually they evolved into what became the Midland standard Class 2 engine which was to be adopted, almost unchanged, as an LMS standard light passenger class during the 1920s. Many commentators feel that the Johnson Belpaire or the Deeley '999' type would have

PLATES 138/139 (above) *The original Johnson 4–4–0 was a beautifully proportioned machine. Few remained that way after Deeley arrived but 306 (left) was one of a handful which remained largely as built. It is seen here somewhere on the Settle-Carlisle in early LMS days with an Inspection Saloon. Some Deeley rebuilds were less offensive, visually, than others and 465 (right), looking rather like a miniature '999' is seen near Cotehill in 1910. (Photos: Shuttleworth Collection, BR, LMR.)*

PLATE 140 *Yet another picture taken by the MR staff photographer at Armathwaite c. 1910 shows Deeley two-cylinder simple Class 4 4–4–0 No. 992 on a southbound express. These '999' Class engines were very much associated with the Leeds-Carlisle services and one feels that had there been more of them, they may have had a much longer post-group life than they did. They were a very successful design and much better load haulers than the rather feeble Class 2 4–4–0s which were so numerous. (Photo: BR LMR.)*

PLATE 141 *This very well known view of a southbound express at Armathwaite c. 1910 is included again in this book mainly because it shows the pioneer Midland compound 4–4–0 No. 1000 almost as originally built by Johnson— although it has acquired a few Deeley trimmings! It was eventually fully rebuilt to the Deeley pattern and is, of course, preserved in the National Railway Museum. Note the many MR lineside features. (Photo: BR LMR.)*

PLATE 142 *The compounds remained at work on the line well after the introduction of more powerful types. In this view, the first LMS built example, No. 1045, is seen southbound at Armathwaite with what looks rather like the 'Thames-Forth Express' in the later 1930s. (Photo: E. E. Smith.)*

been a better choice for such standardisation since, although very numerous, the Class 2s were not particularly outstanding in the context of LMS operations.

Thus, at the close of the Midland era, the Settle-Carlisle line was predominantly the preserve of but two basic types of engine, the 0–6–0 for goods traffic and the 4–4–0 (in all its many varieties) for passenger services. There were, however, still a number of 2–4–0s to be seen, generally reserved for piloting duties up to Ais Gill. At no time were tank engines used to any

great extent although it is quite possible that the odd 0–4–4T or 0–6–0T could have ventured up the line on local passenger or freight workings.

The LMS used the Settle and Carlisle in the early post-group years as a test route for the evaluation of various engines from its pre-group constituent companies and this brought some of the first 'foreign' visitors to the line. In this instance they included LNWR 4–6–0 and Caledonian 4–4–0 types. It was not, however, until several years into the LMS period that any marked changes were apparent in the every-

PLATE 143 *LMS Patriot Class 5XP 4–6–0 No. 5902 'Sir Frank Ree', later No. 5501 'St Dunstans'. This was one of the first two Patriots which were, officially, 'rebuilds' of withdrawn Claughtons. The wheels were certainly of Claughton type but it is doubtful if much else remained. The chassis layout was basically of Royal Scot type and the boiler was of the same design as that which had been fitted to some of the Claughtons. (Photo: BR LMR.)*

PLATES 144/145 *Double heading was very much a feature of the Settle and Carlisle, even after the onset of the 4–6–0s. These two pictures from the LMS period show (right) ex-MR Belpaire 4–4–0 No. 775 piloting as yet unnamed Stanier 5XP No. 5616 (later 'Malta') at Crosby Garrett in July 1935 with the up 'Thames-Clyde Express' while below, LMS compound No. 1148 and an unidentified Stanier 5XP take a northbound express through Armathwaite. (Photos: Corbett Collection, courtesy National Railway Museum; E. E. Smith.)*

day locomotive workings of the railway; but when the LMS changes did begin, they ushered in a period of some 40 years or so during which the Settle and Carlisle was frequently to witness more changes in a decade than the Midland had seen fit to introduce in a lifetime.

This accelerated rate of change on the line may have been because locomotive working on the route during the LMS period tended to be very much a reflection of the overall operating strategy of the new company. As many will know, it took the LMS some time to develop a corporate policy—particularly in the locomotive department—and during the earlier post-grouping years, things tended to remain very much as they had been. The only decision made during the first few years or so after 1922 which really affected the Settle and Carlisle, was that which led to the adoption of certain Midland locomotive designs, virtually unchanged, as LMS standard classes. Thus, although the number of Compounds and Class 4 goods engines continued to increase, it hardly represented a radical change.

It was not until the first generation of specifically LMS locomotive designs went into production that the effect was felt on the Carlisle line and this was sometimes only at second hand. In fact, looking back at the situation, it is now clear that the first changes wrought by the LMS were indicative that the Settle and Carlisle was no longer regarded by its owners as the prime main line it had formerly been. It therefore seems fair to state that the late 1920s mark the beginning of the long decline of this route as a prime traffic mover—at least in passenger terms. However, the run-down was only very gradual and right up to the end of the steam period there was more than sufficient challenge in the passenger workings to tax the new types of engines as they came along.

The first purely LMS design of express passenger locomotive was the famous 'Royal

PLATES 146/147 *Of the many locomotive depots which provided engines for the Settle-Carlisle services, perhaps Holbeck (Leeds) was the best known. The view above, taken from the adjoining signal box, shows Holbeck in July 1939 when the classes on view were dominated by Hughes/Fowler 2-6-0s and MR/LMS standard compound 4-4-0s. There are, however, a few ex-LYR engines in evidence. The picture below is generally believed to be of Carlisle (Durranhill) shed. It shows MR compound No. 1028 taking water in early LMS days. (Photo: BR LMR.)*

Scot' 4–6–0 design of 1927; but in its original form, this type was never seen on the Settle and Carlisle. This was the first time since the line was opened that at least some examples of the most powerful new passenger class were not drafted to the line from the outset—but it was not to be the last. All the Settle and Carlisle received for its main services were those engines displaced by the Royal Scots on the West Coast main line. This brought ex-LNWR engines onto the Midland main line in the shape of a group of Claughton Class 4–6–0s. Althouth nominally considerably more powerful than the Compounds, they were not exactly welcomed with open arms and this was not merely prejudice on the part of the ex-Midland drivers. From all accounts, the ex-LNWR lines did not exactly part with the pick of the bunch as far as the Claughtons were concerned and their work, though good at times, was generally undistinguished and they spent long periods of idleness between days of duty.

It was not until the LMS began to develop its own 'second line' express passenger type in the 1930s as a Claughton replacement for use on all but the heaviest trains, that the Midland lines began to receive a fair share of new passenger motive power. This took the form of the parallel boiler 'Patriot' and taper boiler 'Jubilee' Class 5XP 4–6–0s of Fowler and Stanier design respectively. These machines were put in service on the route in considerable numbers and soon became very characteristic motive power between Leeds and Carlisle. In the form of the Jubilee type, they were represented until the very twilight of steam over Ais Gill. The Class 5XP engines were used on both passenger and express

freight workings and were supplemented in time by the ubiquitous Stanier Class 5 mixed traffic 4–6–0, of which more anon.

As with the Royal Scots, so too with the first LMS 4–6–2s, the Settle and Carlisle was ignored. It is true that certain bridges in the Skipton area would have needed strengthening (and this was done in World War II), but one feels that had LMS policy really decreed a need for more powerful engines on the line, this would have been carried out earlier. So it transpired that whenever loadings over Ais Gill exceeded the capacity of the 5XPs—as was increasingly prone to happen during the accelerations of LMS services during the later 1930s—the company had to resort to the old familiar practice of piloting with its consequent increase in loco-motive operating costs. In the event, the majority of the really heavy LMS trains took the West Coast route and the LMS pacifics never operated over the Settle and Carlisle until BR days and then only on occasional excursions. In fact, as far as is known, the Princess Royal class 4–6–2s were never seen at all on the line.

Nevertheless, the presence of an increasing number of powerful 4–6–2s on the Shap Fell route did, in time, free some of the Royal Scots for work elsewhere; and the need for something more powerful for the most taxing services between Leeds and Carlisle was becoming pressing during the early war years. Thus, as with the Claughtons in the 1920s, a group of Royal Scots was sent to Leeds in 1943. But this time there was a vital difference. The Royal Scots were all approaching their due time for major boiler renewal and other repairs so Stanier took the

PLATE 148. *The taper boilered Stanier 5XPs were very much associated with the Settle-Carlisle line from their introduction in 1934 to their final withdrawal in 1967. In this view, one of the many Leeds examples No. 5573 'Newfoundland', is seen heading north from Skipton in 1947. Interestingly, it was wearing the experimental post-war blue/grey livery applied by the LMS to only two engines—'Newfoundland' and a Duchess 4–6–2.*
(*Photo: Eric Treacy.*)

PLATE 149 *Two more familiar locomotive types are seen here at Hellifield in the late 1950s. On the left is a Stanier 2–6–4T while on the right an express, probably some form of extra working, is seen behind a Hughes/Fowler 2–6–0 —a type generally confined to freight working in this particular area. (Photo: BR LMR.)*

opportunity to completely rebuild them to the latest standards with taper boilers and other significant modifications. Good though they had been in original form, the 'converted' (or 'rebuilt') Scots proved to be a minor revolution and for the first time since grouping, the Settle and Carlisle was the first route to receive what amounted to brand new heavy duty express passenger engines. Increased wartime loads may have been a contributory cause to their being first allocated to Leeds but be that as it may, there was at long last available a machine more than capable of mastering anything likely to have to be lifted over Ais Gill summit.

The Settle and Carlisle line was to be a familiar stamping ground for these magnificent machines (conceivably the finest express passenger 4–6–0s ever to run in Britain) for the rest of the steam age. It is not without significance that the farewell enthusiast tour with the last survivor of the class included Ais Gill in the itinerary; for the rebuilt Scots established their reputation on this route

and were as familiar on it during the 1940s and 1950s as the Compounds had been during an earlier generation.

During the final phase of steam operation, other classes were to be seen on the trains, including both varieties of BR standard pacifics, 'Britannias' and 'Clans'. The first named was the much more commonly seen of the two types and these engines represented the first regular 4–6–2 workings over the line. They were not to be the last; for in 1960/1, there was sent to Holbeck a group of engines which no one in the 1930s and 1940s could ever have remotely imagined in service over Ais Gill and Blea Moor. These were, of course, the famous ex-LNER Gresley Class A3 4–6–2s of 'Flying Scotsman' fame—rendered surplus by dieselisation on the East Coast main line.

Nor was it a case of old warriors being put out to grass as in the case of the LNWR Claughtons. The Holbeck crews took to the Gresleys like ducks to water (it must be confessed that their

PLATE 150 *It was not until the rebuilt Royal Scots appeared that the Settle and Carlisle truly had a frontline LMS express type for its main duties. Here, one of the first five to go to Leeds, No. 6103 'Royal Scots Fusilier' heads past Marley Junction near Keighley with the down 'Thames-Clyde Express' in 1947. (Photo: Eric Treacy.)*

riding was somewhat superior to that of a rebuilt Scot!) and for a few years the A3s worked alongside Jubilees, Scots, Britannias and even the new diesels to give the enthusiast perhaps the most interesting variety of express engines ever to be seen on the line. Diesels finally replaced steam haulage on most expresses during the middle 1960s, but the Jubilees battled on manfully until 1967 amidst ever increasing signs of hysteria amongst some of the more peripheral members of the railway enthusiast fraternity!

Returning now to freight traffic, the motive power situation was rather different than in the express passenger field. The Midland had pinned its faith on the 0-6-0 type and for a while it seemed that the LMS might do the same. It built no less than 575 further examples of the Midland Class 4 freight engine, many going to the Settle and Carlisle and for a while, at least, the Midland 'big goods' engines reigned supreme on all manner of workings all over the LMS system. However, the 4F was not master of

every task nor, in retrospect, was it a particularly good design *per se* and the need was soon felt for something rather more powerful and versatile—especially for the fitted and express freight duties which were forming an increasingly high proportion of the total freight task.

This resulted in the development firstly of the Hughes/Fowler 2-6-0 mixed traffic engines—generally nicknamed 'Crabs'—in 1927 and the ever famous Stanier Class 5 4-6-0 in 1934. These two classes became synonymous with the Settle and Carlisle—particularly on freight workings—for although the LMS may have regarded its passenger services as secondary to those over Shap, the freight traffic was always, as it still is, of considerable importance. One reason for this may be that because of the relatively light passenger traffic—even in the line's heyday—freight trains over Ais Gill are rarely subjected to the same delay as they are over Shap and there is usually the prospect of an essentially uninterrupted run.

PLATES 151–153 THE FAITHFUL FIVES. *All told, 842 examples of Stanier's Class 5 4–6–0 mixed traffic engines were put into service by the LMS and BR and many a hundred of them probably worked over Ais Gill in their time. In the views on this page, some of their duties are depicted. Above, No. 45056 breasts the summit at Ais Gill box with a southbound through freight in the 1950s while below, No. 45081 crosses Dent Head viaduct in July 1960 with a southbound special. Towards the end of the Class 5 'production run' as it were, BR instituted a series of modifications to the basic design, some of which incorporated Caprotti valve gear and double chimneys (left). The tidy outline was not improved by these changes, and the engines enjoyed a mixed reception from their crews.*
(Photos: BR LMR, Eric Treacy, Gavin Morrison.)

PLATES 154/155 *Post-war LMS motive power practice continued in the Stanier tradition. Some of the Patriots were rebuilt into a form very similar to the rebuilt Scots— No. 5530 'Sir Frank Ree' is shown above. The cabside was the main visible difference. In time more utilitarian approach to design came along, and the design replacement for the Class 4F 0–6–0 was the Ivatt Class 4 2–6–0 of starkly functional appearance. No. 43056 is seen (right) approaching Blea Moor tunnel with a Hellifield-Carlisle local during the 1950s. (Photos: BR LMR, Alan Robey.)*

Whatever the reason, the Settle and Carlisle always received its due share of the new freight classes whenever they appeared. The 'Crabs' eventually became outnumbered by the Class 5s which soon began to make the fitteds their almost exclusive preserve and the 4Fs began to make way for larger engines on some, at least, of the other freight hauls. Some use was made of the LMS standard Class 7F 0–8–0 and even the odd ex-LNWR 0–8–0 managed to penetrate the region but the really major step forward in the heavy freight category came with the introduction of the Stanier Class 8F 2–8–0. From the very earliest days of the introduction of this design right until the end of steam, the 8Fs could be seen hammering their way ponderously up the Long Drag from Settle to Blea Moor.

In later years, the wartime 'Austerity' 2–8–0s, the Ivatt Class 4 2–6–0s (the post-war LMS design replacement for the familiar Class 4F 0–6–0) and the BR Class 9F 2–10–0s were all to be seen at work. Indeed, one of the finest sights

of all in the last years of steam was that of a BR Class 9 climbing along Mallerstang to Ais Gill with the heavily loaded anhydrite trains from the Eden valley to Widnes.

As in Midland days, so in LMS and BR times, tank engines in particular and small engines in general were somewhat rare on the Settle and Carlisle. No doubt many classes of smaller engine made sporadic ventures onto the line, especially with local trains, but this was not a general practice. Occasionally the local passenger workings were entrusted to a 2–6–4T or 2–6–2T, but a 4–4–0 or 4–6–0 tender engine was far more likely, even in LMS days. The greater coal and water capacity of the tender engine may have been the telling factor.

Although it was a source of regret that authority did not see fit to transfer any LMS 4–6–2s onto the line in the same way as it had done with the A3s, some recompense could be obtained from the very considerable number of 'distinguished visitors' which took excursions and other special

PLATE 156 *The BR designed 'Britannia' 4–6–2s, and others, continued the functional trend and, in their turn, came onto the line to work alongside Scots, Patriots and Jubilees. No. 70005 'John Milton' is here seen about to leave Skipton on a dynamometer car test run over Ais Gill —a not uncommon occurrence in LMS and BR days for any locomotive class in need of extended test evaluation. (Photo: W. Hubert Foster.)*

PLATES 157–159 *During its lifetime, the Settle and Carlisle has played host to a number of distinguished visiting engines from all parts of the country. Some of the more celebrated types are shown on this page. Above is seen Stanier Coronation Class 4–6–2 No. 46238 'City of Carlisle (an appropriate name!) on a joint SLS/RCTS tour train passing Dent on 29th September 1963. These engines, although they never worked regular schedule services along the route, were quite familiar visitors in the early 1960s and they did have one point of distinction entirely suited to the line. They were the last steam engines to work the line sporting the traditional red livery—and a fine sight they made!*
(*Photo: Gavin Morrison*)

During the severe 1948 floods between Berwick and Edinburgh on the East Coast main line, the Settle and Carlisle was used for a short time by such celebrated trains as the Flying Scotsman. No picture has been located of this train actually between Settle and Carlisle but left (above) is shown Gresley A4 4–6–2 No. 25 'Falcon' on the down Scotsman passing Bell Busk, some five or six miles south of Settle, during the period in question. (Photo: W. Hubert Foster.)

The final picture shows rebuilt SR Merchant Navy Class 4–6–2 No. 35012 'United States Line' heading south near Armathwaite with an excursion train in the early 1960s. On the few occasions when engines of this type visited the line, they gave a very good account of themselves. (Photo: Alan Robey.)

PLATE 160 *The Gresley A3s were regular users of the line in the 1960s and the preserved 'Flying Scotsman' has been a frequent visitor in more recent years. The engine is seen here leaving Moorcock Tunnel with 'The Lord Bishop' special on 30th September 1978. (Photo: David Eatwell.)*

PLATE 161 (below) *The Eden gorge is the most sylvan stretch of the Settle and Carlisle and the line from Lazonby to Armathwaite affords some of the most pleasing scenery of the whole route. In this view a York-Carlisle excursion is seen leaving a tree-girt Lazonby headed by the preserved GWR type Castle Class 4-6-0 No. 7029 'Clun Castle' on 30th September 1967. (Photo: Peter Robinson.)*

PLATE 162 (*above*) *The rather distinctive looking Clayton Type 1 Bo-Bo diesels are somewhat unusual visitors to the Settle and Carlisle. In this picture, a pair of them are seen heading south past Armathwaite signal box with a trip freight working. Note the derelict goods yard tracks in the foreground.* (*Photo: Peter Robinson.*)

trains over the line during the final steam years. Most of the more glamorous engines from all the 'big four' grouped companies were seen from time to time and included ex-LMS Coronation Class 4–6–2s, ex-SR Bulleid pacifics, virtually the whole range of the ex-LNER pacifics (including the streamlined A4s) and even the occasional trip by a GWR Castle. Would that those days could return!

Today the line is, of course, an exclusively diesel preserve. With modern methods of locomotive rostering, it is less easy to say which is the characteristic type of engine to be seen but it is probable that most varieties of BR main line diesel may have been occasionally used. The only noteworthy exceptions, except for the smaller classes, seem to have been the production batch of English Electric Type 5 'Deltics' and, of course, the Western Region diesel hydraulics.

During the transition phase from steam to diesel, when the latter engines were mostly confined to passenger haulage, probably the most commonly witnessed individual class of locomotive was the BR Sulzer Type 4—and perhaps this was appropriate. Bearing more than a passing resemblance to the pioneer LMS main line diesels Nos 10000 and 10001, the Sulzer Type 4 seems somehow to be 'one of the family' on this route; and the bestowal of names like 'Ingleborough', 'Whernside' and 'Pen-y-Ghent' to some of the early members of the class seemed singularly fitting. The pity is that these particular members of the class do not seem to have seen service over the line—somebody was slipping up in the publicity department!

With the final passing of steam on the freights too, much more diesel variety became evident. The pioneer English Electric Type 4s (of the 2xx series) and the Brush Type 4s are familiar visitors while the very fine English Electric DP2 locomotives in the 4xx series can often be seen on diverted West Coast expresses. The prototype 'Deltic' was tested on the route and many of the smaller Type 2 and Type 3 engines have worked the line during recent years.

PLATES 163/164 *In spite of the diesel incursions, while steam was alive it continued to bear a major share of Settle-Carlisle freight traffic and no more hard worked steam engines were to be seen in Britain during the mid-1960s than the willing Stanier 8Fs and BR 9Fs which continued to flog their way over the fell country. In these two pictures, an unidentified 9F is seen above heading across Dent Head in November 1967 while to the right, Class 8F No. 48005 moves off vigorously from Long Meg in the summer of 1965 after a signal check. (Photos: John Whiteley, D. Jenkinson.)*

Chapter 13

. . . and the Future?

Life's but a walking shadow, a poor player that struts
and frets his hour upon the stage,
And then is heard no more; it is a tale
Told by an idiot, full of sound and fury,
Signifying nothing.
Shakespeare: *Macbeth*

The first edition of this book closed with the above quotation, asking whether it was to be the epitaph for the Settle and Carlisle, yet hoping—seemingly against all contemporary logic—that different counsels would prevail. It is a matter of history that events did not bear out the author's worst fears—and how long ago it all seems now that those first stirrings towards a re-think became apparent. Yet the calendar tells us it was only in 1974–5 that the partial revival of the Settle-Carlisle line began to be seriously considered in those high places with the actual power to do something about it. Even so, it is worth reflecting upon some of the reasons why there was a case for retention of this railway line; for it must have been a close run thing.

This book has tried to present an objective view of the Settle and Carlisle line, and the writer has tried to resist the temptation to rhapsodise—perhaps not always successfully. It is too easy to wax enthusiastic about this railway, and it is tempting to look back at earlier times with eyes so blinkered by nostalgia that they are blind to the need for change. Yet it was right and proper that the line today should be judged by the same high standards that its creators brought to bear more than a century ago. The trouble was that in the inmediate post-Beeching era, one could not help wondering whether our actions were not falling somewhat short of the examples set in the 19th Century in terms of vision and imagination.

Perhaps it was true that the Midland route to Carlisle should never have been built, but it was; and for almost a century until the local facilities were closed in the later 1960s and 1970, it played its part in shaping activities in the region. Since it still existed, it did seem to some that every possible opportunity should be taken to discover whether or not it still had a part, albeit of a different nature, to play. But there was precious little evidence that anyone was prepared to see if new uses could be found for what might still be a valuable asset if looked at in a different way.

The cessation of local passenger services did not in any way improve communications in the region, and one seriously wondered whether any meaningful savings had been made. As far as can be ascertained, no economies in signalling or track maintenance were made as a result of withdrawal of the local trains, and one cannot seriously think that the removal of a handful of DMU services made any appreciable difference to the overall line costs.

However, it was and is not BR's responsibility to promote or subsidise socially desirable services so the hopes rested with the local authorities. Were they prepared to do anything other than wring their hands in impotence? No one was sure until it almost seemed too late. The wire was going up over Shap Fell and it was confidently assumed by most observers that once this happened, the Settle and Carlisle's days must be numbered. But then things began to stir—and how they stirred!

Essentially, one feels in retrospect, the partial renaissance of the Settle and Carlisle Railway in the mid-1970s can be put down to two or three major happenings which took place almost simultaneously. They are related here not in any perceived order of importance, but more or less as they seemed to be happening from the on-looker's standpoint.

The first signs came from the Local Authorities in the shape of the Yorkshire Dales National Park. It is quite clear that the officials were becoming concerned about the problems of rural transport both in terms of the lack of public transport in the area and the real risk of spoiling the region if unrestricted private transport was encouraged. The result was a proposal to BR that an experimental, limited re-instatement of local services should start in 1975—fortunately, most of the station platforms had survived.

PLATE 165 *As it turned out, the 1968 'Farewell to Steam' special at Ribblehead on 11th August 1968 was only an 'Au Revoir'. Less than ten years later, they were back. (Photo: John Whiteley.)*

Much to everyone's surprise, the idea was accepted and 'Dalesrail' was born.

The basic idea was to run a monthly stopping train up the line on summer Saturdays in order to bring visitors into the National Park—without motor cars, of course. Buses and guides would meet the trains to help visitors enjoy their trip and tickets would be bookable in advance. More significantly, however, the trains would then be available to allow local folk the chance of making a reciprocal shopping trip to the peripheral towns and cities of West Yorkshire. This, in effect, gave two guaranteed passenger loads in each direction since the process was reversed in the evening (locals back home, visitors back to the towns). No extra rolling stock was needed since there is always a ready supply of DMUs at the weekends, taking their rest from Monday–Friday commuter duties. Dalesrail not only worked but showed an operating profit. The Dales National Park symbol—Rastus the Ram—appeared on new station signs in Ribblesdale, Dent and Garsdale and in due course, the service was extended down the Eden Valley end of the line to Carlisle, thanks to the co-operation of the Cumbrian authorities.

This was indeed a totally new way of looking at the role of a railway in society and its success can only be a source of satisfaction. Full marks then to the Yorkshire Dales National Park officers and the BR operators who went along with the idea.

It was at about the same time that another encouraging move took place. BR clearly began to realise that, in spite of electrification, the Shap route could not absorb all the Settle and Carlisle freight traffic. Moreover, the diversionary capability of the Midland route was still vital; so we heard no more about total closures. Indeed, viaducts and bridges began to receive much more maintenance attention and, wonder of wonders, new mineral sidings were installed to serve the re-opened quarries at Ribblehead. To offset this, the Thames-Clyde Express lost its name and, later, only started its journey at Nottingham; but, in due course, a third day train was added to the existing two which stopped at Settle and Appleby, so matters could have been worse.

By now, it was quite clear that the line would

see its centenary and it was this event which drew by far the most attention—at least to the non-railway minded amongst the population. Led by a highly efficient and hard working Centenary Celebration committee, it seemed during late 1975 and early 1976 that half of North West England—including all the BR staff who mattered—had caught Settle-Carlisleitis! Meetings were held, special trains were planned, BR published a centenary booklet, the National Railway Museum chipped in with a special exhibition and a grand banquet was organised for 1st May 1976 at Settle station. During the Spring of 1976, hundreds and thousands came from far and wide to join the activity—only to be greeted in true Settle-Carlisle style on centenary day itself by the most vile weather imaginable in what was to prove an otherwise rain-free, almost sub-tropical summer. It did not really matter—maybe it was only fitting—and we were all caught up in the events of the day . . . and what a day it was! Bunting decked the stations, bands played, sober folk dressed in period costume and rode the line in vintage

railway coaches brought out just for the occasion and steam engines were seen again—at least as far as Settle. Surely it would not all be forgotten on 2nd May; so we kept our fingers crossed—and we were not to be disappointed.

Dalesrail prospered even more mightily than in 1975 and then, in 1977, BR let it be known that it would allow steam excursions along the whole length of the line from 1978 onwards; steam was, apparently, commercially viable in small doses. Thus it was, less than ten years after BR's own last steam excursion over Ais Gill that the National Railway Museum's 'Green Arrow' set off up the hill on Easter Saturday to inaugurate the return to steam. It somehow seemed quite fitting that the task should be entrusted to a locomotive which, as far as is known, had never been anywhere near the line before!

Of course, the cynics and killjoys muttered about 'living in the past' and 'playing with trains' and, in truth, there was more than an element of nostalgia about it. But the organisation of the trips was first rate, the favourable publicity accruing to BR was enormous and surely of great

PLATE 166 *Gresley V2 No. 4771 'Green Arrow' heralded the return to steam in 1978 on Easter Saturday. On the following Monday she returned to the National Railway Museum and is seen here traversing Dent Head viaduct on the first southbound steam run. (Photo: David Eatwell.)*

PLATE 167 *The National Railway Museum's other famous green engine—Class 9F No. 92220 'Evening Star'—made its first ever assault on the 'Long Drag' on 13th May 1978 with the 'Border Venturer' excursion. It is seen here in typically wild Ribblesdale country near Selside doing battle with the 1 in 100. (Photo: David Eatwell.)*

value; while the writer for one would not mind being the proprietor of a cafe or public house on the days when the steam trains go by—the extra revenue must be quite considerable, judging from the number of spectators.

So, in true British fashion, there seems to have been added yet another unique chapter to the story of what is, after all, a unique railway. For most of the year, the Settle and Carlisle goes about its business as a now accepted part of our somewhat reduced railway system. It has its extra train or two and in the snows of early 1979, as has so often happened in the past, it again provided the only communication link to the outside world when stranded drivers of cars and lorries at Appleby were taken to Carlisle by train. Dalesrail comes to life every spring, and every so often a sense of drama and expectation falls upon the scene when a steam excursion is planned.

If the stones of Ribblehead viaduct were melancholy with Macbeth in 1973, one wonders if they are now musing on Horatio's words outside Elsinore:

But, look, the morn in russett mantle clad,
Walks o'er the dew of yon high eastern hill.

Pen-y-Ghent, perhaps?

THE END

Statistical Significance Testing

The test for significance adopted in Chapter 9 was the Chi-Squared (χ^2) test— familiar to statisticians but probably unknown to most general readers. The mathematics are not relevant to the discussion and have, therefore, been omitted but the tabulated data in Chapter 9 is sufficient for statistically minded readers to calculate the values for themselves should they wish.

Basically, the χ^2 test establishes whether or not the variation between observed and expected values (for given data) is explicable in terms of sampling error only or whether the variation is too great to be thus dismissed. A simple case will probably clarify the situation.

Consider a collection of, say, one hundred parishes grouped into two equal sized categories (A and B) determined by their population changes over a given period. Suppose that one fifth of the total of 100 parishes contain railway stations. Theoretically, if there was no relationship between railway stations and population growth then one would expect to find half the stations in Group A and half in Group B. The values could well be expressed in simple tabular form if desired viz:

	Number of Parishes	Number of Stations
Group A (parishes showing increase in population)	50	10
Group B (parishes showing decrease in population)	50	10

Now, the sheer random factor might well, in fact, cause 11 stations to appear in Group A and only nine in Group B but if one observed 15 stations in Group A and only five in Group B, one might reasonably begin to suspect that there may be some connection between population increase and railway stations. The χ^2 test enables one to establish the mathematical probability of such a division of observed data occurring solely by chance.

If calculated for the example given of a 15:5 division of stations, the χ^2 value would indicate that such statistics would occur by chance less than one in twenty times (or on less than 5% of occasions). We can therefore say that there is a better than 95% probability that the observed figures did *not* occur by chance. Given the same example, a 14:6 split of stations could occur by chance rather more than once in twenty times but a 16:4 split could occur by chance less than one in a hundred times. Thus, when observed data present a pattern which could occur by chance, mathematically speaking, on only very rare occasions, the probability of a relationship between the two sets of data is very high. In this way, by working out frequency of occurrence of stations in relation to the observed changes in parishes one can establish the mathematical probability of the relationship being a chance occurrence.

The important proviso to be made about χ^2 is that it will never produce a certainty—the best it can achieve is such a high degree of probability (in excess of 99%) as to amount to a practical certainty. Furthermore, the χ^2 test should not be taken to imply that one set of figures represents cause and the other represents effect. It can only establish the probability that two sets of data are related in some way—there may be other factors which have caused the relationship.

Although in general, the larger the sample selected for comparison, the better the results are likely to be, the precise number of observations is not important. Thus, for example, if in the case of the above illustration data was missing for ten of the parishes concerned, the comparison would then be between a total of 90 parishes and the number of stations found within this reduced total. If, by good fortune, the missing ten parishes did not contain any stations, then the expected number of 'parishes per station' as it were, would be 4.5 rather than the value of 5 used in the example given. If, however, one or two stations were also missing, then one would have to calculate a new value for 'parishes per station' based on the actual number of stations present in the reduced sample. It would not invalidate the mathematical principles involved.

It should, however, be finally stated that if an expected frequency of occurrence of less than five is obtained, the χ^2 test is unreliable. Thus, in calculating the values for the examples given in Chapter 9, the figures have been so classified that on a strictly proportionate basis, one would expect each group of parishes to contain at least five stations.

Shed Allocations and Train Formations

The author has frequently been asked, generally by modellers but occasionally by others, if he can give details of any specific locomotives (as opposed to class types) which have worked the line. Allied to this is the less often made but still quite common query relating to train formations.

Even were such information readily available in easily digestible form (which it is not), the volume of data involved would be so enormous as to more than fill a book in its own right. To give but one example, the LMS issued new carriage marshalling books three times per year (or more) for each of its four operating divisions. Thus, merely to cover the LMS period of coach marshalling would involve reproducing the essential data contained in some 300 books (if they could be found!). Without such sources, the research involved in merely tracing one particular working may well involve many hours of work. However, much can be done by the individual himself if he is prepared to make intelligent use of the multiplicity of pictures and other data now available from such sources as this book and those listed in the bibliography on page 154. The main ingredients for success are inexhaustible supplies of patience and notepaper!

However, it did seem that some readers, at least, might be interested in a few selected samples of the type of information less easily retrievable. The following details are nothing like exhaustive—in fact, the shed allocations cannot even be guaranteed to be 100% complete for the dates in question— but they are believed to be correct as far as they go. More than that, the writer would not be prepared to guarantee.

I. Sample Shed Allocations

The following data was compiled circa 1948/9 for some five sheds concerned with operating the Settle and Carlisle line amongst their other duties. To save space, LMS running numbers are quoted. In the vast majority of cases, 40,000 should be added to give the appropriate BR numbers.

Leeds (Holbeck)—LMS Shed code 20A		*Total*
LMS standard Class 6P Royal Scot 4–6–0 (rebuilt):	6103/8/9/17/33	6
LMS standard Class 6P Patriot 4–6–0 (rebuilt)	5530/5	2
LMS standard Class 5XP Jubilee 4–6–0:	5562/5–6/8–9/73/87/9/97/ 5604–5/8/11/9/20/51/8–9	18
LMS/MR standard Class 4P Compound 4–4–0:	910/27/32/1020/40/8/68–9/ 87/1144	10
ex-MR Class 3P 4–4–0 (Johnson 'Belpaire'):	720/58	2
ex-MR Class 2P 4–4–0:	351/9/406/55/519/21	6
LMS standard Class 5 4–6–0:	4743–7/53–6—BR built 4774–5/821/8/49/50/3–4/ 6–7/943; 5040/65/8/92/276/ 89—LMS built	26
LMS standard Class 5F 2–6–0:	2795/8/816	3

LMS standard Class 8F 2–8–o.	8067/70/104/26/57–9/283/	
	454/537/641/703	12
LMS/MR Class 4F o–6–o:	3878/931/98; 4044/404/31/	
	501	7
ex-MR Class 3F o–6–o:	3401/665	2
LMS standard Class 3F o–6–oT:	7418	1
ex-MR Class 3F o–6–oT:	7249/54	2
ex-MR Class 1F o–6–oT:	1745	1
ex-MR Class 1P o–4–4T:	1315	1
ex-LYR Class 2P 2–4–2T:	10622/89/880	3

Bradford (Manningham)—including Ilkley—LMS Shed code 20E		*Total*
LMS/MR standard Class 4P Compound 4–4–o:	1004/43/67/137	4
LMS standard Class 2P 4–4–o:	567	1
ex-MR Class 2P 4–4–o:	391; 489; 562	3
LMS standard Class 5F 2–6–o:	2762/91	2
LMS standard Class 4F o–6–o:	4151/400/555	3
ex-MR Class 3F o–6–o:	3351/454/509/783	4
ex-MR Class 2F o–6–o:	22976; 2998; 3078	3
Fowler LMS standard Class 4P 2–6–4T:	2377/80	2
Fairburn LMS standard Class 4P 2–6–4T:	2682	1
Fowler LMS standard Class 3P 2–6–2T:	17; 69	2
ex-MR Class 1P o–4–4T:	1247; 1413	2
ex-LYR Class 2P 2–4–2T:	10630–1/3–4/6/81/714/95/	
	896	9

Skipton—LMS Shed Code 20F		*Total*
ex-Somerset and Dorset (MR type) Class 2P 4–4–o:	323	1
ex-MR Class 2P 4–4–o:	409/14/22/52/84	5
MR/LMS standard Class 4F o–6–o:	3893/904/44/60/84/99/	
	4000/7/41/197/222/76–7/99	14
ex-MR Class 3F o–6–o:	3251/95/337/784	4
LMS standard Class 8F 2–8–o:	8005/145	2
ex-MR Class 2F o–6–o:	3037/477	2
LMS built (LT & SR type) Class 3P 4–4–2T:	BR 41971–4 (ex-LMS	
	2153–6)	4
		(in store)
ex-LYR Class 2P 2–4–2T:	10623/71	2
ex-MR Class 1P o–4–4T:	1249/75/357/8/66	5
ex-LYR Class 2F o–6–oST:	11415/84	2
ex-MR Class 1F o–6–oT:	1767/820/55	3

Hellifield—LMS Shed Code 20G		*Total*
LMS standard Class 4P Compound 4–4–o:	1056	1
ex-MR Class 2P 4–4–o:	459/70	2
LMS standard Class 8F 2–8–o:	8105/89/608/16	4
LMS standard Class 5F 2–6–o:	2770/845/93	3
LMS standard Class 4F o–6–o:	4149/282/579	3
ex-MR Class 3F o–6–o:	3137/86/231/335/79/585–6	7
Fowler LMS standard Class 3P 2–6–2T:	21; 64	2
Stanier LMS standard Class 3P 2–6–2T:	183–4	2
Ivatt LMS standard Class 2P 2–6–2T:	1205–6	2
ex-LYR Class 2P 2–4–2T:	10625/86/842/99	5
ex-MR Class 1F o–6–oT:	1869	1

Carlisle (Kingmoor)—LMS Shed Code 12A—LMS standard main line classes only		*Total*
LMS standard Class 5XP 4–6–o Jubilee:	5564/77/9/80–2/713–6/27–32	16
LMS standard Class 4P Compound 4–4–o:	1129/39–43/6	7
LMS standard Class 2P 4–4–o:	613/5	2

LMS standard Class 5 4–6–o:	4795/877–9/82–4/6/99–903/ 93–4; 5005–6/9/13–5/7/22–3/ 81–4/96/100/18–9/26–7/ 51–2/69/241/66/363–4/ 429/32/43/54–5/82	48
LMS standard Class 5F 2–6–o:	2742–6/8–9/51–2/7/80/93/ 802–3/31–7/50/75–8/ 80–4/99/905–7	35
MR/LMS standard Class 4F o–6–o:	3868/902/22/73/96; 4001/ 8–9/16/181/3/9/99/315/24/6	16

II.   Selected Locomotive Transfers (not complete allocations)

Locos Transferred to Hellifield (20G) during 1936–37

ex-MR standard Class 4P Compound 4–4–o:	1010/44
ex-MR Class 2P 4–4–o:	458
LMS standard Class 5P5F 4–6–o:	5267
LMS standard Class 7F o–8–o:	9554/78/80
LMS standard Class 4F o–6–o:	4201
ex-MR Class 3F o–6–o:	3192
ex-LYR Class 3F o–6–o:	12299
ex-LYR Class 2P 2–4–2T:	10629

Locos transferred to Skipton (20F) during 1936–37

LMS standard Class 4F o–6–o:	4130
ex-MR Class 3F o–6–o:	3137/361
ex-MR Class 1P o–4–4T:	1373; 1402
ex-LYR Class 2P 2–4–2T·	10659

LMS standard Class 5XP 4-6-o Patriots transferred to Holbeck (20A) 1936–37

5525—Un-named (later 'Colwyn Bay')
5534 'E. Tootal Broadhurst'
5535 'Sir Herbert Walker, K.C.B.'
5538—Un-named (later 'Giggleswick')

LMS standard Class 5XP 4–6–o Jubilees allocated at Holbeck (20A) during 1936–37

5560 'Prince Edward Island'
5561 'Saskatchewan'
5562 'Alberta'
5568 'Western Australia'
5598 'Basutoland'
5609 'Gilbert and Ellice Islands'
5619 'Nigeria'
5620 'North Borneo'
5621 'Northern Rhodesia'
5622 'Nyasaland'
5630 'Swaziland'
5642 'Boscawen'
5658 'Keyes'
5659 'Drake'
5660 'Rooke'
5724 'Warspite'
5726 'Vindictive'

III. Selected Express Train formations—Summer 1938

N.B. All trains composed of gangwayed stock.

1. *The Thames-Clyde Express'* (London–Glasgow)

Corridor First Class Brake (16 seats)   Carlisle End of train
Corridor Composite (18 first + 24 third)
Open Composite (18 first + 18 third)
Kitchen Car
Open Third (42 seats)
Open Third (42 seats)
Corridor Third (42 seats)
Corridor Third (42 seats) Monday and Saturday only
Corridor Third (64 seats) Saturday only
Corridor Third Brake (24 seats)   Leeds End of train

Note: Southbound, this train carried an extra full brake at the third class end and also conveyed a two coach portion for Bristol (Saturdays excepted). This portion consisted of a corridor third plus corridor composite brake and was attached at the third class end of the main train.

2. *The Thames-Forth Express'* (London–Edinburgh)

Corridor Third Brake (24 seats)   Carlisle end of train
Corridor Composite (18 first + 24 third)
First Class Kitchen/Diner (24 seats)
Open Third (42 seats)
Corridor Third (42 seats)
Corridor Third (42 seats)
Corridor Third (64 seats) Saturday only
Corridor Third (42 seats) Saturday only
Corridor Third (42 seats) Saturday only
Corridor Third (42 seats) Saturday only
Corridor Third Brake (24 seats)   Leeds end of train

Note: Southbound, this train only carried two extra corridor thirds on Saturdays but it also carried two extra corridor thirds (64 seats) on Mondays and Fridays.

3. *Lunchtime Anglo-Scottish Express* (12 noon from St Pancras)

Corridor Composite Brake (12 first + 18 third)   ⎫
Corridor Third Brake (32 seats)   ⎬ LNER stock—Edinburgh
Corridor Third (64 seats) Saturday only   ⎭
Corridor First Brake (27 seats)   ⎫
Semi-open first (18 dining seats)
Kitchen Car
Open Third (42 seats)   ⎬ LMS stock—Glasgow
Open Third (42 seats)
Corridor Third (42 seats)
Corridor Third Brake (24 seats)
Corridor Third (64 seats) Monday and Friday only ⎭

Note: Southbound, this train carried two 42 seat corridor thirds every day and had no extra coaches on Mondays/Fridays.

4. *10.20 a.m. Leeds-Scotland* (all LMS stock)

Corridor Third Brake (24 seats)   ⎫
Two Corridor Thirds (64 seats) Saturday only   ⎬ Edinburgh portion
Corridor Composite (18 first + 32 third)   ⎭
Corridor Third (64 seats) Monday only southbound ⎫
Brake Van
Corridor Third (64 seats) Monday and Friday only
Four Corridor Thirds (64 seats) Saturday only
Corridor Third (42 seats)   ⎬ Glasgow portion
Open Third (42 seats)
First Class Kitchen/Diner (24 seats)
Corridor Composite Brake (12 first + 32 third)   ⎭

Note: Southbound, this train returned as two separate workings from Carlisle to Leeds.

5. *9.30 p.m. St Pancras–Glasgow Express* (Northbound formation only)

'All Steel' full brake (Leeds–Glasgow)
'All Steel' full brake
Corridor Third (64 seats) Saturday only
Corridor Third (42 seats)
Corridor Third (42 seats)
Third Sleeping Saloon (28 berths)   } London–Glasgow portion
First Sleeping Saloon (12 berths)
Corridor Composite (18 first + 24 third)
'All Steel' full brake
'All Steel' full brake (London–Kilmarnock)

Note: Southbound, the basic Glasgow–London passenger carrying part of the train was substantially similar but the disposition and destination of full brakes was rather more complicated.

6. *9.55 p.m. St Pancras–Edinburgh Express*

'All Steel' full brake
Corridor Composite (18 first + 24 third)
*Composite Sleeping Saloon
*Three Corridor Thirds (64 seat)
*'All Steel' full brake

Note: The portion marked thus: * consisted of LMS and LNER stock on alternate days When LMS stock was used, one of the three corridor thirds (adjacent to the sleeping car) was a 42 seat coach.

IV.   Typical restricted wartime formations (Summer 1941)

1. *10.00 a.m. St Pancras–Scotland* (as worked north of Leeds)

Full Brake (Burton–Boat of Garten) Thursday only
Full Brake   } Leeds–Glasgow
Open Third (56 seats)
Corridor First Brake (27 seats)
First Class Kitchen Diner (24 seats)
Four open thirds (56 seats)—one for dining   } London–Glasgow
Corridor Third Brake (24 seats)
Corridor Third Brake (24 seats)
Open Third (56 seats)   } London–Edinburgh
Corridor Composite Brake (12 first + 24 third)

Note: This train replaced all the daytime Anglo-Scottish workings on the Settle and Carlisle line.

2. *10.30 a.m. Leeds–Glasgow*

Full Brake (London–Carlisle) Monday excepted
Full Brake
Two Open Thirds (56 seat) Monday, Friday,
   Saturday only   } Leeds–Glasgow
Five Open Thirds (56 seat)
Corridor Composite (18 first + 24 third)
Corridor Brake First (27 seats)

Note: Southbound, this train did not carry the two extra open thirds or the extra full brake on any day but on Saturdays it conveyed milk tanks attached at Carlisle (one tank for Cricklewood) and Appleby (five tanks for Cricklewood).

Acknowledgements, Bibliography and Sources

I have been amassing data on the Settle and Carlisle Railway for well over ten years now, during which time many people and institutions have contributed, directly and indirectly, to the information which I have used in preparing this book. Odd letters, chance remarks, photographs, newspaper cuttings and the like have all been either gratefully received or thankfully noted. To all who have helped in any way, be they archivists, librarians, photographers, railway employees, friends or merely chance acquaintances, go my sincere and grateful thanks.

I would, however, like to single out a few names for especial thanks—and in approximately alphabetical order! Firstly, Dr Jay Appleton of Hull University for his help in guiding me in the early stages of my research—originally intended for a higher degree. By now he may have forgotten his help to me but I shall for ever remain in his debt. I would also like to pay tribute to the efforts of John Edgington of BR(LMR) for his untiring efforts in producing photographs, drawings, maps and diagrams from numerous dusty corners of Euston House. Without them, life would have been very hard indeed.

I have mentioned my general indebtedness to several photographers and authors in my introduction to the book but I would like to record my especially grateful thanks to Bishop Eric Treacy. Not only do his pictures provide a constant inspiration but he has gone to a great deal of personal time and trouble to help me prepare this book—not just by providing many hitherto unpublished illustrations and very generously agreeing to write a foreword to my efforts; but also by reading and passing comment on the manuscripts during the final stages. During the past few months, he has heard an awful lot about the Settle and Carlisle line and for his kindness, tolerance and good humoured encouragement I am grateful.

Finally, my thanks must go to my very good friend and fellow enthusiast Arthur Whitehead. Not only has he produced some beautiful artwork in the form of sketches, drawings and the cover design for the book, but over the years he has also suffered much in helping me pursue the Settle and Carlisle in its many moods—Ribblehead Curry, wild strawberries at Dent Head, mushrooms on Birkett Common and all! It is his friendship, however, that I most value and it has stood the test very well indeed!

MAPS AND DIAGRAMS

The maps, station plans, building drawings and diagrams incorporated in this book have all been prepared by the author. Most of the maps and plans are based, with permission, on Ordnance Survey material and are reproduced with the sanction of the Controller of Her Majesty's Stationery Office, Crown Copyright Reserved. The author would like to thank the staff of the Ordnance Survey, Southampton, for their kind co-operation in this project.

Selected Bibliography

BOOKS

The Story of the Settle-Carlisle Line. F. W. Houghton and W. Hubert Foster. Norman Arch Pubs, 1948.
North of Leeds. P. E. Baughan. Roundhouse Books, 1966.
Settle-Carlisle Railway. W. R. Mitchell and David Joy. Dalesman Paperbacks, 1966.
Main Lines Across the Border. O. S. Nock and Eric Treacy. Ian Allan, 1960.
The Midland Railway, its rise and progress. F. S. Williams. Strahan & Co., 1876.
The Midland Railway. C. Hamilton Ellis. Ian Allan, 1953.
English Railways, their development and relation to the State. E. Cleveland-Stevens. Routledge, 1915.
Our Home Railways Vol I. W. J. Gordon. Warne & Co., 1910.
British Railway History Vol I. C. Hamilton Ellis. Allen & Unwin, 1954.
British Railway History Vol II. C. Hamilton Ellis. Allen & Unwin, 1959.
London Midland and Scottish—a railway in retrospect. C. Hamilton Ellis. Ian Allan, 1970.
The Midland Compounds. O. S. Nock. David & Charles, 1964.
Railway Carriages in the British Isles. C. Hamilton Ellis. Allen & Unwin, 1965.
Railway Carriage Album. C. M. Kichenside. Ian Allan, 1966.
The LMS Coach 1923–1957. R. J. Essery and D. Jenkinson. Ian Allan, 1969.
The Geography of Communications in Great Britain. J. H. Appleton. O.U.P., 1962.
British Regional Geology—Pennines and adjacent areas. H.M.S.O.
British Landscapes Through Maps—The Yorkshire Dales. C. A. M. King. Geographical Association, 1960.
Geographical Journal 1950. Royal Geographical Society.

ARTICLES

Many past issues of the various railway journals contain passing references to the Settle and Carlisle Railway and it would be impossible to list them all here. However, particular mention should be made of the three primary magazine sources 'Railway Magazine', 'Railway World' and 'Trains Illustrated' (latterly 'Modern Railways'), back issues of which will repay careful study. A brief list of some more recent articles follows:

The Leeds–Carlisle Road at the close of the Midland Era. N. Harvey. Railway World, Sept., 1961.
Half a Century of Train Travel C. J. Allen. *No 4 Midland Memories.* Railway World, June 1962. *No 41 Midland services of 1905.* Railway World, July 1965.
Locomotive Running Past and Present No 198: The 'Thames–Clyde Express'. C. J. Allen. Railway World, 1968.
The Settle & Carlisle main line. M. C. Reed. Trains Annual—Ian Allan, 1966.
The Men who built the 'Long Drag' over Ais Gill. T. J. Hunt. Railway World, June 1963.
Outpost of the Midland. John Clarke. Railway Magazine, March 1966.
Disaster at Hawes Junction. E. G. Barnes. Railway Magazine, Feb. 1971.
By Rail through Wensleydale. H. A. Vallance. Railway Magazine, Oct. 1950.
Historical Geography and the Beeching Report. J. H. Appleton. Scottish Geographical Magazine, April 1965.

OTHER PRINCIPAL SOURCES

British Railways Archives, Porchester Road and York
British Railways (Headquarters LMR)
British Railways (Barrow-in-Furness)
The Ministry of Agriculture
The Public Record Office
Cumberland County Archives
Westmorland County Archives
West Riding County Archives
City of Carlisle Public Library
City of Leeds Public Library
City of York Public Library

ACKNOWLEDGEMENTS, BIBLIOGRAPHY AND SOURCES

The Craven Herald
The Lake District Herald
Dalesman Magazine
Contemporary papers and documents in the possession of:
  W. Hubert Foster, Esq
  E. F. Haswell, Esq
  A. Robey, Esq
  N. Wilkinson, Esq
  K. C. Woodhead, Esq
  the late W. O. Steel, Esq

The author would like to apologise to any individual or organisation whose name may
have been inadvertently omitted from the above list.

Index